To all the good ghosts
of 200 South Miami Avenue

———————

Contents

Preface

Newspaper ethics is a slippery topic. Defining ethical behavior is a little bit like defining art, and most of us follow the I-know-it-when-I-see-it rule. Collecting horror stories about journalistic misdeeds is easy, but proceeding toward a rational cure for the problems of the profession is much more difficult. The issues are so variable that there often appears to be no recourse but to handle them one at a time as they arise. This, of course, is just what newspeople do—and that makes them particularly susceptible to rapidly shifting fads and fashions. Editors and publishers carry in their heads (and perhaps their hearts as well) what contemporary ethicist Lawrence Kohlberg has called a "bag of virtues." When a problem arises, they fumble around in the bag for whatever virtue seems to fit the occasion. As a result, like Charlie Brown of their own comic pages, they try to please too many conflicting interests and end up pleasing none. It is an easy trap, says Kohlberg. "If we, like Charlie Brown, define our moral aims in terms of virtues and vices, we are defining them in terms of the praise and blame of others and are caught in the pull of being all things to all people and end up being wishy-washy."*

If there is one consistent motive in the way that people in the news business approach ethical problems, it is a desire to please. So ethics is treated not as a striving toward integrity, but as a public relations problem, one that follows the shifting winds of public attention. Newspeople are thus in constant danger of swinging between, on the one hand, recklessly pursuing narrow self-interest and, on the other, being paralyzed into inaction for fear of being judged unethical. They need more ego strength, better self-analysis, clearer values.

Clarifying values is not easy. People who study ethics for the first time are often disappointed to find that neither the ancient nor the modern philosophers can give them principles that will solve their everyday dilemmas. Perhaps the best they can hope for is to reach a better self-

* Lawrence Kohlberg. The philosophy of moral development: Moral stages and the idea of justice. New York: Harper & Row, 1981.

understanding. This process requires developing an awareness of one's values, pulling them up from the gut level to full consciousness, where they can be examined and criticized. Those who have done that can see more clearly the connections between their values and the decisions that they make. When values are examined, they can be made consistent, it becomes possible to tell with some precision where one's values differ from those of others, and a person can do a better job of finding ways to live with those differences.

Since the Watergate scandals of 1972–1975 raised public consciousness about morality in national institutions, the continuing and erratic struggle of the people who report the news to come to terms with their own self-doubts has had special poignance. Watergate reminded everyone that people who make their living by exposing the misdeeds of others have a special need to keep their own behavior beyond criticism. When they discover that it can't be done, that every action will bring criticism from some quarter, many retreat into a superficial tough-mindedness, relying on rigid, knee-jerk responses to mask their brittle uncertainty. But the difficult decisions are still there to be made, whether directly or by default. The truly strong will face the problem of discovering and dealing with their real values. This process of self-discovery is not for the faint-hearted. The study of ethics is not for wimps.

This book is designed to help by documenting the ethical confusion of the press, offering an analytical and historical framework to show how the press became the way it is, and making some suggestions to clear the air and contribute to self-knowledge. Its four parts are organized as follows:

Part One. Because First Amendment ideals underlie most of the ethical positions of the press, these ideals and their historic background are examined in the opening chapter—along with some extreme examples of the application of these ideals to the narrow self-interest of newspapers.

Chapter 2 expands the notion of the journalist as philosopher by examining the codes of journalism. Newspaper ethics are codified on two levels, the visible and the hidden. The written codes of three major professional organizations of journalists are examined and contrasted to the hidden codes—some of which are documented by a survey of newspeople.

Part Two. Chapters 3–6 each detail a major area of ethical concern—pressure from advertisers, objectivity, conflict of interest, and invasion of privacy—to show how newspapers handle these problems and how a certain amount of ethical confusion interferes with efficient resolution of the problems.

Part Three. Chapters 7–9 look at structural and organizational effects on newspaper ethical judgments: how a publisher's management style sets the ethical tone for the staff, the effects of size and type of ownership on ethical behavior, and the influence of reference groups (the people newspaper managers really care about—who aren't always the readers).

Part Four. Finally, Chapters 10–13 examine ways of watching the watchdogs. The first of these constitutes a direct challenge to you, the reader, to judge the newspaper you read most often. Chapter 10 suggests standards to which your local paper ought to be held. Chapter 11 pursues the First Amendment principle that shedding light on troubled areas tends to cure the troubles and examines the resistance to news councils and ombudsmen, two instruments of disclosure that have received only scattered support within the profession. Chapter 12 examines the efficacy of the marketplace in correcting problems and shows how much of a beating the news business has already withstood without moving toward major reform. The final chapter offers a practical approach for self-help: the concept of an ethical audit, which could give a newspaper the benefit of an independent check on its moral condition, just as an independent accountant evaluates its financial condition.

This is my third book about the news business and the first in which I refer to newspeople in other than the first person plural. This does not mean that I have abandoned the business so that I can talk about "their" misdeeds instead of "our" ethical problems. It does signify an attempt to step outside the closed circle for a moment and speak directly to the consumers of news. If you are a practicing journalist or a student of journalism, I invite you to take the same step. Stand out here with me for a while and look at the news business through the eyes of the consumer. Whatever your connection with the news business, you are also a reader, and this book is addressed to you in that role. It is from such a viewpoint that solutions to problems of ethics will have to come, for the news business will be only as moral as the consumers who support it require it to be.

The work on which this book is based began with a phone call early in 1982 from Robert H. Phelps, then the executive editor of the *Boston Globe* and chairman of the committee on ethics of the American Society of Newspaper Editors. ASNE wanted someone to conduct a survey to study the role of the editor–publisher relationship in the resolution of ethical problems in the newspaper business. Being newly established in academe, where I had both the time and the responsibility to think about such problems, I took the job.

That survey provides the basic framework for the book. Other material comes from a series of seminars held over the following three years by ASNE and state and regional press associations in various parts of the country, from additional analysis by students in the School of Journalism of the University of North Carolina at Chapel Hill, and from my own reflections on 25 years of newspaper work in jobs ranging from substitute carrier for the *Clay Center [Kansas] Dispatch* to corporate staff member at Knight-Ridder Newspapers. The initial data collection and part of the writing were funded by the John and Mary R. Markle Foundation through the American

Society of Newspaper Editors and the ASNE Foundation. The writing was completed during my service as a Senior Fellow of the Gannett Center for Media Studies at Columbia University. I had many thought-stimulating conversations along the way with a great number and variety of people both in and out of the news business, including Jack Behrman, Bill F. Chamberlin, Donna Charron, Everette E. Dennis, Deni Elliot, Garrett Epps, Kenneth Goodpaster, Louis Hodges, Laura Nash, and Deborah Wadsworth. Additional thanks are due to my research assistants: Charles Elder, Joyce Jones, James Lee, Sharon Polansky, and the indefatigable J. Walker Smith.

Philip Meyer

PART ONE

Journalists as Philosophers

CHAPTER 1

The First Amendment

Suppose for a moment that you have been accused of a crime—a crime that you sincerely believe you did not commit—yet here you are, on trial, and with a policeman testifying that he saw you perform the illegal act.

Now suppose further that an impartial witness saw what the policeman saw. Not only did this witness see it, he recorded it on film. Better yet, this impartial witness is a newspaper photographer, and his newspaper is well known for its integrity and devotion to uncovering and disclosing the truth.

You are home free, right? Wrong. If that newspaper photographer is your only witness, you may be in big trouble.

Strange as it may seem, many newspaper people consider it a violation of their ethical standards to testify in court about events they have heard and seen. You may get that photographer's evidence eventually, but you and the court may have to subpoena him, threaten him, place him in fear for his own liberty before he will make the slightest effort to help you.

This is not an issue of protecting confidential sources. A few reporters, in highly publicized cases, have gone to jail rather than identify sources whom they had promised to protect. Their tenacity in keeping their promises to those sources is admirable. But in this case the source needs disclosure, not silence, and is not likely to get it, at least not without a struggle. To many news people, the silence itself is the virtue, not any underlying concern for the people who make the news. What was once rational protection of sources has become a law of journalistic *omerta*.

Newspaper people today are ethically confused. Their attitudes toward the moral implications of their work range from humility to arrogance, from total insensitivity to hypersensitivity. Sometimes these conflicting attitudes are held simultaneously by the same individuals. On the one hand, they risk alienating their public through insistence on special privileges not available to the rest of us, and, on the other, they risk locking themselves into timorous paralysis, fearful of acting lest someone cry foul.

This book is an attempt to sort such ethical issues out. News people are good people, and the responsibility they face in bringing us a daily measure of truth out of the noise and confusion of events is an awesome one. Conflict is inevitable.

The example of the reluctant witness is based on a real case. It came to my attention in 1984, at a luncheon meeting of newspaper people who were swapping tales of the tribulations of their craft. The man from the *Dallas Morning News* reported that his paper had a legal problem on its hands. A photographer was being subpoenaed, and the court was determined to make him testify.

The case was straightforward. A woman had been arrested—unjustly, she believed—in a demonstration against nuclear power. She was charged with blocking a public passageway. The photographer had witnessed the event, recorded it on film, and was now being summoned to testify on her behalf and to provide prints of the shots made at the scene to support her claim of innocence. Some of the images had not been published in the newspaper.[1]

"Why are you fighting it?" the young editor was asked. He looked surprised.

"Because of the First Amendment," he said.

One of the troubles with newspapers is this tendency to invoke the First Amendment reflexively to justify their immediate self-interest or even their mere convenience. The First Amendment is such a powerful and integral part of our basic law that this practice is a little like invoking Holy Scripture to avoid taking out the garbage. Newspapers have also invoked the First Amendment to explain why they feel they must publish the names of rape victims, why they should reveal the circumstances of people which, if known, would make them potential victims of crime, and as justification for not allowing persons about whom disparaging things have been said to reply in their columns.

Our concern here is newspaper ethics, not press law. But because many decisions involving moral obligations are justified with First Amendment arguments, we need to start with an examination of those arguments. The legal outcome of a case and the ethical outcome are not always the same. Sometimes an action that is immoral will be within the law, and sometimes a moral action will violate the law. For newspaper people, however, the First Amendment involves an ethical principle as well as a legal one. Indeed, for many the First Amendment is the foundation of an ethical system, and to understand how news people think, it is necessary to understand the structure of that system.

The Texas case turned on a question of fact: whether the woman had or had not chained herself in the doorway. She argued that to prove she had not, she needed the photographer's testimony, his photographs, or both. Her argument, as much as his, was grounded in the Constitution. The Sixth Amendment states, "In all criminal prosecutions, the accused shall enjoy the right. . . to have compulsory process for obtaining witnesses in his favor." And bearing witness is a traditional duty of every citizen, regardless of his or her status. A trial applies the law to facts, and there must be procedures for making the facts known. The right is not absolute. It yields, for example, to the power of the national government to protect its military secrets.

But how does the First Amendment get involved? The First Amendment, of course, says that "Congress shall make no law . . . abridging the freedom of speech, or of the press . . . ." The bridge from that language to the photographer's reluctance to be a witness involves an extrapolation from the freedom to speak to the freedom to discover the truth. Forcing a newsperson to give testimony, the argument goes, interferes with his or her ability to gather news. Protecting that ability is indeed important, as it has been since the birth of our republic.

The Historical Background of the First Amendment

The delegates to the Constitutional Convention of 1787 were keenly aware of the importance of information in a democratic government. The memory of the Dark Ages was fresher to the Founding Fathers than it is to us, and they were but a century beyond Isaac Newton's mechanical model of an orderly and potentially predictable universe. In the eighteenth century the humanistic benefits of an enlightened and scientific world were becoming visible. The value of reason was appreciated as never before. The notion of truth as something to be verified through observation and logic had taken hold, and social philosophers inspired by Newton, including John Locke, had laid the groundwork for applying reason to the political sphere.

Superstition and prejudice were giving way to a new humility, which included the ability to suspend judgment while facts were investigated and evaluated. The idea of the perfectibility of humans and their institutions was taking hold, and truth was seen as something that could only gradually be discovered. If today's belief might be proven wrong tomorrow when more evidence was uncovered, it would be wrong to compel particular beliefs or to persecute unusual ideas. In the middle of the seventeenth century, Roger Williams in this country argued for keeping the state out of religious matters, while in England John Milton pleaded for freedom of conscience and speech. In his *Areopagitica,* published in 1644, Milton argued for an end to government licensing of printers. Censorship, he said, would lead

> to the discouragement of all learning and the stop of truth, not only by disexercising and blunting our abilities in what we know already, but by hindering and cropping the discovery that might be yet further made, both in religious and civil wisdom. . . . Give me the liberty to know, to utter, and to argue freely according to conscience, above all other liberties.

Milton's plea was eventually successful, but printing was still licensed in the colonies long after the practice was ended in England, so the memory of the lifelessness of the licensed product was fresh when the Founding Fathers debated their Bill of Rights. Thomas Jefferson argued vigorously for a bill of rights to make explicit some constraints on government. Writing to James Madison from his diplomatic post in Paris, Jefferson argued that the benefits would outweigh the risks. "The inconveniences of the Declaration (of rights) are that it may cramp government in its useful exertions," he wrote. "But the evil of this is shortlived, moderate, and reparable. The inconveniences of the want of a Declaration are permanent, afflicting, and irreparable. . . ."[2]

Was Jefferson right? Kurt Luedtke, the former executive editor of the *Detroit Free Press*, suggested to a meeting of the American Newspaper Publishers Association in 1982 that the First Amendment has not made much difference. In Britain the press is less free, "but their citizens are every bit as free as we are. The near-absolute freedom which you enjoy," he told the assembled publishers, "is not essential to a functioning democracy."[3]

Harold Evans, who had to work hard to stay out of English jails for activities relating to the hard-hitting investigative reporting of his staff at the *London Sunday Times*, has disagreed. Precisely because the press is not free, he has argued, great damage can be and has been done to the people by governments not sufficiently checked. The thalidomide case is an example. Under British law, courts can prevent newspapers from reporting on litigation in process. The thalidomide cases involved 450 plantiffs and a dozen years. Settlements were shamefully small, on the order of $40,000 per family, and they were being made in the absence of public scrutiny of the facts. Evans eventually led a successful campaign to get better compensation for the victims, but only after waging a long and costly legal battle of his own to get those facts into print.[4] In short, then, Jefferson was right: Government free of public view cannot be trusted.

The Absolutist Position on Press Freedom

Given Jefferson's wisdom on that score, the question then becomes one of exactly how free the First Amendment makes the press. The objection to the absolutist position is summed up in the aphorism that your freedom to swing your fist ends where my nose begins. An absolute freedom to swing your fist would place no protections around my nose. There has been a school of thought, never subscribed to by a majority of the Supreme Court, that the First Amendment freedoms are absolute and therefore must prevail in any conflict—and there will always be conflict—between a First Amendment claim and some other claim under the Constitution. Thus, the accused trespasser in Texas must yield her right to compel testimony on her behalf if the reluctant witness has a First Amendment claim.

The Preferred-Position Theory

Any First Amendment claim? If you think about it, you realize that pure absolutism is impossible, because you can always dream up a hypothetical First Amendment claim that even the most rigid fundamentalists would not accept. It would be absurd to argue, for example, that a reporter should be allowed, in the name of the First Amendment, to pistol-whip a source to make him talk. And refusing to come to the aid of a source who needs a witness is also pretty high on the scale of absurdity. However, we would be making a serious mistake if we were to leap from that judgment to an assumption that the underlying rationale used by a reluctant media witness is also absurd. There is a vital and essential truth at the bottom of it, and the great danger of trying to push this truth to its silliest limits is that the importance of the basic truth itself may be obscured or even lost.

The vital core of this argument is that the freedom to impart the truth must include the freedom to discover the truth. Therefore government should not only refrain from preventing or punishing speech, but it should also refrain from inhibiting the process of discovering and imparting information. There is much historical justification for this position. Following the social-contract theory of John Locke and its later elaboration by Jean Jacques Rousseau of France, the authors of the Constitution believed—as we still do today—that government exists with the consent of the governed, and that this consent must be informed consent.[5] The system can't work unless the public knows and understands what the government is up to. This was not idle theorizing. There were too many examples of despotic governments the world over, and even England, where the notion of individual liberty had been born, was on the edge of darkness under the corrupt Parliament of George III. America seemed the only hope for the future, and that hope lay in an enlighted and knowledgeable public. On these shores, wrote John Adams, must begin "the illumination of the ignorant and the emancipation of the slavish part of mankind all over the earth."[6]

Government, the Founders believed, was essentially selfish, grasping, and abusive of power. So an independent check in the form of the free transfer of information was essential to keep it in line. The connection with some of today's more difficult ethical and legal problems comes as soon as you decide that the free flow of information requires not only noninterference with speech and noninterference with the processes by which information is developed and distributed, but also a ban on any government action that might conceivably lead to such an interference. With each of those successive steps, the case for absolutism grows weaker. The legal and moral problem is one of where to draw the line.

In modern times the debate over just how far the First Amendment extends to protect the press has centered on a few key extensions of the basic need articulated by John Milton in the seventeenth century and written into the U.S. Constitution in the eighteenth. One such extension holds that when the First Amendment is in conflict with some other provision of the Constitution, the First Amendment should generally prevail. The case of the Texas photographer is just such a conflict because the accused person was invoking her Sixth Amendment right to compel testimony when she asked for the newspaper photographer's pictures. The theory that the First Amendment comes first is called the *preferred-position theory,* and it stems from a footnote, in a case about something totally different, that was written by Associate Justice Harlan F. Stone in 1938. Stone elaborated on the idea in later decisions and said that when constitutional provisions are in conflict, there should be special protection for "those political processes which make all other rights in our society possible."[7]

The Chilling Effect and the Slippery-Slope Problem

The process of getting the information out so that the people will know what their government is doing is certainly one that makes everything else possible. And if you walk far enough down that road, you can reach the justification for a photographer's refusal to testify in a criminal case. The justification has to do with avoiding a *chilling effect.*

A chilling effect can be almost anything that has an unfavorable effect on the reward system for journalists or their sources. It raises the cost or decreases the pleasure of discovering and imparting information and so discourages the free flow of information, without necessarily obstructing it outright. If a person responsible for gathering news is required to testify about the things that he learned in that process, the argument goes, it will make the people who tell him things or pose for the pictures less willing to do so in the future.

There was no such chill in the Texas case because the person who was arrested had invited the photographer to be there and hoped to benefit from his testimony. But, say the newspapers, the principle still applies. And here we have an encounter—the first of many in dealing with the way newspapers think about ethics—with the *slippery-slope problem.* Sure, editors will acknowledge, this case does not make any practical difference, but if we give in on this one, we'll have to do it in the next one, too. And that one will be a little bit different and before you know it, we will have slid all the way down the slippery slope to the point where no one will want to talk to or be photographed by a journalist.

In the view of those newspaper people who are First Amendment fundamentalists, the chilling effect begins at the top of that slippery slope. That's why the expression is used so much. "I sometimes think," wrote David Shaw of the *Los Angeles Times,* "that the phrase 'chilling effect'—as in 'This will have a chilling effect on the ability of the press to fulfill its First Amendment obligations'—is routinely administered to all journalists, by injection, along with their first press cards."[8]

The slippery slope is a recurrent theme in ethical thought. My grandmother, for one, believed in it. Consuming carbonated soft drinks from bottles, she warned, was a bad idea because it can lead you to sipping from bottles with wine or beer in them. From there, you may be tempted to try some of the hard stuff, and the next thing you know, you're lying in a gutter somewhere not knowing what day it is. She wasn't far wrong, at least for some people. But the existence of some slippery slopes in real life does not demonstrate either the immutability or the universal application of the theory. Yes, everybody who lands in a heap at the bottom of some slippery slope did indeed have to start with that first step. But lots of others take the first step with no harm at all. In real life, slippery slopes must have handholds, ledges, tree branches, or even golden staircases leading back up.

In application, the image of the slippery slope justifies various kinds of absolutism. "If I did this for you, I'd have to do it for everybody." Or "If we don't fight communism in Southeast Asia, we'll eventually be fighting it on the beaches of California." Or "If we admit one of those (insert any ethnic group, sex, or profession) into the club, they'll soon take over the place." Or Richard Nixon stating that he was worried about the effect on "future presidents" of his potential prosecution in the Watergate scandal.

The moral problem with an absolutist position is that it rejects compromise before discussion even begins. As Walter Lippmann observed, whenever you hold your positions to be "perfect examples of some eternal principle or other, you are not talking, you are fighting."[9] When there is conflict, the absolutist insists that all the adjustment must be made by other parties. In a world where nobody is perfect, that is a difficult position to sustain. Yet journalists sometimes behave as if theirs were the world's only perfect profession. The issue of refusing to take part in other people's legal proceedings is perhaps the clearest example of this claim to preferential treatment. How far will journalists go to defend their claim? Pretty far, it seems.

In 1982 *Washington Post* reporter Loretta Tofani wrote a three-part series about sexual assaults among prisoners in the Prince Georges County, Maryland, jail. She described 12 cases of jail rape. This story was reported at a time when the *Post* was in a mood for reform of its methods. In 1981 Janet Cooke, another *Post* reporter, had received a Pulitzer Prize for her gripping story about an 8-year-old heroin addict. It was later discovered that the story was fabricated and that the child did not exist; the Pulitzer was returned and Cooke was fired. After that episode (discussed further in Chapter 4), the *Post* was jumpy about printing dramatic disclosures that could not be traced back to specific sources. Tofani therefore went to more than the usual trouble to get her sources on the record. Many of them, including prisoners, did allow her to use their names. The series was published and led to a grand jury investigation of the county jail system. The grand jury, not illogically, decided that the place to start was by talking with Tofani—to verify her story, to find out what else she might have learned that didn't get into the paper, and to learn who else might have been present to verify her conversations with the inmates.

The *Post*, through Tofani, fought the subpoena even though no question of protecting the confidentiality of sources was involved here. There was at least the possibility of a chilling effect—modest here, perhaps, but maybe not so modest in future cases. How can there be a chilling effect when the sources allowed the use of their names? Well, it can be argued, they knew their names would be in the newspaper, but they didn't expect the reporter to repeat her information to a grand jury; if they had, they might not have talked. So, if Tofani were to testify, future subjects of jailhouse interviews would find out about it, and that would make them reluctant to talk, and the press's freedom to report would have been damaged.

That's a pretty faint chill, in light of what actually happened. While Tofani was resisting her subpoena, the grand jury went right ahead and indicted several people, and they were eventually convicted. To believe that a lawbreaker would weigh an equation so delicate that he would decide it is safe to admit misdeeds to a reporter and to allow use of his name—but that he won't cooperate if he thinks she might testify—is to stretch the argument awfully thin. It makes sense only on the slippery slope.

It is fear of sliding down the slippery slope that leads newspaper people to balk at giving testimony even in cases where there is absolutely no possibility of a chilling effect. Cases where newspaper people go undercover are a good example. If the source doesn't know he is talking to a reporter, then nothing he believes about the reporter's role can have any kind of effect, chilling or otherwise. Yet, even in undercover cases such as the *Chicago Sun Times*'s famous Mirage Bar operation, where reporters ran a bar in order to observe corrupt city inspectors, newspapers and broadcast media reflexively resist providing evidence when no chilling effect would result from doing so. Again, the slippery-slope argument is invoked—the claim that any instance of cooperation would be the first line in a long chain of events that would ultimately undermine the neutrality and independence of the media.

Leonard Downie, the managing editor of the *Washington Post,* paints a troubling scenario toward the bottom of that slippery slope. Individual instances of newspaper cooperation with law enforcement authorities could, he argues, add up to a public perception that the newspaper is a part of the law enforcement process. This could be true even if no single instance creates a practical chill. If news sources start to equate reporters with cops, they will stop talking. Downie told a meeting of Wisconsin newspaper people in 1984, "The *Post* refuses to cooperate with law enforcement authorities when they request or even when they subpoena testimony, photographs, notes, or documents from our reporters because we strongly believe a free press should not be an arm of the law."[10]

This stance is based less on eternal principle than on the kinds of situations that news people often faced in the 1960s and 1970s, when civil rights demonstrations and antiwar protests were major news. Many of the protesters used civil disobedience as a tactic, and repressive law enforcement was a common countertactic. Police officers were no longer automatically perceived as the good guys, as they had been in the past. Covering those movements, getting those viewpoints heard, was of overriding importance to journalists, and the tradition of cooperation between reporters and policemen was set aside. But the new tradition carried problems of its own, particularly when it was overgeneralized.

In the *Dallas Morning News* case, the photographer finally agreed to testify, but he balked at supplying photos that had not been printed in the paper. He would not even look at the photographs to refresh his memory. Some witnesses claimed that the defendant had chained herself in a doorway. She claimed she had not. The photographer said he couldn't be sure whether she was chained in the doorway, and he admitted that looking at his own photos might refresh his memory. But he refused to do so.

In general, the courts have had very little sympathy with these far-flung extensions of the chilling-effect argument. That newspapers keep fighting anyway suggests that they are being bad legal tacticians. It is never wise to press for a final decision on a legal point that you are going to lose: far better to preserve any ambiguity that might exist in the absence of a final decision. This was particularly true when the Supreme Court under Chief Justice Warren Burger had made a number of rulings against the press and, in the opinion of some observers, had gone out of its way to reach down for and examine lower court rulings that favor the press. If newspapers were truly interested in preserving their First Amendment privileges, they would try to dodge as many contests as possible, postponing final resolution until a more sympathetic majority is created among the nine justices. Sophisticated civil rights groups are very choosy about the issues they attack. They have sometimes—even in cases involving capital punishment—chosen to let an adverse ruling in a state court stand rather than take it to the Burger Court and risk losing and having that rule given national scope. The news media, in contrast, sometimes appear eager to strike out in all directions, litigating everything, even when it is clear that there is a high risk that more antipress decisions will be written into the record.

Arguments for Press Privilege Beyond the First Amendment

News people are not stupid, so some reasons other than refining and enhancing First Amendment law must lie behind their dogged refusals to testify. Indeed, there *are* other interests, more immediate and less noble, that journalists are protecting.

Inconvenience and Expense

One of their concerns is the sheer inconvenience and expense of having to provide evidence. By fighting subpoenas at every turn, they raise the cost to litigants of relying on evidence generated by news people—thereby, ironically, imposing a chilling effect of their own. In any community, a newspaper is just one of many power centers, and its place in the pecking order may depend on how it responds to what outsiders may consider perfectly reasonable requests. Perhaps to be free, strong, and independent, it has to be prickly as well. Yet if the newspaper were truly strong, perhaps it could afford to be more routinely helpful.

Ideally, a newspaper is seen as an honest and neutral chronicler of fact. Its agents would therefore be ideal witnesses because they would be readily believed. And because reporters and photographers always go where the interesting things are happening, they tend to be in those places where litigation arises. If there are 50 witnesses to a crime and one happens to be a newspaper reporter, the prosecutor may find it more convenient to call the reporter than any of the other 49. The reporter is easy to identify, is a trained observer, and is easy to track down. If newspapers did not routinely fight subpoenas, bearing witness in criminal and civil litigation would become a heavy overhead cost—one that they are not prepared to bear and for which they are not compensated.

Some editors make this argument without ever mentioning the First Amendment, and one has to admire their straightforwardness. An economic problem is more amenable to solution than one based on abstract principle. The case of newspaper clipping files or morgues suggests a precedent. Typically, newspapers have barred the public from their files simply because of the inconvenience and expense of maintaining a system accessible to the public. But with newspaper libraries converting to electronic data bases, the possibility suddenly exists of making money from lawyers, businesses, and members of the general public by providing nonintrusive access to those libraries. Some newspapers are following the example of the *Toronto Globe & Mail* and making their morgues available to the public on a fee-for-use basis.

Expert witnesses in civil cases sometimes command fees of $1000 a day or more. If newspapers could work out a way to charge for the time their staff members spend on the witness stand, if testifying were to become part of the revenue stream instead of a nuisance, some pressures on the First Amendment might disappear. But first, news people would have to discuss the issue frankly as a nuisance or as an economic problem, rather than package it in the First Amendment.

Emotional Reasons for Refusing to Testify

Once we set aside the First Amendment argument and look for practical considerations behind the reluctance of newspaper people to be witnesses in court, a number of others appear. An investigative reporter shares some of the methodology of the confidence artist, blind-siding sources with soothing talk, giving subtle psychological rewards for cooperation. A *Washington Post* editor's account of Tofani's method reveals an excellent example. As the editor described the process, Tofani

> warmed them up with softball questions. . . . She knew when to back off if she felt like her source was getting uncomfortable. . . . Then at some point she would usually ask what Francis Bacon called 'the bold, unexpected question that lays a man open.' You wait for a time when they're not expecting anything, then ask it point blank and 50 percent of the time you're going to get an answer that amazes you.[11]

This makes it sound as if a reporter *likes* to "lay a man open" with unseemly zest. But reporters are human, they have some humane reservations about such manipulative behavior, and they have ways of dealing with these reservations. When a source is rendered vulnerable in this way, a news person feels a moral responsibility to do no unnecessary harm, to get the facts as gently as possible, and to remain on as good terms with the source as the circumstances will permit. In such a situation, the reporter truly wants to believe that the information being coaxed from the source will not bring the source undue harm. This is perhaps a necessary side effect of the rapport that arises in the coaxing process. For the confidence man, part of the swindling process is "cooling out the mark," leaving the swindled person feeling as good and as philosophical about being victimized as possible. This process has the twin functions of assuaging the swindler's guilt and reducing the mark's motivation for retribution. Reporters are not swindlers, but there are some parallels in their relationships with sources. And to testify in court against someone whom one has already manipulated and exposed to painful publicity may seem unconscionable at worst and unpleasant at best. The reporter's feeling that he or she should not be forced to do a law enforcement agency's job is a very understandable and strongly felt one. But it may be pushing the First Amendment too far to use it to relieve reporters of such emotional burdens that go with the job.

Reluctance to Help Public Officials Get Off the Hook

There is yet another reason for the reluctance of news people to be party to legal proceedings related to their investigative work. When a newspaper uncovers specific instances of wrongdoing, it is often using those cases to illuminate a more general problem. But public officials will often ignore the general problem and respond to the illustrative cases as though they were isolated incidents. In addition, these officials sometimes behave as though they are more interested in punishing the reporter for revealing the problem than they are in eliminating its causes, and the main function of the subpoena is a punitive one.

In the Tofani case, it was perfectly clear that a general and ongoing problem had been aired by the *Post* series. Nevertheless, according to Downie, the grand jury went after only the people named by the reporter, not anybody else. The true moral of the story, that a reporter could walk in from outside and document a situation that had been ignored by officials inside the system, was lost amid the flurry of official attention to the specific instances. A reporter can't be blamed for not wanting to be a party to that kind of misdirection.

Tofani and her editors had a right to feel resentful. But not even justified resentment over the self-interested maneuverings of public officials is enough to make a First Amendment case. Overuse, particularly ineffectual use, can damage the First Amendment. To understand its particular fragility, we need to examine some other uses of the preferential arguments.

Press Privilege and the Issue of Prior Restraint

As we saw earlier, the preferred-position theory says that when First Amendment rights conflict with other constitutional guarantees, the First Amendment takes priority. It has been further argued that because freedom of speech and freedom of the press are mentioned separately in the Bill of Rights, the authors of the Constitution meant the press to receive special consideration. The latter argument has been received with even less sympathy than the former. And the question of just what the First Amendment basically protects remains to be resolved. Judicial precedents have given the amendment three levels of meaning, with decreasing levels of absolutism. At the most absolute level, the First Amendment means that there can be no prior censorship of the press.

This tradition is rooted in English common law and was well known by 1787, the year of the Constitutional Convention. Sir William Blackstone, in his influential *Commentaries*, wrote: "Every freeman has an undoubted right to lay what sentiments he pleases before the pulic; to forbid this is to destroy the freedom of the press; but if he publishes what is improper, mischievous and illegal, he must take the consequences of his own temerity."[12]

But recent court cases have held that not even prior censorship is absolutely forbidden. In 1971 the *New York Times* was blocked from publishing Neil Sheehan's reports on the Pentagon Papers for 15 days until it received a go-ahead from a divided Supreme Court. In 1979 *Progressive* magazine was restrained for six months from publishing an article that the government said contained information that could be useful in constructing a hydrogen bomb. The government relented after another publication released the same information.[13]

There remains, however, a strong presumption against prior restraint. Other sanctions may chill free speech, the Supreme Court said in 1976, but censorship "freezes" it.

At the second level of restriction, it is claimed that the First Amendment prevents newspapers from being punished for whatever they print. And at the third level, the amendment is held to prevent any government interference with the editorial process,—that is, with the activities of reporters and editors in gathering the news. It is at these two levels that exceptions are most often found and the issue of a chilling effect on free expression is most often raised. Among the exceptions are issues of obscenity, invasion of privacy, subversion, and—by far the most troublesome—libel.

The power of a civil litigant to collect damages for libel represents a very old form of restraint against freedom of speech and the press. A libel is publication that defames or damages the good name or reputation of someone. The main defense is also old: if you publish the truth *and* can prove it, nobody can collect libel damages from you. In 1964 the Supreme Court under Chief Justice Earl Warren handed the newspapers what appeared to be a marvelous gift in the form of a brand new and easier kind of protection. Recognizing the need in a democracy for "uninhibited, robust, and wide-open" debate about matters of public concern, it laid down tough new rules for public figures hoping to chill newspaper coverage through libel actions. The Court's ruling, in *New York Times Co.* v. *Sullivan,* removed from the newspaper the burden of proving the truth of what it had said and instead placed on the plaintiff the burden of proving that the newspaper had printed a falsehood with "actual malice," meaning that it had done so in the knowledge that the statement was false or "with reckless disregard of whether it was false or not."

This ruling removed some inhibitions from newspaper and broadcast reporting, and it helped news organizations become more aggressive in their investigative reporting where public figures were concerned. And how do you think newspapers reacted? Did they receive this gift with appropriate grace and humility, or did they scream for even more concessions from the Court?

You guessed it. It's hard to be a humble journalist. When the *Sullivan* rule shifted the burden of proof from the news writer to the news maker, it gave the press a degree of freedom never enjoyed before, but a new set of burdens was part of that package. If plaintiffs were forced to prove knowing and reckless falsehood to win a case, they had to have some means of getting at the facts. And how do you prove that a reporter knew he or she was telling a falsehood? You can't read the reporter's mind, but you can ask the reporter to tell under oath what he or she was thinking about and what was in his or her notes and what was said in staff conversations about the story in question. In 1979 the Burger Court ruled that a libel plaintiff could inquire into the editorial process to ask such questions about a reporter's state of mind when the alleged libel was written.[14] Such a ruling follows logically enough from the *Sullivan* case, and by itself it seems a reasonable price to pay for the great extension of editorial freedom that the *Sullivan* ruling provided. But the news people's reaction was more than shrill—it was hysterical.

Some editorial writers said the Court had reversed the *Sullivan* ruling. Some said newspapers could not function without a special privilege to protect them from such inquiries. One even said that truth would no longer be a defense in libel suits. Associate Justice William Brennan, Jr., a champion of a free press and a partial dissenter on the Burger Court's ruling, was appalled. Invited to give a speech at the dedication of the S.I. Newhouse Center for Law and Justice at Rutgers University on October 17, 1979, he used the occasion to urge the press to abandon the absolutist tack and face the real world.

"This may involve a certain loss of innocence," he said, "a certain recognition that the press, like other institutions, must accommodate a variety of important social interests. But the sad complexity of our society makes this inevitable, and there is no alternative but a shrill and impotent isolation."[15]

One can argue—and some newspaper people do—that a shrill, nagging, tireless, always adversarial response is the only way to hold the forces of restriction and oppression at bay. Give an inch on the smallest point, in their view, and you start tumbling down the slippery slope toward the bottomless pit of regimented expression. Brennan's point was that such a rigid policy is bad legal strategy. If you raise every argument you can think of, the unsound along with the sound, the sound will go unnoticed amid all the noise. And, legal stratagems aside, the strategy is impossible to defend from an ethical point of view because it depends on a selfish insistence that journalists are so special as to require freedom from the inconveniences that civic duty imposes on ordinary people. This is a lonely and precarious position.

It is also ineffective. Journalists have not been successful in convincing the courts or the public that they should have such privileges, even though they have produced some impressive anecdotal evidence of the existence of chilling effects. The most efficient and effective way for journalists to improve the free flow of information may be to clean up some of their own bad habits—as the *Washington Post* did when Loretta Tofani demonstrated that even difficult sources can be put on the record. Tofani accomplished that with hard work, building her information from the outside in, talking to the most cooperative sources, defense lawyers first, then judges, prison guards, medical workers, and victims. Only when she knew what had happened and when it happened did she talk to the prison rapists. Seeing how much she knew already, they gave the details without any promise of confidentiality from her. In her case, the Pulitzer Prize was well earned.

Fighting to uphold claims of privileged status is also hard work, and it isn't getting the press very far. News people might be better off if they abandoned their claims of privilege and cast their lot with the general public, fighting for their rights as public rights, not for recognition as a privileged class. They might feel better about themselves, too.

NOTES

1. *Ex Parte Randy Eli Grothe,* in the Court of Criminal Appeals of Texas. Application for writ of habeas corpus denied July 1984.

2. Letter to Madison on March 15, 1789, in Thomas Jefferson, *The Portable Thomas Jefferson,* ed. Merrill D. Peterson (New York: Viking Press, 1975), p. 439.

3. Kurt Luedtke, "The Twin Perils: Arrogance and Irrelevance," *Presstime,* June 1982, p. A-4.

4. Harold Evans refuted Luedtke in a meeting with my Seminar in Media Analysis at Chapel Hill, North Carolina, in the spring of 1984. His account of the thalidomide case is given in *Good Times, Bad Times* (New York: Atheneum, 1984).

5. See John Herman Randall, Jr., *The Making of the Modern Mind* (Boston: Houghton Mifflin, 1940).

6. Quoted in Bernard Bailyn, *The Ideological Origins of the American Revolution* (Cambridge, Mass: Harvard University Press, 1967).

7. Justice Stone's footnote may be found in *United States* v. *Carolene Products,* 1938.

8. David Shaw, *Press Watch* (New York: Macmillan, 1984).

9. *Public Opinion,* 1920.

10. Leonard Downie, remarks made at a seminar held by the Wisconsin Newspaper Association at Madison on March 15, 1984.

11. Tofani's reporting methods are described by Virginia Holcomb in "Surviving the Long Haul," *The Quill,* June 1984, p. 38.

12. Quoted in Edward S. Corwin, *The Constitution and What It Means Today* (New York: Atheneum, 1963).

13. *New York Times Co.* v. *United States,* 1971; *Nebraska Press Association* v. *Stuart,* 1976; *United States* v. *Progressive,* 1979.

14. *Herbert* v. *Lando,* 1979.

15. Quoted in *Editor & Publisher,* October 27, 1979.

CHAPTER 2

Codes of Ethics

In the ethos of journalism, there are two kinds of codes. One kind is written by a committee, is made public, and fairly honestly represents how journalists think they ought to behave. The other kind is unwritten, hidden sometimes from the consciousness of journalists themselves. Because it is often unconscious, this latter code is more difficult to describe and analyze, but it is the more powerful of the two.

Written Codes: ASNE, SPJ/SDX, and APME

There is no shortage of the first type of ethical code. The 1982 survey on newspaper ethics for the American Society of Newspaper Editors found that more than half the newspaper readers in the United States are served by editors who are aware of written codes of ethics or guidelines subscribed to by their newspapers.

"Could you," these editors were asked, "put your hands on it right now if you wanted to, or would you have to look around for a while to find it?" And editors serving 91 percent of the newspapers covered by these codes said it was accessible right now.

These codes are so visible because their writing has proceeded at a fairly fast pace in recent years, although newspaper lawyers have begun to advise against the practice. Plaintiffs' lawyers in libel actions, looking for ways to prove actual malice, have taken to citing the newspapers' own written codes as evidence that reporters and editors were recklessly disregarding their own standards. The newspaper lawyers' judgment that it is better to have no written standards than to have them used against you may be sound legal thinking, but law and ethics are not always compatible. When editors and publishers blindly put legal stratagems ahead of everything else, as some appear to do, they are abdicating their ethical responsibility to lawyers. It is a responsibility which lawyers are not particularly well equipped to handle.

Written codes are often criticized for being of little help in making decisions. The values they list are obvious values, the behaviors enjoined are clearly bad behaviors. Ethics is more complicated than that.

Louis Hodges of Washington and Lee University, explaining the problem to a group of investigative reporters, said that ethics is concerned with what one "ought" to do. And "ought," it turns out, is a peculiar word, an auxiliary verb stemming from an archaic form of "to owe." We sometimes owe, Hodges said, different and conflicting things to different people, groups, or ideals.[1] It is when such conflicts occur that ethical decisions have to be made. Having a list of unethical behaviors to pull out of a desk drawer and look at when a decision has to be made is not of much help if the decision involves a choice in which at least one of the caveats on the list will be violated no matter what you do. And the real world puts everyone—particularly news people, it seems—in exactly those situations of conflict. However, a code can be a starting point in defining exactly what has to be resolved.

There have been two great waves of codification amid concern for newspaper ethics. The first came in the 1920s, when newspaper people began to feel enough of a professional identity to form associations. The American Society of Newspaper Editors approved a code at its first meeting in 1923, a year when public consciousness of ethical problems had been raised by the leasing to private interests of government oil reserves at Teapot Dome in Wyoming.[2] The second wave came in a time of parallel concerns after the Watergate burglary. The current ASNE code was adopted as a "statement of principles"—some members objected to having a code per se—in 1975. The Associated Press Managing Editors adopted its code in 1975, and the Society of Professional Journalists/Sigma Delta Chi acted in 1973. In 1984 SPJ/SDX began exploring the possibility of adding sanctions for violations to its code, an unusual step for news people, but not unprecedented. In 1926 the ASNE board of directors declared F. G. Bonfils, editor and publisher of the *Denver Post,* "censured and suspended from membership in the Society" for his participation in the Teapot Dome scandal. While his newspaper was reporting the scandal, Bonfils had obtained a financial interest in the outcome—some said as a blackmail payoff—and thus stood to gain from the success of a transaction that the newspaper was denouncing. "Such a dual relation. . . is conducive to the weakening or destruction of public confidence in the newspaper press," the ASNE resolution said.[3]

The resolution was not publicized. Nevertheless, Bonfils threatened to sue the society and each director for slander and offered a deal. If the society would rescind its action, he would resign. ASNE took him up on it, thus establishing, as its own historian, Nathaniel R. Howard, later said, "that ASNE did not have the muscle and lacked the authority to punish anyone."

Present-day codes are similarly lacking in muscle. They are full of glittering generalities. "A good newspaper is fair, accurate, honest, responsible, independent and decent," says the APME code. Journalists are obliged to "perform with intelligence, objectivity, accuracy and fairness," echoes the SPJ/SDX code.[4]

Concern for Appearances

As if recognizing a major problem of ambiguity, each of the codes of the three major newspaper professional organizations does a peculiar thing. Each warns against the "appearance" of evil as well as the substance. Why this concern for appearances? Are the writers of these codes telling us that appearances are as important as the underlying realities? Perhaps what they are trying to say is that ethical problems are so murky and unfathomable that, just to be on the safe side, a journalist should avoid anything that even looks bad, whether it is bad in fact or not. If this is indeed the intent, it is peculiar advice coming from organizations that are dedicated to discovering and disclosing the truth, because they seem to be saying that in ethical matters, truth is unknowable. Consider these excerpts:

APME: "Even the *appearance* of obligation or conflict of interest should be avoided."

SPJ/SDX: "Journalists and their employers should conduct their personal lives in a manner which protects them from conflict of interest, real or *apparent*."

ASNE: "Journalists must avoid impropriety and the *appearance* of impropriety as well as any conflict of interest or the *appearance* of conflict." (Italics added.)

This concern for appearances has deep roots. In all professions, codes tend to follow the form of past abuses. By reading any organization's code, you can get a picture of its previous sins. And the codes may persist long after the objective reasons for their existence have vanished. Nelson Antrim Crawford, writing on the ethics of journalism in 1924, reported that some large newspapers had a rule against selling large numbers of any one issue to a single buyer without an investigation and approval by the general manager. The reason dated to the early the nineteenth century, when many newspapers were the organs of specific commercial or political interests. Well into the twentieth century, readers were prone to suspect such connections. Thus, when a newspaper contained an editorial defending the railroads, it would be embarrassed if a railroad company bought thousands of copies, marked the editorial, and sent them to opinion leaders. "For this reason," wrote Crawford, "the newspaper would be wholly justified in refusing to sell any copies to the railroad company. It would thus avoid the appearance of evil."[5]

The codes' unanimous concern for appearances suggests a disturbing possibility: that newspaper people basically see ethics as a public relations problem rather than a matter of pursuing good for its own sake. This is a theme to which we shall return often in this book. However, another possibility is that the concern for appearances in the language of codes merely stems from impatience with the amount of time and reflection needed to make fine distinctions. Prohibiting all that merely appears evil along with the activities that are in fact evil can certainly save time and discussion. Such a shortcut may, however, come at some cost. It may be that painstaking reflection and weighing of values is exactly what newspaper people need, and a code of ethics that holds that *looking* bad is as much to be enjoined as *being* bad may short-circuit the process.

The belief that ethical concerns are basically public relations problems is heard often in the news business. "The public doesn't understand us" is a common theme in trade journals, and news people often exhort one another to do a better job of explaining themselves to the public. Editors hold this belief with particular zeal. In the ASNE survey, news people were asked to agree or disagree with the following statement:

Public concern over newspaper ethics is caused less by the things newspapers do than by their failure to explain what they do.

Editors representing 72 percent of total newspaper circulation in the United States agreed with that statement. For publishers, agreement was 68 percent, and for staff members, it was 60 percent. Among all the groups, this view of ethics as mainly a public relations problem was found more often at smaller papers than at large ones. This is one of many interesting differences that will be explored in a later chapter. The finding suggests that big-city news people are either more sensitive to ethical problems or have more ethical problems to be sensitive about.

Because of the ambiguities in codes, it may be that their main benefit is in the process rather than in the final product. All the work of articulating a professional group's values can make the participants think about what those values are. The time spent in analysis and giving the system form and structure clarifies the group's standards for outsiders and for novices in the group, as well as clarifying the thinking of the insiders. But an ethical system that concentrates on appearance for appearance's sake misses even this benefit. The discussion then becomes one not of what *is* bad, but of what *looks* bad. To try to see through the reader's eyes in a search for the detectable sins is to miss the main point.

In all three of the codes, the concern for appearances crops up in the section on conflict of interest. It is in this area that ambiguity looms largest. Discussions can become so abtruse that perhaps the only way to end one is to say, "Well, even if it isn't a conflict, it looks like one, and we shouldn't do it because of the appearance of conflict." That may indeed end the discussion and provide a rationale for a decision to avoid some questionable course of action, but it creates more ambiguity than it resolves, because the possibilities for the appearance of conflict are endless. When it comes down to cases, as will be shown in a close look at the ASNE survey data, the appearance of a conflict depends less on the objective facts of a situation than on the social desirability element in the conflict. Thus, it may seem desirable for a farmer's son to cover agriculture but undesirable for an oil explorer's daughter to cover energy. The structure of the two situations is identical, but farmers are currently more popular than oil explorers. This particular difference was measured when news people were given a variety of situations and asked to assess whether "the reporter's personal history or circumstances are likely to be a help, a hindrance, or make any difference in covering the indicated field." One of the situations was, "A reporter whose parents run an independent oil exploration business is

TABLE 2.1

	Energy	Agriculture
Help	31%	95%
No difference	23	5
Hindrance	46	0
	100%	100%

assigned to cover energy." Another was, "A reporter who was raised on a farm is assigned to cover agriculture." Table 2.1 summarizes the responses among editors, with the percentages representing the proportion of total U.S. circulation for which they are responsible:

Editors are being perfectly rational here, because they know that readers are more likely to complain about the wildcatter's offspring than about the farm kid, even though the reporter's family's financial stake in public policy may be equally great in both cases. Part of the difference is also sheer numbers. There are more farmers than wildcatters, and if you eliminate everyone who ever lived on a farm as a reporter on agriculture, you wipe out a sizable proportion of the potential work force. But appearance—really a shorthand way of expressing concern over how the public might react—is a strong force in editors' attitudes, and the explicit concern with appearances in the codes is understandable even though it often gets in the way of logical analysis.

Other Areas of Concern

The content of the three principal codes gives a useful guide to the kinds of things that news people worry about—and, by omission, to some things that they perhaps do not worry about enough. Each of the three codes has a section on "responsibility." The ASNE statement uses this section to do an excellent job of summarizing the First Amendment theory: "The American press was made free not just to inform or just to serve as a forum for debate but also to bring an independent scrutiny to bear on the forces of power in the society, including the conduct of official power at all levels of government." All three make some reference to the preservation of "the public's right to know" as a part of the press's responsibility.

All three codes give considerable emphasis to accuracy. Each includes a specific provision for running a correction whenever a newspaper has made a mistake.

Each code makes a strong statement of impartiality and fairness. In all three cases, this section includes a requirement for separating news and opinion by clearly labeling material that is the writer's or the newspaper's opinion rather than verifiable fact. The APME code goes somewhat further than the other two with a specific admonition against giving favored treatment to advertisers in news stories. And APME is the only group to acknowledge that newspapers sometimes have a problem in reporting straightforwardly on their own affairs. A newspaper should, according to APME, "report matters regarding itself or its personnel with the same vigor and candor as it would other institutions or individuals."

ASNE and SPJ/SDX acknowledge a right of reply when material critical of a person is published, but APME is silent on this point. A bow to the right to privacy is made by SPJ/SDX and APME, although both are vague about it. APME says merely that a newspaper person should "respect the individual's right to privacy," while SPJ/SDX says that journalists should "show respect for the dignity, privacy, rights and well-being of people encountered in the course of gathering and presenting the news." Two paragraphs later, the subject is brought up again without adding much clarification: "The news media must guard against invading a person's right to privacy." ASNE does not mention privacy at all, settling instead for a general statement that journalists should "respect the rights of people involved in the news."

The three groups differ significantly on the problem of granting confidentiality to news sources. APME emphasizes the importance of avoiding attributions to unnamed sources and, when a source is kept anonymous, explaining the reasons for secrecy. APME's code makes no mention of the ethics of keeping or violating a pledge of confidentiality, sometimes a major dilemma for news people. SPJ/SDX is somewhat cryptic, saying only, "Journalists acknowledge the newsman's ethic of protecting confidential sources of information." ASNE is the most direct of the three, asserting that promises of confidentiality should not be given in the absence of "clear and pressing need" and adding that such pledges, once given, should be honored "at all costs."

On the matter of conflict of interest, both APME and SPJ/SDX go to considerable effort to detail the kinds of situations that are conflicting. Both caution against accepting gifts or employment from news sources, for example. APME goes so far as to caution against writing stories primarily for the purpose of winning awards, recognizing one of the subtle ways that outside influence can affect newspaper content.

ASNE makes no such attempt to detail the nature of conflict, giving only its caution against conflict or the appearance of conflict and adding that newspaper people "should neither accept anything nor pursue any activity that might compromise or seem to compromise their integrity."

What none of the codes does or even attempts to do is provide some guidance on how a news person should proceed when forced to choose between violating one aspect of a code and violating another. Situations occur almost daily, for example, when impartial reporting of all sides of an issue requires invasion of someone's privacy. When such a conflict arises, it is almost always the right to privacy that yields, but nowhere does any of the codes establish such a priority.

To set priorities in advance may be asking too much of a code. Perhaps such fine distinctions can be made only on a case-by-case basis. What is needed, then, is some public discussion of individual cases held up to the light and evaluated according to the codes—and not just in academic seminars. Making public judgments in individual cases is the necessary next step that the newspaper industry has not been willing to take since ASNE's abortive move against Bonfils in 1926.

The Debate over Enforcement

Proponents of ethics codes see them as a defense against regulation of the press. Foes see them as a first step toward regulation. One of the outspoken foes of codes is Michael Gartner, former editor of the *Des Moines Register.* "They all have one thing in common," he told a panel at Duke University in 1984. "They don't work. . . . The main value of the ethics code seems to be that it is something to cite when disciplining a reporter who has done something wrong or stupid."

If the function of a code is to make bad people good, Gartner is no doubt correct. But if, as ethicist Bruce Payne of Duke's Institute of Policy Science, argues, the main value of codes is that they "help the process of discourse," then codes are useful and can be made more useful still. If APME, SPJ/SDX, or ASNE were to add sanctions to their codes, anyone who expected those organizations to then systematically locate all or even most miscreants and punish them would be disappointed. But if the codes were applied in just a few highly visible cases, the intensity of discussion that surrounded the writing of the codes could be maintained. The discourse would continue and consciousness of ethical distinctions would be raised. And that is what is most likely to happen if one or more of the major professional associations does decide to put teeth into its codes.

Because of the lack of examples of code enforcement in journalism, we are forced to look elsewhere to see how the process might work. The experience of the American Association for Public Opinion Research, on whose executive council I served during a code enforcement action in 1983-1984, provides a useful illustration. The goals of AAPOR overlap those of journalists in some respects. Both are dedicated to discovering and imparting the truth with accuracy and impartiality. Like the news organizations, AAPOR has a code. Unlike them, it has an enforcement mechanism. This mechanism is thorough, unwieldy, and exhausting. Because all the work is done by volunteers, the process can accommodate no more than one or two full-blown cases a year. Complaints of possible code violations are received by a committee of the board and, if found worthy of further action, referred to a special investigating committee convened for that purpose. If the special committee finds the complaint valid, the issue is referred to the full executive council. If the council accepts the report, it schedules a hearing at which the person or organization under investigation may appear to respond to the charges.

In 1984 this procedure led to a finding by a divided executive council that Cambridge Survey Research, headed by Pat Caddell, who had been President Jimmy Carter's pollster, had failed to observe a section of the AAPOR code which states, "We shall exercise due care in gathering and processing data, taking all reasonable steps to assure the accuracy of results." At issue was a poll conducted by Caddell's group for a candidate in the June 1982 Democratic gubernatorial primary in Ohio. One of the questions in the poll presented as fact some inaccurate details of an opposing candidate's sexual escapade and arrest on a morals charge. Respondents were then asked if this knowledge made them "more likely, somewhat more likely, much less likely, or somewhat less likely" to support the candidate. There had indeed been an escapade and an arrest, as the candidate freely admitted, but some of the details in the question were wrong; for example, the number of prostitutes involved was less than the three mentioned by the interviewers. Investigators were satisfied that the question had not been intended to spread an exaggerated story but was a genuine attempt to assess the effect of the eight-year-old incident on the campaign. In fact, the survey organization had made a public apology as soon as the error was discovered and the content of the question appeared in some newspapers. What concerned the council was whether, considering the sensitivity of the information, sufficient care had been taken to ensure its accuracy. It decided that "due care" had not been taken.

The formal action of the council was limited to publishing its report in the *AAPOR News Letter*. But many other things happened. The issue was extensively discussed. Council members decided that the code did not adequately cover such cases, and they initiated a review of their standards. Officials of Cambridge Survey Research offered to assist in the review. As it happened, I was in the minority of the council that did not believe a violation had occurred, but I still saw benefits in the procedure. Discourse over ethical standards was continuing, the process of making distinctions was under way, and consciousness was being raised. Nothing focuses your mind on an ethical problem quite so much as the need to decide a particular case. And even if only a very few cases reach that stage, the exercise is valuable.

Application of their codes by organizations of newspaper professionals could follow the same pattern: without attempting to right every wrong, they could pick those cases that seem to represent the most visible or the most flagrant violations of the codes. They could give such cases a thorough airing and let their only action be a simple finding that what had happened was right, wrong, or something in between. This process could clear a lot of foul air.

Unwritten Codes

Analysis of unwritten codes is much more difficult. Unwritten rules can become so deeply embedded in the newsroom culture that they need never be made explicit to be enforced, but can exist simply as a set of reflexes. Finding and defining them must be done by indirect means. James F. Goodpaster of Harvard University's Graduate School of Business Administration suggested to a seminar of New England newspaper people that one way to make them visible would be to interview new staff members. Newcomers would still be in the process of learning the rules, so for them the local peculiarities would still be at a conscious level—and therefore accessible to analysis.

Even among veterans, however, a few of the unwritten rules are fairly freely acknowledged because their application is so obvious. Here are some that come readily to mind.

Rule No. 1: *A story originated by another medium is never as newsworthy as one originated by one's own paper.*

This rule is manifested by what columnist Russell Baker has called "the tendency to piss all over the other guy's story, to hope that the story will go away because it makes you look bad for missing it."[6] J. Anthony Lukas, who chronicled the Watergate period for the *New York Times,* believes that this impulse is one reason the *Washington Post* was alone in its intensive coverage of the Watergate story in the months between the burglary and Richard Nixon's 1972 reelection.

This is a pure example of an unwritten rule in that it is widely followed and it directly contradicts what everyone says is right. In the ASNE survey, editors and publishers were asked to choose among four courses of action in a situation where a paper had been beaten on a key story. None of the publishers, none of the staff members, and only a trivial number of editors, representing about 1 percent of national circulation, said the story should be downgraded or ignored. The only controversy was over whether the opposition should be given credit for breaking the story; a modest majority said it should.

Rule No. 2: *Newspapers are written for other newspaper people, not for the general reader.*

This rule is related to the first one. Thus, if the afternoon paper breaks a good story in a two-paper town, the morning paper may ignore it or give it far less space than it deserves, even though the story would still be news to the great majority of its readers. News people are often victims of the sample-of-one fallacy, in which they generalize from their own peculiar sets of interests and project them onto the public at large. The morning paper's reporter will not be very excited about rewriting the afternoon paper's story because the people he or she cares about—other newspaper people—will have already read it even if the morning readers have not.

In its wider application, this rule makes news people strive for the spectacular at the expense of the basics. They would rather write long, intricate stories that show off their prose skills than provide the simple day-to-day information that readers need most. That is why some newspapers can do a very good job of covering the big breaking story, such as a local storm disaster or an airplane crash, but a poor job on such mundane basics as local crime reports, school activities, housing costs, or what movies are playing within easy driving distance.

Rule No. 3: *Avoid directly admitting a mistake.*

Not nearly as popular as it once was, the rule works like this. If you were elected president of the local Rotary Club and the newspaper reported that you were elected president of the Lions, the paper would find some reason to mention your name again, perhaps in a story on one of your planned projects for the club, and take care to connect you with the Rotary this time. And that is all the correction there would be.

Two additional covert rules related to this one were teased out of the ASNE data. In the survey, editors, publishers, and staff members were asked to judge the best response to each of a variety of ethical dilemmas expressed in brief, anecdotal form. A computer search for patterns in the responses turned up some clusters of responses that can best be explained by the existence of informal or hidden codes. Consider, for example, the following problem:

> A prominent citizen is vacationing in Key West, and his hotel burns down. The wire service story lists him among those who escaped uninjured and identifies the hotel as a popular gathering place for affluent gays. The citizen says he'll commit suicide if you publish his name in the story. Should the editor:
> a. Publish the story in full.
> b. Publish the story, but without mentioning the gay angle.
> c. Publish the story, but without mentioning the local citizen.
> d. Kill the story.

About the only argument among the news people who participated in this survey was between the first two choices. If their views prevailed, you could expect newspapers with about 42 percent of the newspaper circulation in the United States to publish the story in full. Another 49 percent would publish the story without the gay angle. That leaves only 9 percent for the third choice, omitting the man's name, and none at all in favor of dropping the story. (Responses in this survey were weighted by circulation size, which is why percentages are always expressed in terms of total U.S. newspaper circulation.)

This situation is not at all contrived. Subjects of news stories have made such threats, and some have carried them out. When such a threat is made, there is no way for an editor to know whether or not it is sincere. And while no single story can be worth a human life, it is impossible to know which of the many threats of this sort are idle and which will be carried out. An editor who yielded to all of them would be handing over a censorship power to anyone emotionally unstable enough to make such a threat; it is yet another version of the slippery-slope problem. But is the slope so steep and dangerous that an editor should never modify his or her behavior on behalf of a distraught news subject? Most news people, as the survey shows, would make some modification—in the form of suppressing the gay angle—but hardly any would honor the request to omit the name. And a very sizable minority would make no accommodation with the citizen's wishes at all.

This question, then, neatly divides news people into two groups, those who would do something in response to such a request and those who would do nothing at all. Are they following some inner rule or merely deciding on a case-by-case basis? The evidence for an inner rule begins to accumulate when we consider another question whose answers are significantly related to the responses just described.

Under which of the following circumstances should a newspaper publish material from leaked grand jury transcripts:
a. Whenever the material is newsworthy.
b. Whenever the importance of the material revealed outweighs the damage to the system from the breaching of its security.
c. Only if the material exposes flaws in the workings of the grand jury system itself, e.g., it shows the prosecutor to be acting improperly.
d. Never.

On this question, a common one, there is a wider division than in the case of the Key West hotel fire. Across the three groups—editors, publishers, and staff people—there was 20 percent support for the first alternative, 57 percent for the second, 17 percent for the third, and only 6 percent for never publishing. The first alternative rather clearly identifies the First Amendment fundamentalists, those who believe that the democratic need for a free flow of information routinely justifies a breach of the traditional secrecy of the grand jury system. The next, and most popular, response represents situation ethics at work, a belief in weighing the merits and peculiarities of each case.

The third choice involves some fairly subtle thinking on both an ethical and a legal level. An ethical rule or a statute can be valid generally and still be justifiably violated if it is being employed to perpetuate an abuse of the system it is intended to support. Neither law nor ethics likes a Catch-22 situation. This is the sort of fine reasoning, for example, that enabled the Supreme Court to breach its constitutional barrier against interfering in state political processes to attack malapportionment in state legislatures. The question went to the basic democratic operation of the system itself, and only an externally imposed solution could have had any effect. Following similar logic, grand jury secrecy could ethically be violated without disrespect for the system if such a violation is the only way to right a wrong in the system.

What does all of this have to do with the vacationer at the gay hotel? It turns out that there is an interesting overlap between the news people who would not give in at all to the entreaties of the man from the gay hotel and those who think it is always acceptable to publish newsworthy material from leaked grand jury transcripts. Since the content of the two cases is totally different, there must be some underlying factor that is determining the outcome. That factor might be defined as First Amendment fundamentalism, the belief that publication always comes first. Or it might be simply the basic urge to publish; in spite of adverse consequences, in spite of special circumstances, the mission of the newspaper is to publish, always to publish.

Support for this notion comes from a third item in the survey. This one asks about possible actions for an editor to take when a family, through no fault of its own, is suddenly thrust into national attention. A range of alternatives is offered, ranging from doing nothing to organizing pool coverage to ease the burden on the family. Those who would do nothing, representing about 24 percent of total circulation, had a likelihood greater than chance of being found among those who would do nothing for the Key West vacationer and who would routinely violate grand jury secrecy. All of the formal codes say it is a newspaper's duty to enlighten the public. None says it should do so at all costs. But the survey suggests that, for many, this is another hidden ethic.

Rule No. 4: *Always publish, regardless of the costs.*
Some news people have more restraint than others, and a measure of a news person's capacity for restraint can be made from the three items in the survey. In each of the three questions, two of the four alternatives define somewhat more restraint than the majority is willing to accept. By awarding each person in the survey one point for a restraining answer, we can create an index. The distribution of restraint, thus rather arbitrarily defined, is as follows:

Number of situations where restraint is called for

0	1	2	3
63%	28%	8%	1%

The survey found more of a tendency toward self-restraint among older publishers than young ones. Perhaps as a publisher ages, he or she becomes more careful, less willing to take the opprobrium or complaint that results from a publish-at-any-price policy. If age is the only factor, we would expect it to apply to editors as well, but it doesn't. Younger editors tend to be more restrained than older ones.

Something else must be the cause of this restraint-prone quality. And a search through the data does indeed turn up something else. Restraint among editors, publishers, and staff members alike is much higher in smaller towns —and smaller towns tend to have younger editors, the people who are just starting out on the fast track of journalism. The reasons for greater restraint in smaller towns are plain enough. The psychological costs of publication are much higher there. The editor is more likely to be personally acquainted with the traveling homosexual, the grand jury members, the family in the spotlight. When the pain one inflicts is visible, it becomes much more difficult to decide purely on the basis of abstract principles. The effect of city size is,

TABLE 2.2
READERS SERVED BY RESTRAINT-PRONE NEWS PEOPLE

	Small Papers	Medium Papers	Large Papers
Editors	50%	30%	18%
Publishers	57	36	27
Staff	49	37	28

as we would expect, the most pronounced for editors, but it is visible for publishers and staff members as well (see Table 2.2).

The cutoff points for newspaper size in the above table are at circulations of 40,000 and 200,000. These cuts provide a roughly equal division of readers. A third of the newspaper readers represented in the sample are served by papers of less than 40,000 circulation, another third by papers of more than 40,000 but less than 200,000, and the remainder by papers of more than 200,000 circulation. And the reader of a smaller paper is far more likely to have a restraint-prone editor than the reader of one of the larger papers.

If paper size, not the age of the news person, is the most important factor, then the age effect should tend to disappear when we look for it within a single category of newspaper size. And, among the small and medium papers, this is just what happens. When circulation is less than 100,000, city size explains it all.

On larger papers, however, the age effect persists. For readers of these papers, a young (under 47) editor is twice as likely to be high on the restraint scale as an older editor. Do big-city editors get tougher as they age? One big-city editor, William F. Thomas of the *Los Angeles Times,* thinks they just get smarter. "Experience seems to me the more likely factor, not toughness of mind," he says. "All editors learn sooner or later that decisions not to publish can create problems from many directions—internal and external—unless they are based on pretty firm and clearly understood grounds."[7]

One of the costs of not publishing is that somebody else might, and the restrained editor will look foolish for holding back. This risk is higher in competitive markets, and the data show that there is indeed less support for restraint among news people in these markets. However, the risk is accepted under exceptional circumstances. In 1972 the *Detroit Free Press* received an anonymous tip that the Democratic nominee for vice-president, Missouri Senator Thomas Eagleton, had a history of mental illness. Clark Hoyt and Robert S. Boyd of the Knight Newspapers Washington bureau investigated and got enough evidence to write a story. Before publishing, they imparted the details to the Democratic presidential nominee, Senator George McGovern, and waited for him and Eagleton to respond. While they were waiting, McGovern summoned Eagleton to a meeting, and after the meeting Eagleton held a press conference. There he made his own disclosure, running Knight's exclusive. He did it, he admitted, to forestall publication of the newspapers' version. It didn't do him any good. He eventually withdrew from the ticket, and McGovern praised the reporters for acting "responsibly." Boyd and Hoyt, in a significant departure from tradition, won the Pulitzer Prize. The judges felt that it was the investigation and its effect that mattered, not whether the story was exclusive.[8] But there is no evidence that the incident undermined the journalism folklore precept that publishing is the only value.

One predictor of how tenaciously a newspaper person will cling to this value is the level of civic activity in which he or she engages. The more active are also more likely to support some restraint. Civic activity was measured in the survey by the number of local voluntary organizations a news person belonged to—including churches, civic clubs, charitable organizations, veterans' groups, and the like. Publishers belonged to seven such groups on the average, compared to two for editors and one for staff members.

Community size is certainly a factor here. It is easier for a news person in a large town to avoid civic activity by taking the position that it would hinder—or at least appear to hinder—his or her impartiality. Regardless of the size of the town, reporters hate to cover organizations where their editors or publishers are active and highly visible. Doing so can't help their careers, they reason, and it might hurt, because the boss will be paying special attention, perhaps for the wrong reasons. However, those news people who do not participate at all may risk isolating themselves from the community.

At the 1982 meeting of ASNE in Chicago, Judee and Michael Burgoon of Michigan State University spoke of the insularity of many news people and noted survey data of their own indicating that those with few community contacts were more satisfied with their newspapers' professional standards. That can be good news or bad news, depending on how optimistic you are. On the one hand, civic involvement may be a corrupting influence, leading news people to shirk their duty of putting all relevant information before the public. On the other hand, civic involvement may sensitize news people to the consequences of what they do, making them more willing to consider restraint. Whether this sensitivity can be classed as corruption depends on how far it goes. The ethical problem is to find the balance. The knee-jerk response of the First Amendment fundamentalists to always publish, no matter the cost, may be right most of the time. But it does prevent the issue from being considered as an ethical problem.

One other hidden ethic of the newspaper business was found among the computer printouts from the ASNE survey. Consider the following question (the percentages represent all responses):

> Some newspaper companies in Florida donated money to a campaign to defeat a statewide referendum which, if passed, would have legalized gambling. Which of the following statements comes closest to your view on this action?
> a. A newspaper that takes an editorial stand on an issue has a right, and possibly even a duty, to back up its belief with its money. (13 percent)

b. The contributions are justified if the referendum would have a detrimental effect on the business climate in which the newspaper operates. (5 percent)
c. The contributions should not have been made because they might lead readers to question the objectivity of the papers' news coverage. (30 percent)
d. No political contributions should ever be made by newspapers; the news and editorial columns make us powerful enough already, and adding money only indicates inappropriate hunger for more power. (53 percent)

This question was based on a real incident that happened in Florida in 1978, although the four alternatives are oversimplifications of what was, to the publishers involved, a very complex problem. The majority position—that the newspapers should have confined their participation to news and editorial coverage—is consistent with First Amendment fundamentalism, one tenet of which is that newspapers should do their job from a remote and uninvolved vantage point. But there is more going on here than that.

Responses to the above question were correlated with responses to the following:

An investigative reporter discovers a former city employee now living in another state who has evidence of a kickback scheme involving the mayor and half the city council. He appears interested in cooperating with your investigation, but indicates he will want money. Should your paper:
a. Pay an honorarium based on the news value of the story. (6 percent)
b. Put him on the payroll for the time that he spends working with your staff in gathering and documenting the facts, plus expenses. (8 percent)
c. Pay his out-of-pocket expenses only. (33 percent)
d. Pay nothing. (53 percent)

There is no First Amendment issue here. Although it is often discussed as an ethical issue, checkbook journalism may be more a business dilemma than an ethical problem. It is hard to see how the public interest is helped or hurt one way or another, at least directly. If news media have to spend their money in auctions for source cooperation, checkbook journalism may reduce the amount of money that can be spent on other coverage. It may be unfair to media with fewer resources. It may lead sources to exaggerate their stories in the hope of increasing their market value. All of these objections are speculative. No one has demonstrated that these things happen, and the questions really involve the issue of how to get the most bang for a buck in news gathering, which is a business issue.

What is interesting about this particular item is that the people who don't want to pay the source tend to be the same ones who don't want to make a contribution to the anti-referendum campaign. And all these two actions have in common is that they both involve writing a check! Have we uncovered a tightwad element in the newspaper business?

More than that is involved. Two other questions were part of the same cluster. One involved the issue of whether a newspaper should own a sports franchise—as in the case of the *Chicago Tribune,* which owned the Chicago Cubs baseball team when the question was asked, and Ridder Publications, which owned the Minnesota Vikings football team before the company was folded into Knight-Ridder. The news people who think a newspaper should not have a business interest in a sports team (about 20 percent) have a better-than-chance likelihood of being among those who are against writing checks to news sources or referenda campaigns.

One more item fits into this same puzzle. It deals with a hypothetical case in which a reporter finds out about a technological advance in a popular item of home electronics equipment, and advertisers want the story suppressed until they can unload their inventory of equipment made obsolescent by the new development. Hardly anyone was for suppressing the story, of course, but about two out of five thought the ad manager might justifiably ask that the story be double-checked for accuracy, given its sensitive nature. And the news people who did not want even that modest desire communicated to editors tended to be those who did not want the paper to pay sources, contribute to the anti-gambling cause, or own a sports team.

What is the underlying element that ties these diverse problems together? They all involve money. The underlying attitude is similar to one held by my wife's grandmother, the late Helen Gertrude Peppard, who was fond of saying, "If it comes to money, I'm against it." What we seem to have here is an outcropping of the historic antipathy between the news side and the business side of the newspaper. All involve some risk of business-office influence in the operation of the news room. And the taboo against such influence is so strong that it constitutes another hidden rule:

Rule No. 5: *If it involves money, it is probably bad.*
Support for the existence of such a standard is found when we compare the attitudes of editors, publishers, and staff members on these questions. We can create another index, awarding one point for the extreme antibusiness (or antimoney) response in each of the above four cases. If, for convenience, we classify as business-aversive anyone who gave the extreme response at least twice, we find that 61 percent of newspaper circulation is represented by news people with this characteristic. And editors have it more than publishers. The distribution:

	Publishers	*Editors*	*Staff*
Business aversion	51%	65%	67%

A reporter to whom I disclosed this finding in a seedy bar on Biscayne Boulevard in Miami said it was probably true and attributed it to cognitive dissonance. Reporters delight in using jargon from other fields. This was a reference to psychologist Leon Festinger's theory that your emotions can sometimes lead you to hold contradictory views, the contradiction makes you uncomfortable, and your mind seeks an escape from the contradiction by altering its perception. For newspaper reporters, my drinking companion said, it works like a sort of syllogism:

1. Reporters are good people.
2. Reporters never have any money.
3. Therefore, money is bad.

That publishers have less of this business-aversive quality supports this logic because publishers have more money. As business people, they are also more likely to see money in a nonemotional context, thinking of its instrumental value as something to be used as efficiently as possible for the good of the company.

Anyone in the newspaper business who follows the money-is-evil rule religiously is probably going to be right a good deal of the time. The trouble with following it religiously is that it is not going to be right all of the time, and substituting a knee-jerk or gut reaction for analysis and reflection can prevent a news person from recognizing those exceptional cases. This is the problem with all five of the hidden rules: Because they are hidden, they escape analysis.

The root of the anti-money or business-aversion rule can probably be found in the historical separation of editorial and business sides, and that separation was itself the response to another historical problem of newspaper ethics. That history and where it has led us is the topic of the next chapter.

NOTES

1. Louis Hodges, remarks made to a regional meeting of Investigative Reporters and Editors at Richmond, Virginia, March 31, 1984.
2. The 1923 ASNE Code is reprinted in Appendix III, page 247.
3. Quoted in Bill Hosokawa, *Thunder in the Rockies* (New York: Morrow, 1976), pp. 146–147.
4. The ASNE, SPJ/SDX, and APME codes may be found in Appendix III, page 247.
5. Nelson Antrim Crawford, *The Ethics of Journalism* (New York: Greenwood Press, 1956).
6. Quoted in J. Anthony Lukas, *Nightmare: The Underside of the Nixon Years* (New York: Viking Press, 1976).
7. Quoted by Robert H. Phelps in his foreword to my monograph, "Editors, Publishers and Newspaper Ethics," (Reston, Va.: American Society of Newspaper Editors, 1983).
8. "Pulitzer Prizes," *The Quill,* June 1973, p. 28.

PART TWO

The Major Problems

CHAPTER 3

Advertiser Influence

Once in Miami I had a dispute with a car dealer. It was over a trivial matter, whether he or I was responsible for paying a small fee for the paperwork in our transaction. Perhaps it was the tropical heat that made it seem more important than it was. In any event, we were starting to raise our voices. Suddenly, looking at me suspiciously, he said, "Say, what kind of work do you do?"

I jumped at the opening. While I would certainly not use my newspaper connection to put pressure on this guy, I thought, there was nothing wrong with answering his question. Now he would have to watch his step. As casually as I could, I dropped the name of the *Miami Herald*. Then I waited to see how images of investigative reporters, consumer columns, and an outspoken editorial page would throw fear into his heart.

"Boy," he said. "You better watch your step. Do you know how much we spend on advertising in the *Herald* every week?"

I paid up and left, perhaps out of guilt for even thinking of using the newspaper in that way. It was not out of worry about jeopardizing the *Herald*'s advertising revenue. But the belief that buyers of advertising get some fringe benefits with their contracts or can use those contracts as leverage in other dealings with the newspaper or its personnel is a persistent one. It has some historical basis in fact—and, unfortunately, some present-day basis as well.

The first daily newspapers in the United States were established in the coastal cities, and social historian Michael Schudson has described them as "little more than bulletin boards for the business community."[1] They were expensive and contained mostly ads, some editorial comment, and listings of ship arrivals and their contents. The few newspapers that were not business-oriented were the tools of political parties, factions, or candidates. Whether a paper was backed by a political or a commercial interest, an editor was subservient to that interest. And advertisers who bought space were concerned about advancing that interest as well as gaining any direct benefit from carrying their message to the small readership.

Advertiser Influence: The Model

That equation changed when Benjamin Day founded the first of the penny papers, the *New York Sun,* in the late summer of 1833. Within three years, the *Sun*'s circulation reached 27,000, which was 26 percent more than the combined circulation of the 11 traditional papers, which still had their traditional formats and six-cent price. Day's innovations included editorial independence and a strong effort to build reader loyalty, and they were widely copied. Near the end of the fifth year, he was able to boast:

> Since the *Sun* began to shine upon the citizens of New York, there has been a very great and decided change in the condition of the laboring classes and mechanics. Now every individual, from the rich aristocrat who lolls in his carriage to the humble laborer who wields a broom in the streets, reads the *Sun;* nor can even a boy be found in New York City or the neighboring country who will not know in the course of the day what is promulgated in the *Sun* in the morning.
>
> Already we perceive a change in the mass of the people. They think, talk, and act in concert. They understand their own interest, and feel that they have numbers and strength to pursue it with success.[2]

The daily newspaper business had found its market, and the model established by the penny press proved to be a lasting one. This model has two prime virtues. One is that it fulfills the First Amendment obligation to promote the free flow of information. The other is that it is economically sound.

From the business point of view, the model works like this: The newspaper attempts to reach as large an audience as possible, although quantity is not its only concern. It is especially interested in reaching the educated, the opinion leaders, the affluent, but it wants the masses as well. To do this, it sells its product cheaply, often not even recouping the cost of the paper it is printed on from the selling price, and it creates an editorial environment that readers perceive as trustworthy, reliable, and fair. The advertiser is drawn to this medium by three things: the number of people it reaches, their buying potential, and the climate of credibility. The newspaper's product, as Hal Jurgensmeyer of the University of Miami has pointed out, is influence.[3]

In this model, there is no reason for the advertiser to exercise any control or influence over the editorial content. Indeed, to do so would be counterproductive, because it would undermine the independence that creates the trustworthy editorial environment that, in turn, gives the paper its influence. Advertisers pay money to the newspaper not because they support its editorial content, but because they hope to increase their sales. If business people did not profit from their advertising, they would stop doing it. As long as a dollar of advertising returns more than a dollar of increased sales, the rational advertiser will continue to spend that dollar no matter what the newspaper may do or say in its news and editorial columns—unless, of course, its content becomes so extreme that its credibility is damaged or destroyed. Newspapers of extremely low credibility, like the tabloids sold in supermarkets, have to make their money from circulation sales, not from advertising. (Peek inside a supermarket tabloid, and you'll see what I mean. The few ads they do have seem to be directed at people who will believe anything—for example, that there is a pill that will cause you to lose weight while you sleep.) A credible environment is what advertisers pay for, and they therefore have an economic stake in the integrity of the newspaper.

Advertiser Influence: The Reality

That's the model. Unfortunately, it is not always the reality. The literature of journalism criticism over the past 20 years is replete with instances of advertiser influence over what goes into and what stays out of newspapers. In nearly every case, however, the critic asserts that the situation is not as bad as it used to be. Perhaps. In 1984 I was a luncheon speaker at a meeting of the Kansas Press Association, and I recalled with ironic nostalgia my time on the copy desk of the *Topeka Daily Capital* in the 1950s, when brief stories about advertisers typed on yellow paper (meaning that they were not to be edited) and slugged "BOM" (for "Business Office Must") frequently crossed the copy desk. "Must" copy is material that *must* go in the paper, come what may. Of course, I added, that sort of thing doesn't happen nowadays—and the assembled editors and publishers rocked the room with howls of laughter.

Is advertiser influence declining or not? In order to be sure, we need some quantitative measures. There aren't very many. In 1967, the *Wall Street Journal* cited a survey of 162 business and financial editors, in which 23 percent said they routinely had to "puff up or alter and downgrade business stories at the request of the advertisers."[4]

Some more recent data are available from the ASNE survey of 1982. In telephone interviews, editors were asked how frequently various kinds of ethical problems became so troublesome that they had to be discussed in the news room. One of the problems asked about was "pressure from advertisers: blurbs, business office musts, keeping things out of the paper or getting them in." (*Blurb* is newspaper jargon for a news item initiated by the business side of the paper on behalf of an advertiser.)

The responses indicated that advertiser pressure is a concern at least some of the time on papers read by 79 percent of the American public. For 46 percent, the frequency of such episodes is at least several times a year. For 26 percent, it is once a month or more. And for 9 percent, it happens every week. That's a lot of advertiser pressure.

Of course, the fact that such things are discussed may be a good sign. Back in Topeka 30 years ago, we didn't discuss it. We just sailed the copy right into print. In the 1982 survey editors, publishers, and staff members were asked a more specific question in a self-administered questionnaire:

How often, to the best of your knowledge, does your paper publish editorial matter controlled by the business office on behalf of advertisers in the news columns (commonly known as "blurbs" or "business office musts")?

Publishers, editors, and staff members had somewhat different perceptions. The staffers were more likely to report awareness of BOM copy than editors, and the publishers reported the least awareness of all. If you believe the publishers, 21 percent of the reading public is exposed to blurbs in its news columns. According to editors, the number is 24 percent. According to staff members, it is 39 percent.

Such abuses are not, however, a daily occurrence. They happen with a frequency greater than once a month only to between 4 and 10 percent of the nation's newspaper readers, depending on whether you believe the publisher or the staff members.

The mere existence of the term *BOM copy* means that advertiser influence is institutionalized. How about more casual influences? How often, for example, does the publisher stroll into the editor's office and ask for special handling of an article about a company or organization that has some economic clout over the newspaper?

Not often, it turns out, but it does happen. By the publishers' own admission, it happens at newspapers read by 42 percent of the public. By the editors' estimate, it is 46 percent, and by that of the staff, 58 percent. The staff is just guessing, however, because an editor will try hard to keep these incidents invisible to the staff. Rather than pass the blame up to the publisher, most editors would prefer to be seen as arbitrary or currying favor themselves. Blaming the boss would be a mark of weakness. The fact that the editors and publishers are so close in their estimates suggests that a rate in the low forties is in the right ballpark. Remember, this is the estimate for the situation happening just once. According to the information supplied by both editors and publishers, the newspapers where such intervention happens more than once or twice a year reach only 14 percent of the total newspaper audience.

Special Treatment, Special Sections
That is still enough to supply an abundance of anecdotes for journalism critics. It is easier to find examples of puffery than of suppression simply because the former are so visible. Here's a rare illustration of the latter. The *Twin Cities Reader,* a weekly based in Minneapolis, sent its music editor, Paul Maccabee, to cover a jazz festival sponsored by Kool Cigarettes. "Strange bedfellows, cigarettes and jazz," wrote Maccabee. "Duke Ellington died of lung cancer in 1974." He was fired. The publisher said he was afraid of losing the cigarette industry's four to five weekly pages of advertising.[5]

Another example: At the *Houston Post* in the early 1970s, restaurant reviews were written by the advertising department—and only restaurants that advertised in the paper were reviewed. When the reviewer violated that policy and let his readers know about some restaurants that did not advertise, he was fired.[6]

Newspapers have long been wary of using business names in news copy. In 1971 a large Boston department store, Jordan Marsh, was sued by a debtor who claimed undue harassment. When the debtor won a major ruling on a preliminary procedural issue, both the *Boston Globe* and the *Boston Herald-Traveler* reported the story—but without mentioning the name of the store.[7]

The policy at some newspapers is to ban use of all business names, unless absolutely essential to the story, whether the reference is good or bad. The reasoning is that an unfavorable reference may annoy someone, and a favorable one—well, that's free advertising, and anybody who wants something good said about them in the paper should pay for it. The policy at least has the virtue of consistency, but it often makes for awkward writing. Bank robbers make their gateway in "a small car," not a Volkswagen. A news conference is held at "a downtown hotel," not at the Hilton.

Putting puffery into the newspaper is the more visible offense, and it can be demoralizing for staffers, particularly if they have to participate in it. In the late 1950s, when Al Neuharth was an assistant managing editor of the *Miami Herald* and I was a brand-new reporter, he dispatched me to the owners and managers of the Wometco Theater group so that I could gather material to fill the editorial columns of a special advertising section celebrating some anniversary of the company. I still remember the humiliation of being led around by the Wometco press agent, a cheerful little man who kept introducing me to everybody as "Paul." So depressed was I that I never bothered to correct him.

One such special advertising section almost got out of hand at the *Denver Post* in 1966. The business editor felt that he was being pressured by the ad manager to provide editorial coverage of a new shopping center equal to 25 percent of the ad space that the center was buying. He hadn't reached half that amount and had run out of things to say, he complained in a memo to his managing editor, William H. Hornby. It was all a mistake, said Hornby, and there was no policy of one free inch for every four paid.[8]

Some better solutions to the special-section problem have been found: let the advertiser supply the editorial matter and then label it as advertising and use a distinctive type face to make it easily distinguishable from real news stories; or have the newspaper's advertising department write the copy and give it the same labeling.

Where an ongoing section is involved—a Sunday real estate section, for example—the trend today is toward solid, consumer-oriented reporting instead of puffery. Compare, for example, the *Philadelphia Inquirer's* real estate section in the 1960s with its present-day counterpart. Before, the section's front page bannered stories on activities of local real estate developers and brokers. Now the boosterism is gone, replaced by a consumer-oriented approach, with information that house-hunting readers can use.

But a more subtle problem remains: the way in which the market for advertising influences what kind of news readers will get. Consider the weekly business sections that many newspapers began publishing in the late 1970s. The best of these sections cover business news with a depth and thoroughness never attempted before, and in so doing they have closed a historical gap in their service to their readers. What local business does has a visible effect on almost everyone in a community, its activities are news; but until recently, most newspapers behaved as though local government were the only source of power in the community, ignoring business even though it was sometimes a more important power center.

Did these new special sections spring into being because newspaper publishers suddenly awoke to the fact that there was a huge gap in their reporting on their communities? Not at all. What happened was that they awoke to the fact that they were missing out on a good way to make a buck.

The folks who woke them up were entrepreneurs who began utilizing the new technology of publishing, with its lower production costs, to start local business periodicals such as *Crain's Chicago Business Review*. When these independent journals entered a few markets and started selling advertising, the alert newspaper publishers wondered why *they* hadn't been getting that advertising. In direct response, some of the "Business Monday" newspaper sections appeared—and they worked. They provided a brand-new revenue stream that followed the penny-paper model in microcosm. A limited segment of readers, people interested in business, was drawn to the new section, and advertisers who wanted to reach that segment saw an efficiency there that could not be realized by ads that had the run of the paper. A metropolitan daily is so fat that you can't expect every reader to look closely at every page, so it is not efficient for reaching a limited segment unless there is a section of editorial matter that attracts that limited segment. The "Business Monday" concept does this beautifully.

Another advertiser-supported editorial innovation is the zoned neighborhood section. By providing intensive local coverage of neighborhoods, these sections attract retail advertisers who want to reach specific neighborhoods without paying the cost of ads that appear in the full press run. A new service to readers is created, and it is financed by advertising revenue that is new and distinct, not just cannibalized from some other part of the paper. Everybody wins.

That's the good news. The bad news is that something that readers badly need may never be provided in the absence of a visible signal that it can be hooked to advertising. The major disappointment of my time on the corporate staff at Knight-Ridder was the failure of an experimental feature for children that I had helped recruit. It was called the "Dynamite Kids' Page," and the hope was that it would draw national advertising away from Saturday-morning television. It never did, and the page was dropped. An even more ambitious venture, a colorful Sunday supplement called "Three to Get Ready" and placed in a number of papers by a group of New York City entrepreneurs, met a similar fate. Both features would have been good for newspapers in the long run, because they would have taught children that print media can be fun and useful. Given more time, the advertisers might have come around. But business pressures sometimes dictate a short planning horizon, and the immediate attitudes of advertisers—or nonadvertisers—can have an effect on content that undermines the First Amendment theory on which newspapers rest their case for independence.

The Wall of Separation Between Newsroom and Business Office

Joint efforts of news and advertising departments to create innovative products within the framework of the daily newspaper began comparatively recently. The historical pattern of abuses of business-office power on behalf of advertisers had led to the business-aversion rule in newsrooms and, on newspapers with strong editors, to a structural division between the news side and the business side. Under this ethic, the less the editor knew about what happened on the business side, the better. Insulated by this wall of separation from the machinations of the business office, the editor could make judgment calls without knowing how the financial fortunes of the newspaper would be affected. Publishers could be comfortable with this arrangement because it meant delegating ethical questions to the editor. The publisher was responsible only for hiring an editor of high moral standing; having done that, the publisher could devote full attention to maximizing profit. The public interest was somebody else's department.

And so the in-house atmosphere became adversarial, and those of us who worked on the news sides of such newspapers had no trouble believing that we were nobler than those grubby people who brought in the cash with which our salaries were paid. *We* were altruistic, looking out for the community's welfare. *They* were selfish, thinking only of the company's economic well-being. The symmetry of this dichotomy is appealing. Adherence to it is reflected quite clearly in the responses to this survey question, which was mentioned in the previous chapter and is now presented in full (the percentages represent editor responses):

A business writer discovers that TV sets with built-in videotex decoders will be on the local market within 60 days, greatly increasing convenience and reducing costs for people who sign up for the local videotex service—which, incidentally, is not owned by your paper. The advertising manager calls the publisher and says local TV dealers are afraid they will be stuck with an oversupply of obsolete TV sets if the word gets out. Should the publisher:

a. Order the story killed. (0 percent)
b. Explain the problem to the editor with a recommendation that the story be delayed. (2 percent)
c. Suggest to the editor that the story be double-checked for accuracy. (36 percent)
d. Help the ad manager pacify the retailers, but say nothing to the editor. (62 percent)

The majority position (d) reflects the wall-of-separation tradition, in which it is considered best to keep the editor ignorant of business-side problems. But is it the most rational position?

If you step back and look at the situation with the total newspaper in mind, you may arrive at a different answer. The retailers represent an important segment of the community, to whom significant damage could be done. Their interests need to be weighed against those of consumers. The equation is easy enough, particularly when First Amendment responsibilities are considered. When information damages some and benefits others, a strong presumption exists that the information should be provided and that the newspaper's duty is to its readers as consumers, not to the subset who would like to take advantage of those consumers' ignorance. But where is the harm in double-checking for accuracy? And is there not an important ethical benefit to be derived from doing so?

Where wrong information would be damaging to an individual or group, the need for accuracy, always at the top of any journalistic code of ethics in routine cases, is especially strong. If the editor does not know of the potential for damage in this case, he or she is likely to give it routine treatment even though it is normal to double-check where the damage potential *is* known. The wall of separation, designed to ward off evils of another kind, is working against the newspaper here.

There is, of course, the slippery-slope argument. Okay, this argument goes, the publisher would be justified in talking to the editor in this case, but if that conversation takes place, the next one will be more intrusive, the one after that even worse, and the advertising department will wind up dictating news content.

The argument assumes a weak editor and a malevolent publisher. Indeed, so does the wall-of-separation tradition. A principled publisher and a strong editor could work together to maximize the paper's ability to carry out both its profit-making and First Amendment missions. They could manage conflicts so as to minimize the damage to both sides more effectively than if each side were to pursue its own narrow interests. Cases like the example above highlight the weakness in the wall-of-separation tradition. Keeping key functions in separate, watertight compartments is not an efficient way to run a complicated operation like a newspaper. Indeed, the separation keeps the editors weaker than they need to be. An editor who understands the newspaper's financial situation is in a stronger position to fight for the resources needed to produce the kind of newspaper that readers deserve. Chapter 7 examines the various operating styles of publishers; this will give us an opportunity for additional reflection on the editor-publisher relationship.

Advertiser Pressure and Newspaper Economics

If a strong editor is an important ingredient in producing an ethical newspaper, a strong institution is even more important. Edwin A. Lahey, Washington bureau chief for Knight Newpapers in the 1950s and 1960s, put it bluntly when he said, "All I require of my publisher is that he remain solvent."[9] A financially sound newspaper need not fear the whims of any given advertiser, and most advertisers need the newspaper too much to stay away. Most of the horror stories about newspapers knuckling under to advertiser pressure have to do with small, economically marginal publications, the 97-pound weaklings of journalism. Even among small papers, however, examples of moral courage can be found.

In 1969 two right-wing leaders, Fred C. Schwartz, head of the Christian Anti-Communist Crusade, and Benjamin Grob, an industrialist, took offense at a counterculture newspaper called *Kaleidoscope,* which was published in Milwaukee. Unable to attack it directly, they tracked down the printer, who turned out to be William F. Schanen, Jr., the owner of three weekly newspapers in Ozaukee County and a pioneer in the use of high-quality offset printing for small newspapers. They organized a boycott against Schanen's three weeklies, using a direct-mail campaign to urge people in Ozaukee County not to advertise in any of the three papers or to patronize anyone who did.

The boycott was highly effective, costing Schanen $300,000 in gross income during the first year. To save his company, he folded one of the three weeklies and sold another. He refused to stop printing *Kaleidoscope* on principle, although he himself did not approve of its content.

Schanen died in 1971, but his son, William Schanen III, continued the fight. As the counterculture's heyday waned, *Kaleidoscope* shut down for reasons unrelated to the boycott. That and his father's death contributed to bringing "the whole silly business to an end," the younger Schanen recalled. "We limped along, and then our circulation picked up . . . and every advertiser that pulled out was back within five years." But a shopper that had moved into the vacuum is still around, and the *Mequon Squire,* the paper sold during the boycott, is now a major competitor. Schanen looks back on the struggle as a successful defense of First Amendment principles. "I can't think of anything I'm prouder of," he said recently.[10]

A similar boycott, launched at about the same time by a John Birch Society chapter against the *Denver Post,* had much less effect. For a dominant daily newspaper in a large metropolitan market, there is much less susceptibility to advertiser pressure.

The fact that advertiser pressures still exist where there is relative economic security may be related to causes that are as much social as economic. The ASNE survey showed that publishers who intervene in the newseditorial side to get special handling for an organization or an individual are as likely to do it for someone with whom they have strong social ties as they are for someone with economic clout. Table 3.1 shows the relative frequency of the two kinds of intervention as perceived by editors.

The direct fear of economic retribution therefore may be less important than the publisher's desire to be helpful to his or her friends. The

TABLE 3.1
FREQUENCY OF PUBLISHER INTERVENTION FOR ECONOMIC
AND SOCIAL REASONS

	Economic	Social
At least once a month	3%	3%
Several times a year	11	16
Less often	31	33
Never	54	48

temptation is a strong one. Almost anybody who has worked for a newspaper in any capacity has felt it at one time or another. And this brings us to another large category of problems that comes under the general heading of fairness and balance—goals that are almost universally sought but are extremely difficult to attain.

NOTES

1. Michael Schudson, *Discovering the News: A Social History of American Newspapers* (New York: Basic Books, 1978), p. 16.
2. The *New York Sun*, June 28, 1838, quoted in George Henry Payne, *History of Journalism in the United States* (New York: D. Appleton and Company, 1920).
3. Conversation with Hal Jurgensmeyer, Miami, Florida, 1978.
4. Cited in A. Kent MacDougall, ed., *The Press: A Critical Look from the Inside* (Princeton, N.J.: Dow Jones Books, 1972).
5. *Columbia Journalism Review*, July–August 1982, pp. 8–9.
6. Bruce Swain, *Reporters' Ethics* (Ames, Iowa: Iowa State University Press, 1978), p. 44.
7. MacDougall, *The Press*, pp. 150–151.
8. "News for Advertisers: A Denver Case," *Columbia Journalism Review*, Summer 1966.
9. This is one of many Lahey aphorisms that remain part of the corporate culture of what is now Knight-Ridder.
10. "The Wisconsin Boycott," *Columbia Journalism Review*, Fall 1969, p. 3; "Wisconsin Publisher Folds Papers in Boycott," *Chicago Journalism Review*, April 1970, p. 15; telephone interview with William F. Schanen III, June 19, 1984.

CHAPTER 4

The Objectivity Issue

The masses cause a lot of the trouble for the mass media. The masses of people contain many diverse interests and conflicting viewpoints. Striking a balance among the differences and treating everyone evenhandedly is the editor's most difficult job.

When interviewers in the ASNE survey read a long list of categories of ethical problems to the sample of editors, the one that evoked the most response was this:

> Fairness, balance, and objectivity: allocating space to opposing interest groups or political candidates. Providing right of reply to criticism.

The editors who said such problems were discussed in the newsroom at least once a month represented 64 percent of daily circulation in the United States. No other general category scored as high as 40 percent.

In our diverse society, the problem of fairness is so complex that a direct solution is impossible. What is fair to one group will seem like bias to another. Action taken to solve a problem in one area will create new problems in other areas. But some rules of thumb have been developed to try to minimize the damage. One of them is rooted in the notion of isolation that First Amendment theory, as interpreted by many news people, imposes. This is the objectivity rule. The reporter seeks to adopt a "man from Mars" stance, seeing each event afresh, untainted by prior expectations, collecting observations and passing them on untouched by interpretation.

It doesn't work, of course. The world is far too complex, and readers are far too impatient to wade through and analyze raw data of this sort. Some structure has to be imposed on the data, and, as Walter Lippmann observed in 1920, this means dealing to some degree with fictions:

> By fictions, I do not mean lies. I mean a representation of the environment which is in lesser or greater degree made by man himself. The range of fiction extends all the way from complete hallucinations to the scientists' perfectly self-conscious use of a

47

schematic model or his decision that for his particular problem, accuracy beyond a certain number of decimal points is not important. A work of fiction may have almost any degree of fidelity, and so long as the degree of fidelity can be taken into account, fiction is not misleading.[1]

Take away the creative structure, and what do you have? "Direct exposure to the ebb and flow of sensation," said Lippmann. And we can take only so much of that. "However refreshing it is to see at times with a perfectly innocent eye, innocence itself is not wisdom, though a source and corrective of wisdom."[2]

The Distorting Effect of Perceptual Models

The real world is so complex and subtle that we can't manage it without some means of selecting, rearranging, and tracing patterns in its elements. The need for such simplifying perceptual models is inescapable. The notion of objective reporting is itself a fiction.

So writers, whether they are newspaper reporters, screenwriters, or novelists, adopt models into which they can fit their objective facts. These models help both the writer and the reader to understand and make sense of the facts, but this benefit comes at a cost. In addition to being guides to interpretation, these necessary models—or stereotypes, as Lippmann called them—also help us to select which aspects of the objective world to look for. If something is truly new and different, it may not fit into the existing model, and we may not see it—or not believe it even if we do see it. Or we may so distort it to make it fit into the existing model that it can only steer us away from, not closer to, the truth.

This kind of modeling created newspapers' blind spot for blacks before the civil rights movement made blacks visible to them. For example, crime stories, no matter how dramatic, were reduced to a routine listing of names and charges if both victim and accused were black. When I was an education reporter setting up a routine first-day-of-school photograph in Miami in the 1950s, I would always choose a white school. In the South, when statistics were reported showing how the home city or state compared with others across the nation in infant mortality or literacy, newspapers would lighten the dismal result by quoting some statistician to the effect that if blacks were not counted, the home town or state would compare much more favorably.

Blacks became visible in the 1960s when the civil rights boycotts and other protests began to affect white readers. However, the problem of inappropriate models remained. After the major urban riots of the mid-1960s in the Watts section of Los Angeles, Newark, Detroit, and Washington, D.C., the National Advisory Commission on Civil Disorders (the Kerner Commission) delivered its report in the spring of 1968. The report's thesis sentence was a succinct, almost poetic summary of the prevailing perceptual model of the time: "Our nation is moving toward two societies, one black, one white—separate and un-equal."[3]

This is the model by which newspaper reporters—and some social scien-tists—governed their perception of the events of those years. Guided by the model, they focused their attention on the noisy extremists of both races, and, sure enough, blacks and whites could be seen to be moving further apart. Like most perceptual models, this one was self-reinforcing. The model draws your eye to the elements that support it, and once you see these elements, you believe in the model even more strongly and continue to look for more such elements.

If the model happens to be wrong, both press and public can eventually work their way out of this trap because the model's bad fit with reality even-tually becomes obvious. But it can take a long time. The Kerner Commission's model was, as it turned out, wrong from the start. But it was so strong that when some social scientists with hard, objective data pointed that out, no one paid any attention.

The two social scientists with the best evidence were Angus Campbell and Howard Schuman of the University of Michigan, and they came upon it almost by accident. Michigan's Survey Research Center, then as now, ran national attitude surveys every presidential election year, and in 1964 they had included some racial-attitude questions in their interviews. Now, 1964 was a pretty good year: The Civil Rights Act was passed then, and Watts hadn't happened yet. By the time the fall of 1968 rolled around, however, the burned-out neighbor-hoods in Watts, Newark, Detroit, and Washington had been on front pages around the country. So had the assassination of Martin Luther King, Jr. The Michigan researchers repeated their questions in 1968 and found just the op-posite of what the newspapers were saying. The two races were reporting in-creasing tolerance of and contact with each other.

Take this finding: In 1964 the Michigan investigators found that 81 per-cent of the national sample of white adults had only white friends, no black friends. Four years later, whites who had only white friends had dropped to 70 percent.

Or this, among blacks: In 1964 those with only black friends were 40 per-cent of the total. After the major riots, the period when the two races were supposed to be moving further apart, blacks with only black friends were down to 25 percent.

Both whites and blacks reported more contact than previously with members of the other race where they lived and where their children went to school. The number living in all-white or all-black neighborhoods was down significantly. Among whites, attitudes toward blacks improved the most where they had previously been the worst, in the South. The strongest surviving con-centrations of racial antagonism were in rural areas—which is not where the media were focusing for their picture of increasing separation.

How to reconcile what the data say with what everyone believes is true? I put this question to Campbell at the time. "I believe our data," he said. "It isn't as though there's no backlash at all. There is undoubtedly some citizen in

Hamtramck who's gone sour on Negroes because one has moved into his block. But when you look at the picture nationally, where is it? I just don't see it!"[4]

Campbell and Schuman were hired by the Kerner Commission to survey 15 major cities to double-check on trends in racial attitudes. Theirs was one of three supplementary reports released in the summer of 1968, four months after the main commission report. A press conference was held to announce the results of the three reports. Although this was a snapshot study with no time comparisons, it was guardedly optimistic. The evidence of massive black radicalism and separatism was not there, Campbell and Schuman said—but it was as if they were speaking to an empty room. "Man bites dog" is not necessarily news; if an event departs too far from existing stereotypes or perceptual models, it may simply be ignored.

"Human readiness to disregard the importance of facts, even when significant issues are involved," wrote Nelson Antrim Crawford 60 years ago, "is disclosed again and again in political controversy."[5]

The moral problem for newspapers is that by clinging so tenaciously to popular stereotypes that are contrary to fact, they reinforce those stereotypes and may even retard desirable social change by denying it reinforcement. One of the functions of a newspaper, as George Herbert Mead pointed out long ago, is to help people interpret their own lives and relate them to the larger society.[6] If the world becomes what newspapers say it is, then newspapers must be very careful about what they say it is.

Pragmatic Rules for Objectivity

The need for fairness, balance, and objectivity, then, is driven by even more than the democratic need to treat every person or cause evenhandedly. It is related to the newspaper's ability to see matters afresh, to view the world at least some of the time with the "perfectly innocent eye" that, as Lippmann correctly noted, is the source and corrective of wisdom. And this means that conventional wisdom, on which perceptual models are generally based, needs to be reexamined from time to time. To conduct such an examination, a journalist needs to think in a scientific mode: suspending judgment, examining data, constructing alternative models. It is not easy. It cannot be done every day. And so news people have opted for some easier ways of striving for fairness, balance, and objectivity. These pragmatic rules amount to operational guidelines for the "man from Mars" role.

The Attribution Rule

The attribution rule is an example. This rule requires a reporter to give the source, whenever it is not obvious, for every important fact in a story. Thorough sourcing can clutter up a story, break its rhythm, slow it down. But it lets the reader know exactly where he or she stands, how much credulity to put into each statement of fact. Like most good things, the attribution rule can be dangerous when carried too far. When applied compulsively, it can lead the reporter to forget the journalist's responsibility to go behind the sources and make an independent check of their validity.

The Get-the-Other-Side-of-the-Story Rule

Then there is the get-the-other-side-of-the-story rule. Whenever someone makes a claim that is not verifiable by direct observation, and for which other points of view exist, the reporter is expected to include those other points of view. This practice tends to yield a story pattern in which there are always two points of view, no more and no less. Reality is often quite different. In a complicated situation with many points of view, some viewpoints are inevitably going to get lost when the reporter assumes a model with only two contrasting views. In national politics, for example, the interesting things said by third parties are often ignored while news people concentrate on Republicans and Democrats as if those two sides encompassed the universe.

Another unconscious assumption in the get-the-other-side rule is that both sides are equally credible. If the surgeon general says cigarettes cause cancer and heart attacks and the Tobacco Institute says they don't, a newspaper's compulsion to get the other side and to preserve a balance may lead it to give both of those sources equal weight and leave the reader with the feeling that there is about as much to be said for one side as another, when, in fact, the overwhelming weight of the evidence is on one side. Media critic Ben Bagdikian, in fact, blames the media for the slow rate of change in public attitudes toward smoking.[7] However, natural human inertia is part of the cause as well, and a lag of a generation between new information and a resulting behavior change is not at all unusual. And even when a news story brings in the by-now-ritualistic responses of the Tobacco Institute to the latest medical finding, readers can distinguish between disinterested and biased sources without a great deal of guidance. And the equal-weight-to-both-sides rule has a practical limitation when one side runs out of new things to say, as has generally been the case with the tobacco people.

A special case of the get-the-other-side rule involves the right to reply. Whenever a person or institution is criticized, that person or spokesperson for the institution is routinely given the opportunity to respond. And if the person can't be located or refuses to respond, the newspaper will let the reader know that an attempt was made. Sometimes the effort is a perfunctory one, and sometimes it is purposely delayed so that the affected individual has no time to come up with an effective reply. There is a reason for this tactic. If a public official with a hand in the cookie jar learns that public exposure is imminent, he may decide to go public in a friendly medium with the hope that its story will take the edge off the unfriendly exposure. So a newspaper that has the goods on him will wait until just before press time to let him know what it has and ask for his side of the story. He doesn't have time to get a defense in order, much less take it to a friendly medium, and the newspaper is assured of a clean beat on the story. One newspaper I know about went further than that. In an undercover investigation, its reporters had caught a lawyer in an illegal immigration scheme. He was confronted with the evidence and given his obligatory chance to respond late in the afternoon before publication. The city editor then assigned reporters to call the lawyer, pretend to be representing various other media and, in a harassing, browbeating manner, demand self-incriminating facts of his case. The idea was to convey the notion that no medium would be in the least bit sympathetic and to keep him from cooperating with any of them, thus preserving the exclusive nature of the story for the originating newspaper.

The Equal-Space Rule

Another rule of thumb is that conflicting groups should be given equal space in the newspaper. In an election campaign, some editors will keep track of the column inches given each of the major candidates to make sure that none is slighted. The simplistic nature of this solution becomes obvious if one of the candidates is clearly less newsworthy than the other by virtue of being inactive or having little to say.

The Equal-Access Rule

The equal-space rule deals with news the paper actively seeks. It has a passive counterpart, the equal-access rule, which holds that all interests in the community should have an equal opportunity to have their views and their situations made known through the newspaper. However, equal access is subject to variations in newsworthiness, which is in turn colored by the perceptual models employed by the news people. These models may make some groups invisible, others too visible.

The Fairness Problem: Survey Results

Some items in the ASNE survey illustrate the complexity of the fairness problem, particularly in a diverse community. Consider this question (and the percentage responses by editors):

> Easter Sunday is approaching, and the editor plans the traditional page-one recognition of the holiday: a banner, "He Is Risen." Then a new publisher, who happens to be an agnostic, points out that the latest religious census shows the community to be 6 percent non-Christian. Should the editor:
> a. Keep the Easter banner. (50 percent)
> b. Reduce the size of the headline in deference to the non-Christians in the community. (4 percent)
> c. Limit the paper's coverage to specific religious-oriented events scheduled for that day. (53 percent)
> d. Avoid any mention of Easter. (1 percent)

The problem here is that the function of the banner is not to report the news, the resurrection in question having taken place some time ago (unless the editor has a *really* big story), but to take part in a religious celebration. Publishers favored this practice more than editors (62 percent to 50 percent), and staff members were the least supportive group, at 42 percent. Those who chose any but the fourth option were asked what the proportion of non-Christians would have to be before they would further curtail the paper's Easter coverage. The average response for editors was around 44 percent.

Because it divides news people into two large groups of fairly equal size, this question has promise as a general indicator of sensitivity to the fairness problem. So does the following question, with which it is moderately correlated.

A local boy who grew up in poverty makes good by educating himself, working hard, and becoming a successful businessman. This effort culminates in the opening of the fanciest restaurant the town has yet seen. His younger brother has also made good, in a way, by becoming an editorial writer, and he salutes his brother's Horatio Alger story in a folksy and appealing signed column. To ward off any charge of conflict of interest, he identifies himself as the brother of the subject of the piece in the opening paragraph. Should the editor:

a. Kill the column. (22 percent)
b. Have the column rewritten to eliminate the brother's name and the name of the restaurant. (0 percent)
c. Move the piece to some less conspicuous part of the paper. (3 percent)
d. Let it stand. (75 percent)

There is not a lot to criticize in this case, although a similar situation did receive a dart from the *Columbia Journalism Review* several years ago. By reporting his connection with the subject, the columnist is being honest with the reader, who then can make allowances for what is said. However, a case can be made that the principle of equal access is being denied. Restaurant operators whose brothers are not editorial writers do not get the same treatment. Complicating matters still further is the fact that restaurants are advertisers, and this restaurant owner is getting free space that might reduce his need for paid space. That perhaps explains why, in this particular case, publishers were every bit as sensitive to the possibility of an ethical problem as were editors and staff members. Publishers representing 23 percent of circulation (and staff members with 20 percent) wanted to kill the story, compared to the editors' 20 percent.

Respondents generally shunned the alternatives of moving the piece to some other part of the paper or of disguising the names. The identities would be recognizable to many readers anyway, and an attempt to conceal them would just make the columnist look foolish. Moving the column to some less conspicuous part of the paper solves nothing, although that is not an infrequent compromise when an editor truly does not know what to do—or must reach some sort of compromise with his publisher or with a staff member whose good will he or she wants to preserve.

Another aspect of the fairness problem involves situations where the newspaper's own interests, real or emotional, are involved. If a newspaper is edited in a truly detached and evenhanded manner, it will evaluate each story on its merits, and whether the story is an exclusive or a follow-up on someone else's exclusive will not matter. In fact, however, it usually matters quite a bit and has since the days of the penny press. Newspapers tend to inflate the importance of stories they have developed through their own enterprise and downplay those developed through someone else's enterprise. They do this even though, according to the ASNE survey, nobody approves of the practice:

> A scandal is unfolding in city government, and your paper is getting more than its share of the news beats. But, today, your paper is beaten by a competing medium on a key element of the story. Should your paper:
>
> a. Treat the new element just as though the competition had never mentioned it. (39 percent)
> b. Acknowledge the competition's beat in print and cover the story according to its intrinsic news value. (61 percent)
> c. Downgrade the importance of the new element. (1 percent)
> d. Ignore the new element. (0 percent)

What we have here is more a measure of values than of behavior. But the question does serve to sort out two sets of attitudes toward ways of dealing with competing media: Act as if they didn't exist or treat them as part of the environment, to be reported on like any other part. Some newspapers will mention their opposition only in euphemisms, such as "another paper" or "an afternoon paper." The fairest reaction is, of course, to acknowledge the existence of the competition and cover the story according to its intrinsic news value. This survey item can be combined with the previous two to produce an overall scale of sensitivity to fairness issues. Points for fairness are awarded for modifying the Easter banner, taking some action on the restaurant column, and frankly acknowledging the competition. Roughly four news people out of 10 in the survey scored two or more points. For our purposes, we can classify these people as sensitive—or hypersensitive, depending on your point of view—to issues of fairness and balance.

People working on larger papers were more likely to register high scores than those on smaller papers. The difference was especially great for editors. The numbers in Table 4.1 are the percentages of readers represented by news people who scored high on this measure. It shows that 18 percent of the small-paper publishers scored high on the fairness scale, compared to 29 percent of the publishers of medium-size papers and 53 percent of the large-paper publishers.

TABLE 4.1
HIGH SCORES ON THE FAIRNESS SCALE, BY NEWSPAPER SIZE

	Small	Medium	Large
Publishers	18%	29%	53%
Editors	25	38	65
Staff	36	50	47

Does this mean that big papers are more ethical? Not necessarily. It may mean only that small-town news people, serving more homogeneous communities, have less of a balancing act to perform. The assumptions that everyone is Christian and that everyone knows the restaurant owner and his roots come closer to reality in small towns. News people in bigger towns work harder at striking balances because the pressures caused by diversity are stronger there.

Publishers were far more likely to score high on fairness sensitivity if they had previously worked on the news-editorial side of the paper. Indeed, the longer the period of such service, the greater the likelihood that a publisher would demonstrate this sensitivity. For readers whose publisher has no such experience, the probability is only 20 percent that the publisher will be in the fairness-sensitive group. When the publisher has some news experience, that probability jumps to 39 percent. If he or she has more than 22 years of news background, it rises to 50 percent. Sensitivity to issues of fairness and balance is, then, a response to real-world problems of covering the news in an environment of many conflicting interests.

When news people think about the ethics of their business, they tend to focus on everyday problems like the three examples cited above. But solving such problems is not nearly as difficult as deciding what to define as a problem in the first place. Once a situation reaches the stage where the news people involved have decided that it is a problem, and that it requires some analysis and discussion before it can be solved, the difficult part of the ethical issue has already been resolved. Overcoming this tough part means learning to recognize a problem when it appears. It requires developing a capacity for self-criticism and analysis, among all the other difficult and time-consuming things that need to be done to produce a newspaper every day.

Some news people are too busy with crisis management to reflect on such issues. They have to wait for problems to define themselves—as when a reader calls to complain or the newspaper office is picketed, a reporter subpoenaed or a libel suit filed. Those with the skills or the resources to exercise better management of their time can be more reflective. They can continually assess their actions in terms of their First Amendment responsibilities—to improve the flow of information that the people need to meet their own democratic responsibilities. Such reflection may focus not only on the ethics of what is reported, but on how it is reported—how well, in other words, the important information is communicated.

And this can lead to another kind of ethical bind. This one, too, involves the problem of objectivity.

The New Nonfiction

At the beginning of this chapter, we saw how objectivity in its purest form, approaching the data with a kind of innocence and willingness to experiment with different perceptual models, is needed to perceive situations that are truly new and unexpected. We used the improvement in race relations during the period of the riots as an example. To make such explorations effectively requires borrowing some of the methods of the social sciences, an approach that has been called "precision journalism" because it uses statistical analysis, computers, and formal sampling methods. Newspapers have made sporadic efforts to embrace its methods since the 1960s.[8]

Another movement in reporting has taken a totally different tack, concentrating on the problem of communicating what the journalist has found out, giving it a form that will enable the reader to relate it to his or her daily life. This approach helps a reader to experience an event intuitively as well as intellectually. Everette E. Dennis (who coined the term "precision journalism") and William L. Rivers call this other branch "the new nonfiction."[9]

Advocates of this form of journalism despair of achieving true objectivity. Since objectivity is impossible, they reason, shouldn't journalists abandon it as a goal altogether and instead devote all their resources to the problem of conveying truth as they perceive it? Lippmann's admonition to impose structure and pattern on events to make them understandable is embraced wholeheartedly. That this structure is composed in part of certain kinds of "fictions," as Lippmann put it, is freely acknowledged. The ethical problem arises when the degree of fidelity to verifiable fact is not taken into account and communicated to the reader along with the central message—when, in other words, fiction is passed off as fact.

Journalists disagree on how far they can go in this direction.

At one level, the writer investigates a situation, decides what is true, and then selects the elements of the story that do the most efficient job of portraying that truth. The decision of what to select and which of alternate "truths" to present is subjective. In the presentation, however, every fact is verifiable, and the writer can make that known by attributing each fact to its source—a person, a document, or the writer's direct observation. Broadcast reporting works in this mode with great efficiency. The film itself is the documentation, but the choice of what to show and what to leave out is highly subjective. Edward R. Murrow's classic documentary on Senator Joseph McCarthy in 1954 conveyed truths about the Red-baiting senator that had eluded the print reporters hamstrung by conventional concepts of surface objectivity.

At the next level—and we are talking about print once again—the writer decides that all the attribution slows the story down, obscures the truth by making it hard to digest. So he or she leaves it out, assuming a fly-on-the-wall or omniscient stance as a fiction writer would. The resulting story may even include interior monologue—what a person in the story is thinking about at a critical time. How does the writer know what someone else is thinking? By asking. This is the new nonfiction in its purest form, and it is very hard work because of the extreme pains the writer must take to collect the details. A very large number of details must be collected in order to provide an inventory from which those that move the story the most effectively can be selected. Fiction writers can make them up as they go along, but journalists must go to the trouble of collecting them. The possibilities for error are, of course, proportional to the number of facts one needs to collect.

A few newspaper reporters have been so successful at this kind of writing that they have been able to write themselves right out of the newspaper business. Tom Wolfe, one of the ablest practitioners, went from reporting for the *Washington Post* to writing magazine articles to writing books, including *The Right Stuff,* the most readable and intimate history of the U.S. space program you could ever hope to find. The technique produces riveting copy, but it may be too demanding for daily journalism.

When the nation's college campuses were in a period of upheaval over civil rights and the war in Vietnam, reporter Jimmy Breslin visited one of the nation's most placid and conservative campuses, my alma mater, Kansas State University. It was the spring of 1969, a year after the death of Robert Kennedy, with whom Breslin had visited this same campus, covering Kennedy's brief run for the Democratic presidential nomination. The piece he wrote is loaded with nostalgia and constructed like an O. Henry short story, about the clean-cut, sincere Kansas kids, so far away from the currents and controversies of the day. And Breslin unveils little hints that the winds of change are reaching even this isolated, inland place. The punch line comes after he describes his visit to the field house, now empty, where Kennedy had denounced the war to the applauding, screaming students. He recalls Kennedy's private premonition that "If we don't get out of this war, I don't know what these young people are going to do." Then Breslin walks with a group of students across the campus, and they come to a burned-out shell of a building, with twisted girders and charred stones. Breslin asks the students what used to be in that building. The ROTC, he is told.[10]

The timing and construction of the piece were beautiful. After 16 years, my eyes still mist when I read it. Most of the facts were correct. But Breslin stretched too far. The burned-out building was Nichols Gymnasium, used for physical education classes and the student radio station. Its military connection was ancient and minor: The ROTC had stored its rifles there before the Military Science Department got its own building in 1942. That building was not harmed, and the arsonist who destroyed the gym, as far as anyone was ever able to determine, chose it because it was convenient and not because it had any connection with the war in Vietnam. Breslin's story is so beautiful that one wishes that it *had* been the ROTC building that burned. He needed the ROTC in that building to give his piece its construction as a short story, with scene building, foreshadowing, and an ending that picked up the point and drove it home. The problem with the new nonfiction is that the world is not designed as a series of short stories.

This example brings us to the next and most perilous level of the new nonfiction, where the desire to communicate at an entertaining and gut-satisfying intensity overshadows everything else. The reporter may combine aspects of different scenes and present them as a single episode, build composite characters, invent dialogue—in short, write fiction without letting on that it is fiction. Though it might seem unethical on its face, there is a surprising amount of support for such tactics in print journalism, although not very much among newspaper people.

The *Wall Street Journal* in 1984 quoted Alastair Reid, a writer for the *New Yorker,* as admitting having done all those things over the course of his career:

> In fact, Mr. Reid, who has been appearing in the *New Yorker's* prestigious pages since 1951, says he has spent his career creating composite tales and scenes, fabricating personae, rearranging events and creating conversations in a plethora of pieces presented as nonfiction. He insists that his embellishments have made his articles that much more accurate in spirit, if not in fact.[11]

Newspaper people have tried the same sort of thing. Consider the following two leads from two different newspapers, ten years apart:

> Jimmy is 8 years old and a third-generation heroin addict, a precocious little boy with sandy hair, velvety brown eyes and needle marks freckling the baby-smooth skin of his brown arms.[12]

> Walter Vandermeer—the youngest person ever to be reported dead of an overdose of heroin here—had been identified by many of the city's leading social service agencies as a child in desperate need of care long before his body was discovered in the common bathroom of a Harlem tenement on Dec. 14, two weeks after his twelfth birthday.[13]

The first lead is gripping. Its omniscient perspective enables the reader to visualize the social problem of child drug addiction in a very direct way. The second is more traditional but also packs a vigorous emotional effect. And by giving a full name and a date, it signals that it is going to be fully documented, which in itself gives it a certain power not present in the first lead.

The first lead, of course, is from Janet Cooke's famous "Jimmy's World," which won the 1981 Pulitzer Prize for feature writing and was later proved to be fiction. The prize was returned, and Cooke's career was destroyed. The editors whose careless procedures let her get the piece into print survived.

The second story, by Joseph Lelyveld of the *New York Times,* was published in 1970 as the result of painstaking investigation by Lelyveld and Charlayne Hunter-Gault, and it demonstrates that the choice is not between fictionalizing and forgoing the conveyance of certain kinds of insights to the reader. Objective truth can be found. It just takes more work, and more time—more than the pressures and limited staffing of daily journalism will often allow.

The furor over the Cooke incident sensitized newspaper managements sufficiently to force some other cases of fiction writing to the surface. Michael Daly was a reporter at the *New York Daily News.* Dispatched to Northern Ireland to cover the unrest there, he wrote nine columns in eight days. One of them described the shooting of a young boy witnessed by a British soldier named Christopher Spell. The story described Spell's life in some detail; where he had grown up, when he had joined the army, what he had seen in the war. The British army complained, and British reporters discovered that there was no Christopher Spell nor even a soldier who fit Daly's description. The story may have told an essential truth, but, if so, it was a constructed truth.

"The question of reconstruction and using a pseudonym—I've done a lot of it," said Daly. "No one has ever said anything."[14]

Daly resigned, something that might not have been necessary if his trouble had not occurred at a time when the Cooke case had made news people jumpy. The rule spoken often in jest, "Don't let the facts stand in the way of a good story," does not quite get at the underlying attitude that lets such events happen. News people value facts, but they are rewarded for productivity, and events that have the structure and feel of a short story simply can't be found and written at the rate of one or more a day. When the pressure is on to produce, the subjective approach can get out of hand.

The tension between the two approaches—sticking to objective fact and taking a shorter route to perceived truth—shows up clearly in a daily and mundane dilemma: whether or not to clean up a source's quotes. Few people speak spontaneously in graceful, complete sentences. Most of us converse with false starts, redundancies, "aws," and "ums," with frequent unclear connections between subject and verb. But our listeners know what we mean. When a news source speaks in this manner, and a reporter knows what the source means, should the reporter give the exact words or an easily understandable translation? We're talking about material used in exact quotes, now, not the obviously permissible paraphrasing and summarizing of indirect quotation.

The *Associated Presss Style Book* recommends limited clean-up activity. Here is an example collected in the *Columbia Journalism Review.* Ronald Reagan was asked in 1979 why he expected to be more successful in seeking the Republican presidential nomination in 1980 than he had been in 1976. He said the electorate was changing, and added, "And . . . uh . . . it's kind of encouraging that more of the people seem to be coming the same way, believing the same things." In the AP story, that quote came out: "It's remarkable how people are beginning to see things my way."[15]

This practice is dangerous. But even using exact quotes can be a potent weapon when used selectively. In the early 1960s, I attended a gathering of correspondents called by an aging Representative Mike Kirwan to promote a barge canal he wanted built in Ohio. Kirwan had a distracting speech mannerism in ordinary conversation. He would punctuate every few phrases with, "You see the point I mean?" Other reporters left that out. I put it in, may Kirwan's ghost forgive me, hoping that this evidence of the congressman's dottiness would clue readers in to the folly of his canal plan, a classic example of objective fact used subjectively. The fact that objective fact can be manipulated so unscrupulously leads some news people to denounce objectivity as a myth that ought to be abandoned. I strongly disagree. There must always be subjective interpretation, but the risks of distortion are greatly reduced if the interpretation rests on a basis of solid fact. The first duty of a newspaper is to be accurate, and if it cannot be that, it cannot be fair, balanced, or useful to the society it serves.

The fact that a literal objectivity is impossible should not discourage news people from striving for it. Most of the ideal values prized in our society are impossible to attain in pure form. We always have to settle for something less. Truth is difficult to come by, verifiable fact is hard to discover and communicate, and that is exactly why we should try so hard, and why news people should resist temptation to abandon the quest and try some easier route. The new nonfiction pushed journalism too far toward art. Now it needs to be pushed toward science.

NOTES

1. Walter Lippmann, *Public Opinion* (New York: Free Press, 1965), pp. 10–11.
2. Ibid.
3. *Report of the National Advisory Commission on Civil Disorders* (New York: Bantam Books, 1968), p. 1.
4. Interview with Angus Campbell, 1968.
5. Nelson Antrim Crawford, *The Ethics of Journalism* (New York: Greenwood Press, 1965).
6. George Herbert Mead, "The Nature of Aesthetic Experience," *International Journal of Ethics* 36 (1925–1926): 382–393.
7. Ben H. Bagdikian, *The Media Monopoly* (Boston: Beacon Press, 1983), pp. 170–175.
8. Philip Meyer, *Precision Journalism: A Reporter's Guide to Social Science Methods,* 2d ed. (Bloomington, Ind.: Indiana University Press, 1979).
9. Everette E. Dennis and William L. Rivers, *Other Voices: The New Journalism in America* (San Francisco: Canfield Press, 1974).
10. Jimmy Breslin, "Last Year in Manhattan (Kansas)," *New York,* June 9, 1969.
11. Joanne Lippmann, "At the *New Yorker,* Editor and Writer Differ on the 'Facts'" *Wall Street Journal,* June 18, 1984.

12. Janet Cooke, "Jimmy's World," *Washington Post,* September 28, 1980.

13. Joseph Lelyveld, "Obituary of a Heroin User Who Died at 12," *New York Times,* January 12, 1970.

14. Quoted in Michael Kramer, "Just the Facts, Please," *New York,* May 25, 1981, p. 19.

15. Ronald Turovsky, "Did He Really Say That?" *Columbia Journalism Review,* July/August 1980.

CHAPTER 5

Conflict of Interest

For public officials, conflict of interest is perhaps the most visible ethical problem. The county commissioner who votes for a road project affecting his own land is a common example. The federal official who comes from a private industry to regulate that industry—and eventually goes back to it—is another. Because journalists are very much aware of conflicts of interest among public officials and tend to report them vigorously, they are sensitive to conflict in their own affairs most of the time.

The problem is that conflict of interest can be extremely subtle. Few cases are as clear-cut as that of R. Foster Winans, a *Wall Street Journal* reporter who used his position on the paper to find out what stocks were going to be mentioned in a column called "Heard on the Street" and passed that information on to friends in advance of publication. Such information has very high potential value, because the column discusses the outlook for individual stocks and groups of stocks. Once published, the information tends to affect the prices of the stocks mentioned, favorably or unfavorably, depending on what is said. An investor who gets that information a day ahead of anyone else can buy or sell accordingly and make a lot of money.

Winans's friends not only used the information to make a lot of money but also shared the proceeds with Winans. This violated the *Journal*'s strict conflict-of-interest rules and, as it turned out, was against the law. It led to a jail sentence.

That is an example of a perfectly straightforward case. The conflict was wrong, and everyone knew it, including the participants. Money doesn't always complicate matters. Its involvement often has the virtue of making a case clear.

The psychological effect of such horror stories on journalists can be to create a knee-jerk aversion to every kind of imaginable conflict. That is the only explanation I can think of to the response in the ASNE survey to the following problem:

Your company receives a special rate from a major hotel chain for your traveling employees. A staff member goes out of town for a three-day business meeting and, because the site of the meeting is a major cultural center, decides to stay through the weekend at his own expense. He pays his own hotel bill for Friday and Saturday nights, but at the special commercial rate. Your company has a conflict-of-interest policy against employees accepting any kind of favor or reward from suppliers. Should your company:

a. Fire the traveling employee.
b. Require him to reimburse the hotel the difference between the commercial and regular rate and warn him not to repeat the practice.
c. Warn him not to repeat the practice, but not worry about reimbursement because the amount is so small.
d. Make a ruling that such discounts are not considered favors or rewards under the conflict-of-interest policy.

This is a commonplace occurrence, and you may wonder why it was included in the survey at all. It was inspired by the Minnesota Multiphasic Personality Inventory, which includes a "lie scale" consisting of questions designed to detect whether test takers are trying to make themselves sound too good. A person who says his or her sex life is always fine and that he or she never worries about money gets flagged by the lie scale, because nobody's sex life is perfect all the time and even millionaires worry about money some of the time. The lie scale tells the evaluator of the test how much credence to put in the other answers.

A lie scale seemed an appropriate safeguard in a questionnaire on ethics because it is so much easier to make an ethical response to a hypothetical case than a real one. And I was troubled by what seemed to be an unthinking response pattern among some journalists who will argue against any activity that has the slightest hint of an ethical taint without stopping to weigh the costs and benefits of the particular action.

Nevertheless, I was amazed at the responses to the hotel discount question. Hardly anyone wanted to fire the traveling employee, but the most frequent response among editors and staff members was (b): warn the employee and require him to reimburse the hotel. This was one of the few questions in the survey that showed sharp differences among publishers, editors, and staff members. Table 5.1 summarizes the responses.

TABLE 5.1

	Publishers	Editors	Staff	Total
Fire him	0%	1%	0%	1%
Warn with reimbursement	24	44	65	44
Warn only	27	16	14	19
Rule no conflict	49	40	21	37

Half the publishers, three out of five editors, and four-fifths of the staff members believe it is wrong to make personal use of company discounts. That is far too many to dismiss as liars or social-approval seekers. What is going on here?

We have tapped at least a piece of the old conflict between business office and news side that leads to the money-aversion principle discussed in Chapter 2. The responses are linked with those given to other cases involving money in some way. That would explain the difference between publishers' responses and those of the editors and staff. News-editorial people tend to be suspicious of money and its power, while a publisher is more likely to evaluate expenditures in instrumental terms. Money is a tool, in the publisher's eyes, and one uses it as efficiently as one can. The hotel chain's discount is made to attract a large-volume customer, and the hotel people do not care whether the errands that bring the customers to the city are personal or business. The publisher may perceive the transaction as a fringe benefit that costs the company nothing and that the employees might as well share.

The editors and staff may, in contrast, feel that the discount will make the traveler want to write nice things about the hotel. That is reading a lot into the case, which does not mention a writing assignment, much less one about the hotel. And if that were the problem, it would apply to company discounts as well as those for personal use.

The more likely source of conflict in this kind of situation is that it could lead to an inefficient allocation of the company's resources. This is generally the reason for prohibiting favors from suppliers in the first place. If individuals receive a personal benefit from a supplier, they may use their influence to continue the company's relationship with that supplier even when competing suppliers offer the company better deals. The obvious example is the extensive reward system used by airlines to attract frequent fliers. Bonuses of free trips, based on mileage flown on the providing airline, are given to the flier, even though the company paid for the trips the employee took to "earn" the bonuses. The practice has led to some severe distortions in purchasing behavior, with employees traveling out of their way and wasting company time and money to utilize the airline whose credits they are collecting. If newspapers observed slippery-slope ethics in their business transactions, they would ban such bonuses or require that the free travel be used for company business.

Confession time. For two decades, I have carried a rental car sticker with a corporate-rate identification affixed to my American Express card. And I have always accepted the corporate rate—still do, in fact, even if it is a vacation trip with no university business at all. And while I was at Knight-Ridder headquarters, I bought photo supplies for personal use from the *Miami Herald*'s supplier at the paper's discount. The supplier made frequent deliveries to the *Herald*, and the practice of photo hobbyists in the building was to call in their orders and have them added to the next delivery but billed to the individual. There was no cost to the *Herald*, and the supplier was glad to get the business. Knight-Ridder has a written conflict-of-interest policy, and it includes a ban on accepting benefits from suppliers. Executives are required to sign a statement every year to certify that they have read the policy and to disclose any problems they have with it. When I mentioned the photo-supply situation on my annual statement, my bosses ruled the discounts out of bounds. I appealed. The appeal went all the way up the chain of command to the outside director in charge of ethics, Clark Clifford, the Washington lawyer. He ruled in my favor. Such discounts should not be considered favors or rewards under the conflict-of-interest policy, he said—correctly, I thought, since, at the practical level, neither business-side nor news-side decisions were affected.

A Conflict-of-Interest Sensitivity Index

My case illustrates a key problem in analyzing conflict-of-interest issues: It is extremely hard to be objective, and how you feel about any given situation depends on your direct interest in the outcome. Editors and publishers are more likely to be tough with a staff member's problem than are those to whom the problem might also apply, namely fellow staff members, as the following problem in the survey illustrates:

> An investigative reporter does a thorough and praiseworthy exposé of inequalities in tax assessment practices. In the course of investigating for the story, he looks at his own assessment records and finds that a value-enhancing addition to his property was never recorded, and as a result, his taxes are $300 less than they should be. He reports this fact in the first draft of his story, but, later, at the urging of his wife, takes it out. Should the editor:
> a. Insist that he leave the information in, even though it will raise the reporter's taxes.
> b. Talk to the wife and try to persuade her that the reporter's honesty at leaving it in will be rewarded, someday.
> c. Leave it to the reporter to decide, but appeal to his conscience.
> d. Don't interfere.

Editors were much tougher on that reporter than were publishers, and the reporter's fellow staff members were the most lenient. As Table 5.2 shows, 74 percent of the editors would make the reporter leave the information in. Only 58 percent of the staff members would do so.

Responses to this item correlated with answers to two others in the financial area—a sign that the items are measuring the same underlying sensitivity to financial conflicts. That means we can combine them to make an index and see what kinds of news people have the greater sensitivity on

TABLE 5.2

	Publishers	Editors	Staff	Total
Insist he leave it in	63%	74%	58%	65%
Persuade the wife	2	4	2	3
Let reporter decide	29	17	29	25
Don't interfere	6	5	11	7

this score. There is not much subtlety in the other two items. Both describe behavior that is clearly wrong. The only dispute is over how severe the penalty should be. The first deals with the behavior of a business manager, and it describes a common situation, a junket, which is a trip paid for by someone else:

> The business manager of the company has developed close friendships with Canadian newsprint suppliers, reinforced by regular hunting trips in the north woods, as their guest. The company decides to prohibit managers from accepting favors from suppliers. The business manager continues to take the trips. Should the publisher:
> a. Fire the business manager.
> b. Impose discipline short of firing and extract a promise that it will not happen again.
> c. Advise the business manager to pay his own way on these trips or reciprocate by hosting the suppliers on equivalent outings.
> d. Decide that the no-favor rule should not apply to such long-standing and clearly benign activities.

You might think that business-office aversion would make the staff come down especially hard on the business manager in this case—but you would be wrong. Staff members were considerably more lenient than either publishers or editors. Why? Perhaps the memory of their own junkets—which used to be commonplace for news-side people—softened their judgment. The opinion breakdown is shown in Table 5.3.

Junkets are fun. I took a junket in 1960, with Guest Airways on its maiden jet flight from Miami to Mexico City. A number of local government officials went along. We were wined and dined in the best Mexico

TABLE 5.3

	Publishers	Editors	Staff	Total
Fire him	20%	28%	18%	22%
Lesser discipline	58	51	48	52
Have him pay	17	18	32	22
Okay the trips	5	3	2	3

TABLE 5.4

	Publishers	Editors	Staff	Total
Fire him	44%	47%	49%	47%
Stop moonlighting	13	16	15	15
Don't use position	43	36	37	39
Be more discreet	0	0	0	0

City restaurants. At one point during the festivities, I slipped out to the University of Mexico City to write a story about a student uprising. The airline publicity people were unhappy when that proved to be the major story of the trip. I never took another junket, unless you want to count a 20-minute ride on the Goodyear blimp. But the practice persists among journalists.

The third item in this series deals with a clear case of staff malfeasance:

The chief photographer moonlights as a wedding photographer. The father of a bride calls the editor and says the photographer had made a sales pitch to his daughter and included a sly hint that if he is hired for the job, her picture has a better chance of making the society page. The editor investigates and confirms that this is the photographer's regular practice. Should the editor:

a. Fire the photographer.
b. Impose lesser discipline and order the photographer to stop moonlighting.
c. Allow the photographer to continue moonlighting, but order him not to use—or pretend to use—his position to gain favored treatment for clients.
d. Ask the photographer to be more discreet.

Editors, publishers, and staff members were in close agreement on this one. In each group, respondents representing close to half of the newspaper circulation in the United States said they would fire the photographer who traded on his paper's good name for personal gain (see Table 5.4).

These three items can be combined into an index by awarding one point for the extreme action in each case. The extreme actions were firing the moonlighting photographer and the junketing business manager and insisting that the investigative reporter reveal his own tax break. And the range of possible scores is 0 (no extreme actions) to 3 (extreme action in every case). Across the three groups, the distribution was as follows:

0	1	2	3
20%	39%	28%	13%

So it turns out that news people representing 41 percent (28 plus 13) of total circulation are fairly tough on financial conflict, opting for the extreme solution in at least two out of the three cases.

On this traditional value, there was a pronounced age difference. The editors, publishers, and staff members were all more likely to be in the highly sensitive group if they were young. As newspaper people grow older, gain in responsibility, and come into increased contact with their communities, they appear to learn how to compromise, and they take less of a hard line on financial conflict. They become, in short, less absolutist.

Financial Conflict of Interest

Because money erases the ambiguity from a transaction, one might suppose that if absolutism is justified anywhere in the ethics of journalism, it would be in an absolute ban on news people taking things of value from people who want to influence the content of the paper. The practice violates the clearly defined model of First Amendment fundamentalism, in which the newspaper is viewed as totally detached while it collects its observations of the rest of the world. The fact is, however, that not even the large and well-respected papers that take pains to pay their own way on everything find it possible to be completely pure.

Junkets, Speaking Fees, and Inside Information

For example, the practice of allowing travel writers to take trips paid for by airline, passenger ship, and hotel companies has disappeared from the larger papers—but only where staff travel is concerned. Many of the same papers continue to buy travel stories from free-lance writers who accept the freebies. The practice is mitigated in some cases by requiring writers to disclose in their stories the nature and the source of the free services.

Movie and theater reviewers still sometimes get in on free passes. In its 1977 ethics code the *Washington Post*, a paper close to absolutism in other areas, specifically allowed an exception to the "we pay our own way" rule for reviewers of cultural events. Book and record reviewers still rely on free copies. Because a newspaper can review only a small fraction of the books and records it receives, the problem arises of what to do with the surplus. Bea Washburn, who reviewed books for the *Miami Herald* in the 1950s, used to hold free-book days, on which she would dump the largesse onto a table for the rest of the staff to help themselves. The *Des Moines Register & Tribune* disposes of surplus books at an employee sale and gives the proceeds to charity. Other reviewers sell the surplus to cut-rate book dealers. (So do some professors who accumulate free "examination copies" from publishers hoping for textbook adoptions.) Charles W. Bailey, former editor of the *Minneapolis Tribune*, reported that some book reviewers have been fired for this last practice, which seems a little extreme when no effect on newspaper content is evident.[1] This may be an example of the money-is-evil reflex.

Junkets are still taken by reporters for smaller papers, which are less likely to have the wherewithal to pay the fare for their people. Even larger papers will sometimes allow a government—our own or a friendly foreign nation's—to pay for a trip. And it is considered less of a problem if the reporter is on leave from the newspaper at the time of the trip. Until recently, the highly respected Nieman Foundation brokered junkets sponsored by foreign governments for its fellows.

There is also considerable uncertainty about what to do about fees offered to reporters for public speaking. Consider the following case from the ASNE survey, which, like many others in that study, is based on a real incident. Because there was not much disagreement among publishers, editors, and staff members, only the percentage responses of editors are given:

> An investigative reporter uses a computer to analyze criminal court records and writes a prize-winning series. A major computer manufacturer then offers to pay him $500 to speak at a seminar for reporters which it is sponsoring at a university. Which of the following best describes your view?
> a. The reporter should be allowed to make the speech and accept the $500 from the computer manufacturer. (24 percent)
> b. The reporter should be allowed to make the speech, but accept the $500 only if the honorarium is paid through the university. (18 percent)
> c. The reporter should be allowed to make the speech but not to accept the honorarium. (51 percent)
> d. The reporter should not be allowed to make the speech. (8 percent)

Another confession, of sorts: As one of the early users of computers in journalism, I received such an offer from IBM in the early 1970s. I turned it down. As a national reporter in Knight-Ridder's Washington bureau, I drew almost every story assignment involving computers that came along. Undaunted, IBM went to a local reporter in a smaller town, himself a pioneer in computer applications, and he accepted the offer. I think we were both right. In my case, the danger of conflict of interest was obvious, and the ethical cost was too high. In his case, the possibility of conflict was neither clear nor present.

The above item illustrates the need to weigh balances and the difficulty of writing rules that can be generalized to all cases, as the absolutists would do. Notice also in this item the utility of laundering. If the computer company's money is paid through a university, approval of the reporter's taking it climbs from 24 percent to 42 percent (24 plus 18). If your main concern is the appearance of conflict rather than its reality, a university can provide a virtuous disguise.

Columnist Neal Peirce told Bailey that his specialty, state and local government, attracts speaking engagements that bring in as much income as he earns on his column. His policy: "to charge for the speech what the market will bear and trust my own principles to keep my coverage objective."[2] It would be strange indeed to write a rule that confined a professional communicator to a single medium, and Peirce's principles are far more likely to make sense than a blindly applied money-is-evil rule.

But rules are often blindly applied. Bruce Swain reported the case of a *Milwaukee Journal* reporter who was fired for purchasing stock in a company he had written about. There was no indication that he had used inside information, nor did he write about the company after he bought the stock. But he had acted on information collected while in the act of reporting. It was the problem of apparent conflict again. The paper required, his editor said, that "reporters avoid any situations which might lead the public to believe they have a conflict of interest."[3]

Now, one of the side effects of being a reporter (or a teacher, for that matter) is that in the process of discovering and imparting the truth, you learn a lot of things yourself. And if the rule is that you create an apparent conflict of interest every time you act for personal benefit on the basis of something learned while reporting, then a lot of reporters have a lot of apparent conflict. If such conflict were barred, I would not have quit smoking in 1968—a decision I made while in the act of writing a story on smoking and health. I would not have purchased a home in Reston, Virginia, a decision traceable to research for a story on the new town's early development. In fact, a lot of us, including me, would have had to choose different spouses, having married people we met on company time.

The Ambiguity Trap

And that brings us to another philosophical trap whose argument resembles that of the slippery slope but leads to an opposite conclusion. The argument of the slippery slope, remember, is that if you take one modest and seemingly harmless step in its direction, you are doomed to tumble all the way to the bottom. The parallel when dealing with nebulous conflicts is what Professor Cecil Miller at Kansas State used to call the argument of the beard. If you pull one whisker out of a beard, he would tell his students, it is still a beard. If you pull out two whiskers, you still have a beard. No one can say exactly how many whiskers have to be removed before it is no longer a beard. Therefore, is there no such thing as a beard?

You hear that argument in discussions about ethics. Because there can be no precise rules, it is said, there can be no rules. Anything goes.

No. The beginning of ethical wisdom in the newspaper business, and perhaps elsewhere as well, is to accept a certain amount of ambiguity. Rules can be written without being simplistic on the one hand or overly general on the other. But the best rules may be a little bit fuzzy, may allow for some battlefield decision making, even where money matters are involved. If you are not convinced of that, you will be by the time you read the remainder of this chapter, which is about nonfinancial conflicts. Without money as the measuring tool, the ambiguity problem becomes severe indeed.

Nonfinancial Conflict of Interest

It is this ambiguity that causes journalists to worry about apparent conflict as much as real conflict. "There is no difference between *real* and *perceived* conflict," wrote Bailey; "the one is as damaging as the other."[4] And each of the codes of the three major organizations of journalists enjoins the appearance of conflict as well as actual conflict. The trouble with that, as Bailey acknowledged, is that perceptions differ.[5] What appears to be conflict to one observer may appear to be civic duty to another. Since almost any action may appear to be a case of conflict to somebody, the problem then becomes very much one of judgment: How big must a conflict be before it is enjoined, and which of a newspaper's many constituencies are entitled to have their perceptions considered? The rules against apparent conflict, intended to simplify matters, will, if observed, complicate things enormously.

This point will become clear in a moment, when we look at some specific cases. Start with the premise from the SPJ/SDX code: "Journalists must be free from obligation to any interest other than the public's right to know." There is the ring of First Amendment fundamentalism in that statement. It assumes the man-from-Mars stance, the state of total detachment. Enter the profession of journalism and cut your ties with everything else. As Katherine Carlton McAdams has noted, that can't be done. There are no men from Mars. "Journalists are real people who live in families, vote, and cheer for the home team," McAdams wrote. "It is hoped that all personal loyalties are set aside when one is performing in a professional role—but . . . journalists never can be sure to what extent they are influenced by personal factors which control perceptions and predispositions."[6]

To find out how news people really resolve problems of nonfinancial conflict, the ASNE survey asked its respondents to react to a list of simple but lifelike situations. The instructions for this set of situations were as follows:

> One of the topics that often comes up in the newsroom is whether a reporter with a history of personal activity in a given area is more or less qualified to cover a related field because of that history. Here are some examples, and in each one, please assume that the reporter is otherwise well qualified. Please decide whether the reporter's personal history or circumstances are likely to be a help, a hindrance, or make any difference in covering the indicated field.

And here are the items, ranked according to their order of acceptability as judged by respondents in the poll. The number that follows each item represents the percentage (based on circulation) who said the reporter's background was a help, minus the percentage who said it was a hindrance. A positive value means that, overall, it was considered more a help than a hindrance; a negative value means that it was considered more a hindrance than a help.

1. A reporter with a law degree is assigned to cover local courts. (+94 percent)

2. A reporter who was raised on a farm is assigned to cover agriculture. (+94 percent)

3. A black is assigned to cover civil rights. (+8 percent)

4. An assistant city editor who has married an heiress and undertaken the task of managing her investments has been promoted to business editor. (−4 percent)

5. A Washington bureau chief's daughter becomes secretary to a Cabinet officer. (−11 percent)

6. A reporter whose parents run an independent oil-exploration business is assigned to cover energy. (−25 percent)

7. A reporter who has served on the current mayor's staff returns to the paper to cover local politics. (−36 percent)

8. A reporter who took a leave of absence to work in the vice president's successful election campaign is assigned to the Washington bureau. (−37 percent)

9. An atheist is assigned to cover religion. (−51 percent)

10. A reporter with a history of vigorous union activity is assigned to cover big business. (−62 percent)

11. A reporter whose best friend is elected mayor is assigned to cover city hall. (−74 percent)

12. A copy editor whose wife runs a public relations firm sometimes edits stories which mention his wife's clients. (−74 percent)

Not all of these cases are strictly nonfinancial, it turns out on close examination. The farm reporter may hope to inherit the south 40, and the heiress's spouse may treat her money as his own. But at least there are no immediate financial transactions involved.

It is possible to get some clues to the thinking behind these judgments by looking at their cluster patterns. McAdams did that and found four underlying influences.[7] First, items 7, 8, and 11 were intercorrelated, meaning that a person who disapproved of one of the three activities had a greater-than-chance likelihood of disapproving of the others as well. Since they all involve political connections and all ranked low on the list in acceptability, the underlying viewpoint is easy to see: conflicts of interest involving political connections are generally, although by no means unanimously, thought to be bad.

Another group of three similarly connected items includes items 4, 5, and 6, the cases of the heiress's spouse, the secretary's parent, and the oil scion. News people tend to be consistent in their attitudes toward family connections. There is less disapproval here than in the case of the political connections, but whether they approve or disapprove, news people tend to be guided by an underlying attitude toward conflicts involving family connections. There is a consensus that such connections are harmful, but it is not nearly as strong as the taboo against political connections.

And that brings us to a very interesting finding. The case of the farmer's son who covers agriculture did not cluster with the other family problems at all. Moreover, it was almost unanimously viewed as a non-problem. The cases it did cluster with were also low-priority problems: the black covering civil rights and the lawyer covering courts. What is the unifying thread among these three cases? McAdams called it "affinity for sources." Lawyers like courts or they wouldn't be lawyers. Farmers like farms, and blacks like civil rights activists. This affinity brings with it some expertise, some sensitivity to nuances, some access that a reporter without such affinity might not get. So affinity is another yardstick that is used to judge potential conflicts of interests. And the consensus is that it helps more than it hurts.

Two remaining items formed a fourth cluster and they represent the mirror image of affinity. The former union activist who covers business and the atheist who covers religion have histories that could give them antagonistic relationships with their sources. These cases drew strongly negative reactions from the news people in the survey. What McAdams has uncovered here is a little-noticed principle applied to conflict-of-interest cases, and it goes a long way toward explaining how the handling of these cases turns on the appearance of conflict as opposed to the reality. This is a principle that we can add to the list of hidden codes or unwritten rules, that we began in Chapter 2:

Rule No. 6: *The seriousness of an apparent conflict increases in proportion to the degree that it antagonizes news sources.*

Without this principle to explain them, the above answers make no sense. Objectively, an atheist should be an ideal reporter of religion because he or she will be as close to the position of the man from Mars as it is possible for a human to get. A religion reporter who has a faith of his or her own has to have a particular faith, and that faith will conflict with some of those being covered. The atheist, however, has no temptation to interpret events from a sectarian viewpoint. A case could even be made that the labor activist would approach business news as a man from Mars because his or her labor activity has imposed the needed psychological barrier between the reporter and management.

The data suggest a corollary to the rule that affinity is better than antagonism: The utility of affinity (or the disutility of antagonism) varies directly with the general popularity of the source. If the source is unpopular, then affinity is not as relevant. Farmers are popular, oil companies are not. Thus the farm reporter is judged on the basis of the affinity rule, while the energy reporter is judged on the sterner ground of family conflict—even though the structure of the two cases is exactly the same. The disparity demonstrates that ethical judgments made by news people have much to do with the popularity of the causes or institutions that are affected. This finding is no surprise, but it does clearly document the inadequacy of the vision of the First Amendment fundamentalists. If the man-from-Mars standard conflicts with public relations considerations—which is what the concern for the "appearance" of conflict is all about—then it is the standard that gives way. Appearances come first.

This ordering of priorities is not necessarily a bad thing. A newspaper's influence is its most precious asset. It should not spend that asset lightly. Holding a double standard for the children of farmers and the children of oil explorers may not be too great a price to pay. It can be logically argued that following the principles outlined above is both rational and ultimately beneficial to society because it preserves the newspaper's influence and its ultimate ability to meet its First Amendment responsibilities. What is wrong with this picture is covering it with the rhetoric of absolutism. That rhetoric, with its fundamentalist, black-or-white approach, hides from view the shadowy areas where the real ethical struggles are waged.

To go a step further, it may be unrealistic to think of nonfinancial conflict of interest as an ethical problem at all. If what gives the treatment of these problems consistency is their effect on the newspaper's credibility with its community, then they should be treated as business problems, for that is what they are. If we think of these dilemmas as business problems, the patchwork of seeming contradictions in their treatment suddenly resolves into an underlying consistency. "News people," McAdams wrote, "resolve most conflicts of interest in ways that make good business sense. . . . News people may be unconsciously sensitive to what the traffic will bear in their communities, and they may step around the conflicts of interests they know they must avoid, all the while preserving the quality of the news product."[8]

This view provides a rationale for treating apparent conflict with the same intensity as real conflict. "So as a practical matter," wrote Bailey, the former editor, "it is not enough for journalists to satisfy themselves about their behavior—they must also convince their readers, listeners and viewers."[9]

What confuses many journalists when they discuss conflict-of-interest problems is that they do not realize that they are discussing it on two levels: the ethical level, at which they need to satisfy themselves, and the business level, at which they need to satisfy an audience that has its own concerns. At the purely ethical level, one's formal alliances, kinships, and fraternal or business ties do not matter as much as how these connections affect one's work. The code of ethics of the North Carolina Press Association recognizes this when it says, "Honesty demands objectivity, the submergence of prejudice and personal conviction." No matter how much a news person tries to isolate himself or herself from formal ties, there will always be some that require an effort of submergence. This effort, inner and personal, is of more intrinsic importance than any rearrangement of the external and visible world, although it is the latter that gets the attention.

Edwin A. Lahey once confided to a colleague that he didn't think he could ever write anything bad about Robert Kennedy because of a favor Kennedy had done for a member of his family. Yet those who knew Lahey, perhaps better than he knew himself, were confident that he would put duty first. Lahey was a reporter whose values came straight from the heart.

For every such situation, there is one action, perhaps not taken often enough, that can mitigate a conflict problem on both the personal and the public levels, and that is to disclose it. Les Carpenter's column peaked in popularity when his wife worked in Lyndon Johnson's White House. Everyone knew that Liz Carpenter was press secretary to the First Lady, and some editors and readers may have thought the tie would give her husband insight or gossip not available to less well-connected writers. Columnist George Will's tie to the Reagan administration—he helped Reagan prepare for the 1980 debates—was less well received, and it probably cost him some clients; but it is well known. Ann Landers was criticized by the *Columbia Journalism Review* for failing to disclose that her son-in-law was a funeral director when she wrote a column defending the funeral industry, describing it as "unjustly maligned." Disclosure heals, as First Amendment theory says it should. Give the people the facts and let them weigh them as best they can. Even if George Will is a Reagan partisan, at least he's a known partisan, and readers who wish to can discount his opinions even while enjoying his wit.

Disclosure is one form of protection for the public. Another is built into the system: good, old-fashioned American pluralism. The fact that there are so many conflicts of interest, real and imagined, manifest and potential, minimizes the likelihood that any one will cause serious problems. Pluralism makes room for writers, like Les Carpenter and George Will, who are close to sources because there are plenty of other writers without this affinity or with loyalties to opposing points of view. It is the duty of editors to keep the pluralist pot bubbling by attending to the variety of viewpoints and interests represented in their spaces. They need to do this in addition to keeping an ear attuned to the marketplace to determine what the traffic will bear. If conflict of interest cannot be eradicated, it can at least be managed.

NOTES

1. Charles W. Bailey, "Conflicts of Interest: A Matter of Journalistic Ethics," *National News Council*, 1984, p. 14.

2. Quoted in ibid., p. 23.

3. Bruce Swain, *Reporters' Ethics* (Ames, Iowa: Iowa State University Press, 1978), pp. 10–11.

4. Bailey, "Conflicts of Interest," p. 9.

5. Ibid., p. 15.

6. Katherine Carlton McAdams, "Non-Monetary Conflicts of Interest for Newspaper Journalists," graduate winner of the Carol Burnett–University of Hawaii–AEJMC prize for student papers on journalism ethics, 1985.

7. Ibid.

8. Ibid.

9. Bailey, "Conflicts of Interests," p. 9.

CHAPTER 6

Privacy

The problem of balance in ethical decision making is particularly acute where the issue is protection of privacy or other values that require some restraint in publishing. A newspaper's First Amendment duty to get the facts, shed light so the people can find their way, and publish despite pain and discomfort is in direct conflict with the right to privacy. This conflict has become sharper in recent years, with growing judicial recognition and public support for a common-law right of privacy. Nowhere in the constitution is there a mention of right to privacy, but judicial decisions, many of them dissents, began to recognize such a right in this century. "The right to be let alone," said Associate Justice William O. Douglas in a 1952 dissent, "is the beginning of all freedom,"[1] Ironically, Douglas was one of the rare First Amendment absolutists on the Court.

Journalists often behave as if they are not aware of the conflict. The codes of SPJ/SDX and APME both cite a right to privacy as if respecting it or even defining it were no problem, given the other things a newspaper must do. Editors denounce intrusive and deceptive reporting methods by media other than their own, but find justification for such behavior on the part of their own staffs. Much of the new sensitivity over privacy stems from Watergate. The Nixon administration used some obviously unsavory tactics to promote its ends, including illegal wiretapping, the break-in and theft of records from the office of Daniel Ellsberg's psychiatrist, and the Watergate burglary itself. Surreptitious recording, illegal entry, and false identities had also been occasional tools of reporters, and these were seen in a different light after Watergate.

Privacy problems generally fall into two categories: one is the use of questionable and intrusive reporting methods to obtain information that would not otherwise be forthcoming. The other is the unnecessary revelation of embarrassing or painful private facts, regardless of how they are gathered. The latter is by far the more common, although the former cases often make for more interesting discussion. In the ASNE survey, a sample of editors representing 39 percent of total U.S. circulation said that cases involving injury to feelings or embarrassing private facts reached the discussion level in their newsrooms at least once a month. Questionable reporting methods came up less often: Only 8 percent of circulation was represented by editors in whose newsrooms the problem was discussed at least once a month.

Questionable Reporting Methods

Going undercover to get information that would not otherwise be available is an ancient tradition in the fields of espionage, police work, sociology, and journalism. In espionage, there are no rules: whatever works, goes. In police work, there are constitutional and legal constraints, the chief one being the rule against entrapment: A suspect is entrapped if an undercover law enforcement officer entices him to commit an illegal act that he otherwise would not do; but setting up a situation where the suspect can be observed while he commits the crime of his own volition is not entrapment.

In the social sciences, projects where the observer blends with the background as much as possible are common. William Foote Whyte's study of Italian street life in the Boston area during the Depression is the classic example. Some of the people in the neighborhood knew that Whyte was at Harvard and that he was planning to write a book about his observations. But during the four years he lived in the neighborhood, Whyte did not take pains to explain his purpose to everyone he met. Instead he concentrated on fitting into the society he was studying. He got elected secretary of the Italian Community Club and made field notes while pretending to record the minutes. He involved himself in local politics, even participating in fraud by voting more than once in the same election in order to ingratiate himself with his subjects.

Whyte disguised the location and the names in his book, but this did not do much to mitigate the invasion of privacy. "The people in the district, of course, know it is about them," he said later, "and even the changed names do not disguise the individuals for them. They remember the researcher and know the people with whom he associated and know enough about the various groups to place the individuals with little chance of error." For some, he acknowledged, "it could hardly be pleasant reading."[2]

Social scientists have spent a good deal of time agonizing over the ethics of deception where there is a possibility of direct physical or psychological harm to the people they are studying, as in the famous obedience experiments of Stanley Milgram.[3] There is not so much agonizing over the effects of simple participant observation, where the only harm comes in the effects of publication. Whyte's work has been widely imitated over the years.

Intrusive Deceptions

Until Watergate, journalists were similarly uninhibited. Kurt Luedtke, who highlighted deceptive reporting practices in his screenplay for *Absence of Malice,* occasionally engaged in deception himself in his reporting days. In the 1960s he and a female reporter once posed as a brother and sister seeking an illegal abortion in order to gain entry to the abortionist's office. Once inside, they revealed their true roles.[4] Journalists have posed as schoolteachers, longshoremen, whorehouse customers, military service-men, law enforcement officers, high school students, physicians, and many other things that they were not in order to observe behavior and hear statements that they would not otherwise have been able to observe and hear. John Connors of the *Miami Herald* was so casual about deception that he routinely placed a "Dr." in front of his name when he made restaurant reservations, believing that physicians got better service. Once, at a classy restaurant in Coral Gables, he was called upon to attend an emergency: an elderly woman was choking. Unabashed, he slapped her on the back and cleared her windpipe.

When Eugene L. Roberts, Jr., later executive editor of the *Philadelphia Inquirer,* and Jack Nelson, later Washington bureau chief for the *Los Angeles Times,* were young reporters covering the civil rights movement in the South, they contrived an ongoing deception for areas where big-city journalists were less than welcome. Each developed the habit of wearing a coat and tie and stuffing a bulky notebook in the inside coat pocket to create a bulge resembling that created by the shoulder holsters then worn by FBI agents. Seeing that bulge, people in crowds were more likely to leave them alone. Years later, Roberts would recall with relish the reaction of a teenage boy in a Bogalusa, Louisiana, drugstore when he and Nelson walked in. "Look," the boy had said as he jabbed his girlfriend, "It's the FBI."

"We had perfected our whole act," said Roberts.[5]

The *Detroit Free Press* once sent a reporter to visit abortion clinics and present urine samples for analysis. The clinics told her the samples showed she was pregnant—but, in fact, the samples had come from her male colleagues. A great variety of consumer stories, such as those based on taking a car with a loose sparkplug wire to be evaluated by repairmen, have been based on concealed identity.

After Watergate, there was a tendency to classify all forms of journalistic false identity as unacceptable. The *Chicago Sun-Times* missed a chance at a Pulitzer Prize when some members of the Pulitzer board decided that its entry had been based on an unethical violation of privacy. A team of undercover reporters had operated the Mirage Bar for four months in 1977 in order to expose bribery and tax fraud among building inspectors and other municipal authorities. "In a day in which we are spending thousands of man-hours uncovering deception, we simply cannot deceive," said Benjamin C. Bradlee, the executive editor of the *Washington Post,* who was a member of that board.[6]

This is the absolutist, black-or-white mentality in new guise. It does not allow for weighing the costs and benefits of a clandestine intrusion.

In fact, Bradlee's own reporters are allowed to conceal their identities, so long as the concealment is not elaborate. "Here is one of the many areas in which ethical lines are blurred at the *Washington Post* and elsewhere," admitted Leonard Downie, now managing editor, at a meeting of Wisconsin newspaper people, adding:

> What the *Post* has allowed is for reporters to engage in activities in which it may appear to others that they are not reporters. One *Post* reporter worked among migrant workers to witness their exploitation. Another rode regularly on a minibus that took relatives of prisoners for visits at the local prison to witness drug smuggling. They were not allowed to lie if asked to identify themselves, and they did eventually in each case identify themselves in later interviews with all whom they observed. But they did not volunteer their identities before that point. For me, this is a difficult scrambling of the lines between ethical and unethical conduct for a reporter.

In looking for a place to draw a line, news people, with their characteristic low tolerance for ambiguity, tend to gravitate toward highly visible cues, such as the distinction between passive and active deception. But even this distinction can be strained and artificial. In 1951, as a student editor, I covered a controversy over the quality of the design of new buildings at Kansas State University. Members of the faculty of the department of architecture had been especially critical, and they were summoned to a meeting with the dean of the School of Engineering and Architecture. I put on a clean white shirt and a black knit tie and attended the meeting. Members of the faculty knew who I was because I had interviewed most of them. The dean, however, could not tell me from a junior faculty member, and he proceeded to commit a clear violation of academic feedom by instructing the faculty not to criticize publicly the work of the state architect. I published the story and got away with it, although the administration of the university came very close to suppressing the student daily that day. Was my deception active or passive? Some news people would argue that it was passive because I did not claim to be anything but a reporter. I believe it was active, since I did not normally wear a necktie on weekdays and therefore had actively donned a disguise. Was it justified? A case can be made that it was. A breach of academic freedom is a serious enough event to justify extraordinary measures.

Some news people argue that deception should not be used if a story can be obtained by more conventional means. But the tradeoff is more complicated than that. In most cases where deception is used, conventional means are available, but they carry a greater risk of error. And if the story is damaging to someone, the moral burden to minimize error is greater. In the case of the repressive dean, accuracy was especially important.

I could have waited outside the meeting and interviewed faculty members, particularly the dissident ones, afterward. That might have led to another ethical dilemma, the problem of the anonymous source. Participant observation is straightforward, enabling a reporter to see and hear things with his or her own eyes and ears, and that is a virtue. In fact, given that accuracy is journalism's fundamental objective, it is an extremely important virtue, one that should not be readily sacrificed to a rigid rule against deception. And if the participant observer has the transaction wired for sound, accuracy is even better served. "It is not a question of the press having a First Amendment right superior to a right of privacy," the University of Georgia's Kent R. Middleton has reminded us; "rather, it is a question of the press or another private citizen or any other participant in public business documenting transactions where legitimate privacy claims cannot be made."[7] News people, in their eagerness to appear ethical, may accept too many privacy claims too readily.

In the Mirage Bar case, the activities under investigation were clearly public business, and there was no clear right to privacy. So what was really bothering the critics of the *Sun-Times*? What we may have here is another of journalism's unarticulated rules. Coming as it did in the wake of the elaborate chicanery of Watergate, the story may have triggered a new rule, which can be stated as follows:

Rule No. 7: *The morality of deception by reporters is inversely proportional to the complexity of the deception.*

In other words, the news business is following an unconscious rule that offhand, casual deception is okay, but elaborate and carefully planned deceptions are wicked.

There may be yet another unconscious rule operating here: that new reporting methods are suspect simply because they are new. No newspaper had ever gone to the trouble and expense of buying and operating a bar before. If there is indeed such a hidden rule, it would also explain some reporters' resistance to taping their telephone interviews. It is an emotional response to a new technology.

Most editors are uncomfortable at the thought of reporters using tape recorders on their telephone without advising the other party.[8] In most states and the District of Columbia, it is legal to tape your own conversation without notifying the person at the other end. (It becomes illegal wiretapping only when the recording is made with *neither* party's knowledge.) Nevertheless, the *Washington Post,* like many other large newspapers, does not allow its reporters to tape calls without informing the other party.

The recording does nothing to change the reporter's function. It is not sneaky so long as the interviewee knows that the conversation is for the record. It should not be necessary for the interviewee to know the precise means by which the record is being made, although in the past it was often obvious. Reporters working the telephone used to take notes on manual typewriters, which gave a loud clue to the person being interviewed. Now they are more likely to use computer terminals, whose keyboards are nearly silent. So is the scratch of pencil on paper. To my knowledge, no one has suggested that reporters taking down a person's words by these methods should notify the interviewee that they are doing so. So what distinguishes a tape recording? Merely this: It can later be used to contradict a source who has a change of heart and decides to lie about what was said. A tape recorder's evidence is not easily denied. In this respect it is an extremely powerful tool, and perhaps it is its power that makes some journalists uncomfortable. But can there be such a thing as moral duty to preserve for one's sources the ability to lie? Of course not. "The use of a concealed tape recorder," Theodore L. Glasser has written, "is not nearly the moral quandary its opponents would have us believe: It is not an invasion of privacy, it is not an act of deception, it is not a form of eavesdropping, and it does not constitute entrapment."[9] It might be a tactical dilemma, because the practice could scare off some sources. But to try to decide the issue on moral grounds complicates it unnecessarily. And arbitrarily to ban all tape recording deprives news people of a much-needed technological solution to the ever-present problem of accuracy. Always important, verifiable accuracy becomes crucial when litigation or denials create a need for corroboration of the reporter's account. Much tape recording by journalists is done for this sort of self-defense—although the same journalists who do it would probably refuse to submit the tape as evidence in a legal proceeding unless they themselves were the defendants.

A reasonable balance has been urged by editor Anthony Insolia of *Newsday,* who says the use of surreptitious taping is justified in those cases where there is a risk of having to defend in court the accuracy of what has been published. However, he adds, "We should not feel that every effort we undertake automatically justifies such tape recording."[10] Another possibility is to make taping routine—at least in telephone interviews, where the mechanical device is not distracting—and to announce to the public that all conversations with reporters are recorded unless the reporter states otherwise. That would constitute notification by default.

Arguments over intrusive methods sometimes follow utilitarian logic, which is a way of thinking about ethics that goes back to the ancient Greeks but was most clearly codified by British thinkers Jeremy Bentham and John Stuart Mill early in the nineteenth century. This viewpoint holds that actions can be evaluated by their known consequences. Ends do justify the means if the utility of the ends outweighs the disutility of the means. With this logic, it is easier to justify the intrusions when there is a chance that some important ends will be served. Absolutist thinking, in contrast, can lead to stern and unrealistic resolutions against such behavior in any circumstances. Most editors are against concealed intrusion as a general principle, but there are always cases where its use is appealing, and these cases sharply divide the news business. Here is a situation that raises the ethical ante by introducing a highly intrusive form of deception. The ASNE survey asked the following question:

A just-nominated presidential candidate is meeting with state party chairpersons to discuss his choice for vice-presidential candidate. The meeting is closed to the press. A reporter, pretending to be a party staff person, hands a briefcase to one of the people going into the meeting and asks him to leave it on the table for his boss. The briefcase contains a tape recorder, and the reporter retrieves it after the meeting. Should the editor:

a. Admonish the reporter and kill the story. (45 percent)
b. Admonish the reporter, but use the information as background for conventional reporting. (29 percent)
c. Admonish the reporter, but use the story. (7 percent)
d. Reward the reporter and use the story. (20 percent)

The percentages are editors' views, adjusted for circulation. Staff members had about the same views, but publishers were less inclined to reward the reporter and more likely to limit the use of the information to background for conventional reporting. If this were a real situation and not an abstraction in a survey, I am fairly confident that the proportion of journalists who would use the story would be higher. Even in the survey, a majority would use it in some form. Intrusive methods continue to have a fair amount of respectability, despite Watergate.

Here we have a case of pure eavesdropping by electronic means, and that carries a heavier moral burden than an undercover operation where one meets the deceived person face to face. The invasion of privacy is flagrant, and the deception is greater. To get that bugged briefcase into the room requires an outright lie. Deception, or at least the withholding of relevant information, is a common reportorial trick. Robert Woodward and Carl Bernstein admit to a number of instances of lying to sources in *All the President's Men*. They pretended to have information in hand that they actually only hoped to get. They told some sources that others had said things about them when in fact they had not. One of them even pretended to be Donald Segretti on the telephone. In journalism the stakes are often so high that the utilitarian approach leads too easily to abuse. As Sissela Bok has noted, deception can become a habit that is invoked so casually that it is done without consideration or analysis, even in cases where the information is available without deception:

> The absence of such reflection may well result in countless young reporters unthinkingly adopting some of these methods. . . . The impression gained by the reading public is that such standards are taken for granted among journalists. The results, therefore, are severe, both in terms of risks to the professional standards of those directly involved, the public view of the profession, and to many within it or about to enter it.[11]

It is the presence or absence of reflection that is crucial, not whether or not intrusive deceptions are ever made. If the absolutists followed their own logic, they would have no restaurant critics, and many other kinds of consumer stories would remain unwritten. Here again the solution, not so paradoxically, is a dose of openness. Give notice: Publish in the newspaper on a periodic basis fair warning that conversations reporters have with members of the public are routinely recorded. Publish notice of planned undercover investigations. Before a consumer investigation, write to all the possible targets of the investigation and advise them that it is being contemplated. Won't this put targets on their guard and ruin the story? Not necessarily. Editors who have given notice several months in advance have still found malpractices to expose. Even police departments have granted that courtesy. The Chapel Hill, North Carolina, police department announced its intention to use undercover agents to document cases of liquor sales to underage buyers before it actually began collecting evidence and making arrests—yet there was no shortage of violations. Even Bok, who eschews the easy rationalizations of the utilitarian approach, gives guarded approval to such deception with fair warning when the function is the monitoring of social services. The function is important, and the subjects are not totally unsuspecting.[12]

Subtle Deceptions

Cases of bugged meetings and concealed identity represent one extreme of the use of deception to get information. The ASNE survey also included an extremely subtle example, an item in which the reporter's identity and mission are not concealed, but his or her political views are. If a reporter's views relate strongly to the subject being covered, is it best to conceal them, to be forthright, or to bow out of the picture altogether?

A reporter is assigned to find out about the activities of a political action group whose objectives are in sharp contrast to his own strongly held views. To get the story, he needs the cooperation of group members. Should the reporter:

1. Ask the editor to assign someone else to the story. (35 percent)
2. Take care to explain his own views to the sources so that they can take them into account in deciding how to deal with him. (1 percent)
3. Keep quiet about his own views, but be frank and forthcoming if asked. (45 percent)
4. Adopt the stance of a sympathetic neutral. (20 percent)
5. Pose as an advocate of the action group's objectives. (0 percent)

These are editor percentages. Staff members were less likely to favor giving the assignment to someone else, favoring instead some modest, preferably passive deception. The clear consensus for deception shows that deception is indeed sanctioned by news people when it is not dramatic.

Journalists here have something in common with social scientists, who often try to collect data in the field without letting the act of collecting change the nature of those data. They have found that the stance of sympathetic neutral works best, and I have not found any evidence in the social science literature of concern for the ethics of instructing interviewers who are neither sympathetic nor neutral to behave as if they were.

The problem, as Bok suggested, is to avoid making deception an unanalyzed habit. Those who decry it in all cases are being more absolutist than analytical.

Revelation of Embarrassing Private Facts

For the second major category of privacy problems, the utilitarian solution is particularly inefficient. These are cases where the revelation of embarrassing or painful private facts causes intense pain to a few while the immediate benefit for the many is both slight and diffuse. How do you assign weights in a cost–benefit equation when only one person may bear an intense cost while the benefit is spread over millions and may be so slight as to be not noticeable?

The case of the person who threatens to commit suicide if certain information is published is an example. The cost to the affected individual is extreme. If the editor heeds the threat and fails to publish, the world will not notice and will not be measurably poorer. There will be a cost, however, and, in the long run, it could become visible. The editor would have established that he or she could be manipulated by emotional blackmail and was willing to yield some editorial control to external and perhaps nonrational forces. Editorial decision making, as much as any other professional activity, needs to be handled as rationally and as evenhandedly as is humanly possible, and an editor should not abdicate that responsibility. In part, this is a slippery-slope argument: If I do it for you, I'll have to do it for every nut who calls and threatens to kill himself. And once you introduce the slippery slope into a cost–benefit equation, you have already made up your mind, because the slippery slope, by definition, is open-ended; its cost is infinite. Privacy cases deserve more subtle analysis than that. They involve a weighing of conflicting responsibilities: the obligation to print the news, on the one hand, and the obligation to deal compassionately with readers and sources, on the other. The notion of obligation taps the other great stream of ethical thought, the one that involves our hearts more than our brains (or at least the quantitative portions of our brains), telling us to do our duty. The Judeo-Christian injunction to treat others as you yourself would want to be treated or Immanuel Kant's admonition to let your actions set a standard for the world, or John Rawls's proposal to make decisions as if you were ignorant of which role you would ultimately play in the transaction under consideration—any of these might prove a better guide to such cases than utilitarian thinking.

Remember the story in Chapter 2 of the traveler whose Key West hotel had burned down? The wire story had identified him as a guest and indicated that the hotel was frequented by gays. He told his hometown paper he'd kill himself if it published his name in the story. And news people representing 9 percent of total U.S. circulation said they would have complied and kept his name out. Another 49 percent would have used his name but omitted the gay angle—not a guarantee of complete protection for the citizen, since the gay angle would be sufficiently unusual that the national media would be sure to highlight it, and some of the man's neighbors would be likely to find out and make the connection. And fully 42 percent of the newspaper audience is served by people who said they would ignore the plea and print the story in full.

Such threats are often idle, but not always. In 1976 the *Dallas Times-Herald* learned that Norman J. Rees, a former oil company engineer, had been a spy and a double agent, working for both the FBI and the Soviet Union. Rees said he would kill himself if they published the information. They did, and he shot himself the same day.

Attempts to manipulate editors with suicide threats are not unusual, the *Times-Herald* said later in a published statement. "In our judgment, if a story is newsworthy and supported by the facts, it is our policy to publish."[13] A more balanced rule would require that the story be newsworthy and in the public interest, as this one was because of the nature of the subject matter. But the knee-jerk urge to publish does in fact consider only newsworthiness. Most news people, as the survey results indicate, leave some room in their personal equations for other elements.

Editors' Concerns Versus Readers' Views

News people sometimes feel that they are alone in feeling the pressure of conflicting obligations in such cases, but editors who have sought feedback from their readers have been surprised at how closely reader concern resembles their own. Michael J. Davies of the *Hartford Courant* published six case summaries of the type used in the ASNE survey and invited readers to tell what they would do. While the 690 who responded were a self-selected sample and not necessarily representative of readers in general, the exercise showed that editors and these highly motivated readers thought much alike. This was one of the cases used by Davies:

> A prominent businessman who has long been associated with many charitable causes is discovered to have embezzled $10,000 from one of the charities he heads. There is no question about his guilt, although police haven't yet filed charges. No one else knows about the story. When your reporter contacts him for comment, he begs for a chance to make restitution without a story appearing. He says there are extenuating circumstances that he can't explain now. He also says his wife is in critical condition at a local hospital after suffering a heart attack, and that publicity resulting from such a story would surely kill her.

1. Would you run the story now?
2. Would you wait until you have had an opportunity to talk with the hospital's doctors and are confident the woman is out of immediate danger, then run the story?
3. Would you give him an opportunity to make restitution and, if this is done, write nothing?[14]

Editors were as likely to choose the first as the second, more moderate course. But a plurality of readers, 47 percent, would make sure the woman was out of danger before proceeding. Letting the man make restitution was the readers' second choice, but only a weak third choice for editors. Nevertheless, the differences between the readers and the 10 editors were not great; no more than 20 percentage points on any of the three choices. And differences were greater within the two groups, editors and readers, than between the two groups.

Perhaps the sharpest division in the newspaper business comes on the question of whether to report the names of rape victims. There are two schools of thought, and both tend to use utilitarian, cost–benefit analysis. Most papers avoid printing the names of rape victims in the absence of some compelling reason to do so. Their reasoning is that rape, unlike other crimes, places a special stigma on the victim, and she should be spared the additional trauma of being publicly identified. Women are reluctant to report rapes anyway, and by keeping their names out of the paper, newspapers can encourage the increasing number of victims who do report.

The counterargument is that the secrecy only reinforces the social stigma, that greater openness would yield to more realistic responses to the crime and its victims. By giving the victims anonymity, says sociologist Gilbert Geis, the media are "further imparting to the act of rape a particularly dirty, shameful nuance, rather than serving to portray it and its victims as no more than part of the criminal scene."[15] Michael Rouse, former managing editor of the *Durham* (N.C.) *Morning Herald,* agrees and also cites the problem of balance. The accused person is named, although presumed innocent until proven guilty, and he has the constitutional right to confront his accuser. "When there are two people in a court, one of whom is accusing the other, we think we should treat them alike," Rouse says.[16]

The *Durham Herald* does not use the victim's name until she becomes an accusing witness, and, in response to protests by the local Rape Crisis Center, it stopped publishing victims' exact addresses, which might aid a rapist or his friends in tracking down a witness for revenge. Many newspapers in recent years have reconsidered their general policies on running the exact addresses of crime victims because the information might lead other criminals to the same victims. But there is a potential cost to any departure from the policy of keeping public information before the public. David Shaw cited the case of a man whose rape conviction was reversed after the name of the complaining witness was published. A man who knew her led the authorities to evidence that established her unreliability as a witness, which would not have happened if a policy of strict secrecy had been followed.[17]

The Relentless Urge to Publish

There are, however, many newspaper intrusions into privacy where no reasonable benefit to society can be identified other than blind adherence to the virtue of publication as an abstract principle. On January 6, 1960, I was awakened around 4:00 A.M. by a call from my city editor, Derick Daniels, who told me that a National Airlines flight to Miami was missing and that I should interview the pilot's family, who lived on my block in south Dade County, Florida. Is there any social benefit to reporting that the families of dead pilots suffer? I don't know of any now, and I didn't then. Sleepily, I dressed and stumbled over to my neighbor's house. Another neighbor, Bill Henderson, who was also a National pilot, was already there, sitting up with the wife while search planes traced the southbound route. I've been assigned to the story, I said. The other media are coming, and I might as well keep you company and fend them off for you when they do. I was welcomed inside. We passed the time by talking about the missing pilot, his life, and his plans, and I was sitting there in the familiarly shaped kitchen— the tract house was a duplicate of my own—when the phone rang. Henderson answered, spoke a few words, hung up, turned, and made the dreaded announcement: "They found wreckage." When the *Miami News* and the television crews came to the door, I spoke with them on the porch, giving names, ages, and backgrounds of the family. After they left, I went home, sat at the typewriter, and, as the sun rose, wrote what I knew of the lost pilot, his family, and what had happened in the kitchen that morning. And then I broke one of the strongest taboos in the newspaper business: I showed the story to my source before turning it in to my editor. That day's newspaper would soon be forgotten, but I would still have to face my neighbors. There was no objection, and the story ran. What would I have done if the pilot's family had objected? I don't know for certain, but I probably would have rationalized publication in some form. Utilitarian, cost-benefit ethics had no part in the decision to carry out that assignment. The other impulse was operating, the search for a universal rule—and the rule that reporters with difficult assignments usually heed while the clock is ticking toward a deadline is that publishing is better than not publishing, and a way must be found. Even today, I might hold to that value just as relentlessly.

Twenty years later, I faced a somewhat different situation. Two University of North Carolina students were killed when the Volkswagen in which they were riding smashed into a tree. The driver had been drinking. Local papers ran a few paragraphs from the police blotter and then shelved it as just another routine drunk-driving story. I challenged the students in my advanced reporting class to dramatize the problem of drunken driving by tracing the last day in the lives of the dead students in minute detail to show how UNC's heavy-drinking social climate put students at risk for such disasters. The story was painful to the dead students' families. I know because I had long talks with members of one of the families. But this time a case could be made that there was an overriding social benefit. The story helped to place drunken driving on the community's agenda of problems to be solved.

The relentless urge to publish can produce strange and unexpected benefits, and it can do strange kinds of harm. Oliver Sipple had carefully protected his family in Ohio from knowledge that he was gay and an active member of the homosexual community in San Francisco. Then he saved a president's life, lunging for Sara Jane Moore's gun hand, spoiling her aim at Gerald Ford. This heroic act drew national attention to the details of his private life. His family found out about his sexual preference and, he claimed when he sued the *Los Angeles Times,* disowned him. In reporting that story, was it necessary to mention Sipple's sexual orientation? In fact, more than prurient interest was involved. There was a time—brief, as it turned out—when it appeared that President Ford might not publicly thank Sipple because he was gay. Some believed that disclosure of his sexual preference would help dispell the stereotype of gays as ineffectual sissies. A utilitarian analysis might reasonably assign enough weight to those benefits to justify a decision to publish.

There is, however, another cost, and those who fear slippery slopes ought to consider this one as well. Such decisions to publish can reinforce the habit of attributing too much value to publication; can lead to thoughtless, reflexive decision; can produce an obstinate, compulsive behavior pattern that will lead the public rightly to perceive newspapers as uncaring. Every horror story pushes the entire industry a step closer to that slippery slope. Arthur R. Miller, a Harvard law professor who has made privacy his specialty, has a collection of them. One, which he does not document, is about "a newspaper's decision to publish the name and location of a robbery victim who pleaded for anonymity, because she was on the terrorist hit list in another country."[18] He cites the case of Leonard Berkowitz, arrested as New York's "Son of Sam" killer in 1977. The day after he was captured, three photographers and a reporter were arrested and charged with criminal trespass for breaking into his apartment.[19]

"In my judgment," Miller wrote, "if journalists continue to push the outer limits of the law and fail to exercise restraint, society, speaking through its courts, may find it necessary to expand the right of privacy. The same courts that have interpreted the First Amendment so expansively can contract those rights."[20]

The Expansion of Privacy Rights

Some states have tried to expand privacy rights, with some bizarre results. In several state legislatures, concern for the rights of persons accused of crime has led to laws requiring that arrest records be sealed and permitting conviction records to be expunged after the guilty parties have paid their debt to society. In 1975, the Oregon legislature closed criminal records so tightly that police officers could not reveal who was arrested, charged, tried, sentenced, or released. Within 24 hours after this law was enacted, the jails started to fill up. In Pendleton alone 175 suspects were being held. "We're having a hard time getting rid of them, because we can't tell their friends and relatives they're in here," a deputy explained. The legislature quickly repealed the law.[21]

In 1973 the Missouri legislature decreed that if a person was arrested but not charged within 30 days, all the records of the case must be closed. If there was no conviction within a year, the records must be destroyed. That sounds harmless enough, but it turned out to provide a curtain behind which official abuses could occur unseen. The *St. Louis Globe-Democrat* tried to investigate reports that a magistrate was routinely and arbitrarily dismissing drunk-driving cases. Ordinarily, it would be a simple matter to check by reviewing the court records. But the relevant records in this case were precisely those that were not available. The investigation got nowhere.[22]

If privacy is a slippery and difficult problem when considered at the ethical level, it is even worse as a legislative or judicial problem. Better legislation might bypass problems like the two just cited, but tampering with public records and, in effect, rewriting history carry large costs of their own. It would be far better for newspapers to deal with ethical problems well enough themselves that legislative controls would be obviated. Where problems are so difficult as to be insoluble, then it would pay news people at least to keep them ambiguous wherever possible rather than to force every issue to a resolution. Ambiguity is underappreciated by journalists, yet it is the great lubricant of democracy.

Some editors will agree to this need for self-discipline, but others will cry, "Chilling effect!" The First Amendment fundamentalists are in the latter group, and they perceive self-restraint as the first step on a slippery slope that will lead to worse kinds of restraint. Impatient with ambiguity, they seek to resolve even the silliest issues, on the theory that by defending the marginal cases, they strengthen their hands on the ones that really matter. In a way, this is an application of a very primitive bargaining theory. If you exaggerate your demands, you are more likely to get what you really want. Never give an inch until you are forced to. Miller attributes this view to the press in general: "Journalists apparently think that they are challenged by one Goliath after another and they, media Davids, must sally forth to slay the enemy. This strikes me as a distorted and egocentric view of the universe."[23]

His description can fairly be applied to those of the fundamentalist persuasion, but, despite the high visibility of their excesses, they are not representative of news people in general. Most are trying, and even the most aggressive newspaper will sometimes find a situation where restraint is called for.

A Case of Restraint

In 1959, when I covered the first school desegregation in Dade County, Florida, for the *Miami Herald,* we used restraint to abet the school board in a diversionary tactic designed to outwit the White Citizens Council and the Ku Klux Klan. The board focused all its overt attention on Orchard Villa Elementary School in an older neighborhood that was rapidly changing from white to black. As the school's opening approached, it was clear that only four or five white students would show up at the formerly all-white school. Meanwhile, the non-token integration would take place at a new school in the rural southern part of the county, near Homestead Air Force Base. To distract attention from it, the board had named it Air Base Elementary School, giving the impression that it was in federal rather than local jurisdiction. Blacks and whites would be represented there in rough proportion to their numbers in the population.

We reported the plan to desegregate Air Base Elementary, but kept it low-key and never let a reference to it get so high in a story that a headline needed to be based on it. The diehard segregationists ignored that school, wasted their venom in an unsuccessful effort to stir up resentment over the obviously token effort at Orchard Villa, and unwittingly allowed desegregation to make a smooth start in the Miami area. Audiences of younger journalists become indignant when I tell this story, insisting that we sold out by going along with the school board's ploy. Perhaps you had to be there to appreciate it. The memory of the 1957 violence at Little Rock's Central High and the bloody clashes between citizens and federal troops was very fresh then. Protecting our town and our children from that kind of uproar seemed more important than protecting traditional news values. All these years later, it still does.

One factor that sometimes gets in the way of self-restraint is the intense competition among news people. Although head-to-head competition among major dailies is gone in all but a few cities, there is still competition among different forms of media and among newspapers at the state, regional, and national levels. Competition has many positive effects, but it also leads to what columnist Tom Wicker calls "wild swings." He cites the Son of Sam case as an example. The intense competition between the *New York Daily News* and the *New York Post* built up the frenzy of interest in that case in the first place. Both papers were represented in the trespass charges mentioned earlier, and so were the *Washington Post, Time* magazine, and some national media that were trying to catch up. The pressure comes when a competing medium has something that another doesn't. Editors of the losing paper don't want to ignore the story, but they don't want to cite the competition, either. So they sometimes put tremendous pressure on their reporters not just to catch up, but to find a way to top the opposition, develop a new aspect, improve on its story in some way. As Wicker noted, "Just as the urge to compete—that is, to win—can lead a football player to jump offside or even slug an opponent in the heat of battle, so the urge to compete—to get ahead—can cause newspapers and broadcasters to breach their standards in ways that would never happen in conditions of calm reflection and unhurried judgment."[24]

The task for news people is to find incentives for calm reflection and unhurried judgment that are as powerful as the competitive pressures that drive them toward unthinking publication. The incentives should be internal —at the level of the individual or the organization. Much depends on the kinds of people who work in the news business and the kinds of organizations they work for.

NOTES

1. From the Douglas dissent in *Public Utilities Commission* v. *Pollak* (343 U.S. 451). 1952.

2. William Foote Whyte, *Street Corner Society,* 2d ed. (Chicago: University of Chicago Press). First published 1943.

3. Stanley Milgram, *Obedience to Authority: An Experimental View* (New York: Harper & Row, 1974).

4. The series of reports by Kurt Luedtke and Eleanor Kruglinski appeared in the *Miami Herald* beginning January 4, 1964.

5. Telephone interview with Eugene L. Roberts, Jr., September 18, 1985.

6. Quoted in David Shaw, *Press Watch* (New York: Macmillan, 1984), p. 139.

7. Kent R. Middleton, "Journalists and Tape Recorders: Does Participant Monitoring Invade Privacy?" *Comm/Ent Law Journal* 2, no. 2 (Winter 1979–80); 287–331.

8. S. Elizabeth Bird, "Newspaper Editors' Attitudes Reflect Ethical Doubt on Surreptitious Recording," *Journalism Quarterly* 62, no. 2 (Summer 1985); 284–295.

9. Theodore L. Glasser, "On the Morality of Secretly Taped Interviews," *Nieman Reports* 30, no. 1 (Spring 1985); 17–20.

10. Quoted in Alan R. Ginsberg, "Secret Taping: a No-No for Nixon—but OK for Reporters?" *Columbia Journalism Review,* July/August 1984, pp. 16–18.

11. Sissela Bok, *Lying: Moral Choice in Public and Private Life* (New York: Vintage Books, 1978), p. 128.

12. Ibid., p. 212.

13. Quoted in Bruce M. Swain, *Reporters' Ethics* (Ames, Iowa: Iowa State University Press, 1978), p. 72.

14. Michael J. Davies, "In Editor's Chair, Readers Face Tough Choices," *Hartford Courant,* 1 April 1984, p. B3.

15. Gilbert Geis, "The Case of Rape: Legal Restrictions on Media Coverage of Deviance in England and America," *Deviance and the Mass Media,* ed. Charles Winick (Beverly Hills, Calif.: Sage Publications, 1978).

16. Michael Rouse, "Rape," *ASNE Bulletin,* February 1982; also telephone interview, July 9, 1984.

17. David Shaw, *Press Watch* (New York: Macmillan, 1984), p. 109.

18. Arthur R. Miller, "The William O. Douglas Lecture: Press Versus Privacy," *Gonzaga Law Review* 16, no. 1 (1980): 852.

19. Cary Winfrey, "'Son of Sam' Case Poses Thorny Issues for Press," *New York Times*, 22 August 1977, p. 1.

20. Miller, "Press Versus Privacy."

21. Quoted in Paul R. Clancy, *Privacy and the First Amendment* (Columbia, Mo.: Freedom of Information Foundation, 1976), p. 32.

22. Ibid., p. 39.

23. Miller, "Press Versus Privacy," p. 849.

24. Tom Wicker, *On Press* (New York: Viking Press, 1978), p. 171.

PART THREE

Ethics and the Organization

CHAPTER 7

Publishers

Organizations have ethical values, just as people do, and likewise some of their values are visible and some are hidden. An individual has to resolve conflicts, and so do organizations. An organization is the projection of the people who work in it. These people create the organization's values and its culture—and its sometimes conflicting subcultures.

This "principle of moral projection," to use Kenneth Goodpaster's term, creates a personality for a newspaper.[1] To some readers, this personality is so clearly defined that the newspaper seems to be a monolith whose every act and moment is planned by some central directing authority. In fact, however, newspapers are quite decentralized. Large ones are run not by individuals but by committees—and not even by single committees, but by groups of committees. If you believe with Freud that the human personality is created by different aspects of the psyche that are frequently at war with one another, then the parallel is even better.

Power in an organization is not, of course, evenly divided among its members. A strong publisher creates a corporate culture that can leave its mark on an organization long after he or she is gone. But he or she does this not so much by dictating every detail and policy as by setting examples and by choosing the people who help run the place. Some publishers are highly visible to the people who gather the news. Others are remote and even sinister figures, moving in different worlds with different values. Murray Kempton once referred to this distance in a newspaper column, asking rhetorically, "Which of us has not sat one lonely night in the dirty lofts where we work and just once cursed the owner of the property?"[2]

Defining the Publisher's Role

The fact that ultimate power lies with someone else can be frustrating to journalists for whom power is one of the chief rewards of their profession. The best publisher, in journalistic folklore, is one who never shows up. The tradition of separation of news and business sides, in its extreme extension, is interpreted by a few to mean that not even the publisher should have anything to say about what goes into the newspaper. In reality, however, the two functions have to be integrated at some level, although the integration is often ambiguous or concealed. The main goal of the ASNE survey was to describe what actually goes on between editors and publishers, and it ran into difficulty from the very start over the problem of first defining the role of publisher and then identifying the person in that role. The editor was defined as the highest-ranking person in the organization who had full-time responsibility for the news operation, and the *publisher* was defined as the person to whom the editor reported. To find out who that person was, we simply asked the editors. In a simple, one-owner, privately held company, that was straightforward. In some more complicated organizations, the editor had to stop and think about it. In a few cases, the editor insisted that he or she did not report to anybody. Anticipating those cases, we had primed our interviewers with a few follow-up questions—for example, who sets your salary, reviews your budget, hires and fires the person in your job? That jogged their memories and elicited the name of someone we could define as publisher.

Sometimes one person has the title of editor and publisher, and that title implies a full integration of business and news functions. Under our definition, such a person was classified as a publisher, the news product not being a full-time responsibility. If it was a group newspaper, the publisher might be a corporate executive in some other city. In other group situations, the publisher is based locally but has a boss in a remote group headquarters. The central reality is constant in all these situations: the editor is responsible to someone, and that someone has to worry about the financial health of the newspaper. And, despite the wall of separation, financial health has something to do with a newspaper's ability to meet ethical responsibilities. To be moral, one must first be strong.

The tension between business goals and news gathering can be a built-in source of conflict. However, despite journalistic folklore's invisible publisher, most news people in the 1980s could generally see the need for publisher involvement. Editors, publishers, and staff members were asked this question in the survey:

> If an editor could set any rule he or she wanted for defining the relationship with the publisher, which of the following rules would result in the best newspaper?
> a. Don't ever talk to me about what I put in the paper.
> b. Make suggestions about the content if you want, but don't give orders, unless to fire me.
> c. Play a major role in the big decisions—creating new sections, targeting new markets, and major design changes, for example—but don't get involved in individual stories.
> d. Be the boss, all the way.

Staff members turned out to be the most faithful to folklore, preferring a smaller role for publishers than did either editors or publishers themselves, but the differences were not extreme. All three groups yielded a majority for the third option, publisher involvement in strategic but not tactical decisions, much like the role of a general in an infantry campaign. The following percentages are based on circulation.

	Publishers	Editors	Staff	Total
a. Don't talk	0%	0%	2%	1%
b. Suggestions	11	26	36	24
c. Major role	82	72	61	72
d. Be the boss	8	2	1	4

The same people were then asked,

Which of the above rules comes closest to describing what actually happens at your paper?

The distributions were roughly the same except for a big increase—on the part of everybody but the publishers—in the choice of the fourth option, "Be the boss, all the way."

	Publishers	Editors	Staff	Total
a. Don't talk	0%	2%	2%	1%
b. Suggestions	13	25	29	23
c. Major role	80	63	50	64
d. Be the boss	7	11	19	12

This difference in perception appeared at several points in the survey. In general, editors and publishers disagreed very little on matters of ethical substance. They did disagree on procedures—questions of who should be responsible or how the final decision should be made—and they disagreed in their perceptions of who actually makes the final decisions, with publishers giving higher estimates of their roles than editors. There was even a difference of perception on the straightforward factual question of how often the publisher visits the newsroom. Publishers said they visit much more frequently than either editors or staff members reported. Are publishers such mild, retiring personalities that nobody notices them when they walk into the newsroom? I doubt it. Yet publishers representing 49 percent of national circulation said they walk into the newsroom at least once a day, while editors reporting that much publisher presence accounted for only 32 percent and staff members 27 percent.

Publishers are a force on the news side, and to evaluate that force, we shall rely mostly on the editors' perceptions. But, because of the major difference noted above, we shall also contrast the editors' view with that of the publishers from time to time, hoping that truth will emerge as we go.

The Ethical Influence of the Publisher

To evaluate the publisher's influence on the ethical positions of a newspaper, we must first find out what the publisher does. The ASNE survey asked about a number of specific behaviors, some of them obviously good, wholesome things to do, and others not so wholesome. The responses to these questions were subjected to factor analysis, a computer-assisted procedure for teasing out the underlying patterns in survey responses. It shows which items are related to one another and therefore are probably measuring some aspect of the same factor.

The Index of Benign Publisher Participation

Here, we are getting very close to the heart of the trouble with newspapers, the crucial editor–publisher relationship. The substance of what we are looking for is too important to risk on a single question in a survey. There is too much room for error in the response to one question. What the questioner had in mind and what the respondent thinks is being asked about may be quite different. The safe thing to do is compile a number of questions that measure pretty much the same thing, ask them all, and then combine them into an index; one number that summarizes the content of the whole group of questions. Factor analysis identifies the individual items that will work in an index because of their shared relationship to whatever nebulous thing is being measured.

The following four items formed such an index. They came from a series of questions about the frequency of certain kinds of behavior. The reported frequencies, as in the rest of this book, include the automatic adjustment for circulation.

1. The publisher suggests "a major investigation or series of articles but leaves the final decision to the editor." Fifty-seven percent of the editors said their publisher did this at least once or twice a year, and that earns those publishers one point on this index.

2. The publisher "demonstrates, by selective use of praise or criticism, what he wants the editor to do." This happens at least once or twice a year, according to 70 percent of editors, and where it does, the publisher gets another point.

3. The publisher walks into the newsroom. Approximately 53 percent of the nation's newspaper readership is served by publishers who appear in the newsroom, with a presence sufficiently striking

TABLE 7.1
INDEX OF BENIGN PUBLISHER PARTICIPATION

Points	Frequency
0	8%
1	14
2	26
3	28
4	23

that the editors notice them, nearly every week or even more often. For thus showing up, another point on the index.

4. The publisher questions or otherwise participates in the assignment of a particular reporter to a story or a beat. For 45 percent, according to editors, it happens some of the time, and this is worth another point.

So here we have a laundry list of behaviors that describe a certain trait of publishers. They are not, on the surface, particularly harmful behaviors, although those who favor absolute separation of news and business functions might find them so. But, for an active publisher, these are relatively benign forms of involvement. So we can call this collective measurement the index of benign publisher participation. Scores range from 0, for a publisher who meets none of the four criteria above, to 4, for a publisher who meets all of them. If we were to combine the judgments of editors, staff members, and the publishers themselves, award points to each publisher on this basis, and add them up, we would get the distribution shown in Table 7.1.

The total is less than 100 percent because of rounding error. This distribution provides a handy way to classify publishers. Fifty-one percent score 3 or higher and can thus be classed as high in benign participation.

The Index of Malign Publisher Participation

If we are going to have an index of benign participation, our natural desire for symmetry requires an index of malign participation as well. No problem. The same factor analysis that gave us the benign index also produced a set of malign indicators. Because the behaviors on this list are much less frequent, a publisher scores a point if he commits one of them with any frequency at all. These are the indicators:

1. The publisher sometimes asks for special handling of an article about a company or organization that has some economic influence over the newspaper. According to editors, this happens, at least once in a while, at papers with 46 percent of the nation's circulation.

TABLE 7.2
INDEX OF MALIGN PUBLISHER PARTICIPATION

Points	Frequency
0	30%
1	22
2	23
3	18
4	7

2. The publisher sometimes asks for special handling of an article about an organization or individual with whom he has strong social ties. Here the frequency is a little greater, 52 percent.

3. The publisher sometimes asks the editor to send a reporter on a non-news mission for the company: to influence legislation, for example, or gather information on a competitor. This is relatively rare. Editors with 19 percent of total circulation have seen it happen.

4. The paper publishes, in its news columns, editorial matter on behalf of its advertisers. This material, commonly known as "blurbs" or "business office musts," is controlled by the business office. As we saw in Chapter 3, this hoary practice is still alive. It affects 24 percent of the nation's readership, according to the editors.

As with the other index, these four items are intercorrelated, meaning that a publisher who does one of these things has a better than random chance of doing the others, too. So, scoring each publisher by awarding one point for each of the four behaviors, we get the distribution shown in Table 7.2.

As with the benign index, we have combined the judgments of editors, staff members, and the publishers themselves to make this index. A natural cutoff point occurred between one point and two points, with 48 percent scoring two or higher and qualifying for classification as high in malign participation. We cut the cases there because we like to have categories of roughly equal size. Following the same logic with the benign index, we cut it between two and three to get categories of roughly equal size.

Types of Publishers

Now comes the fun part. We have two categories for each of two dimensions. That's four categories in all. And they define quite different styles.

1. Publishers who are high on both the malign and benign scales are very much involved in the operation of their papers, and they

FIGURE 7.1
PUBLISHER TYPES

Benign Participation

		High	Low
Malign *participation*	*High*	Politician	Fixer
	Low	Statesman	Absentee

FIGURE 7.2
PUBLISHER TYPES

Benign Participation

		High	Low
	High	Politician 26%	Fixer 19%
Malign *participation*	*Low*	Statesman 19%	Absentee 36%

apply their energy in both good ways and bad ways. We'll call them "Politicians."

2. Publishers who are high on the malign scale of activity but low on the benign scale are involved only for bad purposes. "Fixers" is not too unkind a label.

3. Their opposite numbers are the publishers who are high in benign activity and low in malign involvement. A complimentary label is called for here: "Statesmen."

4. That leaves the publishers who do so little that they are low on both scales: "Absentees," obviously.

We can make this classification model easy to visualize with a diagram; see Figure 7.1.

How many publishers fit into each category? Because of the way the categories are created, the four cells should be roughly equal in size. However, when we consider only the editors' responses to the questions, they are not equal at all. Figure 7.2 shows how they break down when only editors' responses are considered.

According to editors, the Absentee is the most common type of publisher, with the Politician in second place. The fixers are mercifully rare, but so are their opposite numbers, the Statesmen. When we consider only

FIGURE 7.3
PUBLISHER TYPES: PUBLISHER RATINGS

| | | *Benign Participation* | |
		High	*Low*
Malign participation	*High*	Politician 28%	Fixer 10%
	Low	Statesman 38%	Absentee 23%

FIGURE 7.4
PUBLISHER TYPES: STAFF MEMBER'S RATINGS

| | | *Benign Participation* | |
		High	*Low*
Malign participation	*High*	Politician 26%	Fixer 19%
	Low	Statesman 19%	Absentee 36%

publisher ratings, however, the frequency distribution changes. As Figure 7.3 shows, for publishers themselves, the Statesman is the modal type, and the Fixer is almost nonexistent. The proportion of Absentees drops, as well.

For yet a third view, let us consider staff members' view of the publisher. Staff members have perhaps the poorest vantage point from which to judge, but the distance can also make them more objective. They are less inclined to be kind to the publisher than either the editor or the publisher himself. In Figure 7.4 the Statesmen almost disappear. In staff members' view, the newspaper industry is dominated by publishers who are Fixers and Politicians.

Comparing Publisher Types

These differing viewpoints are illuminating in themselves, but they should caution us against treating these definitions of publisher types as absolutes. The exact percentage in any category is not as important as the question of whether publisher type makes any difference in ethical outcome. There are several ways to measure this.

One way is to see whether each publisher type shows more or less sensitivity on various sets of ethical problems than the other types. If the Statesman is really better than the Fixer, as one might infer from the behaviors that define these two types, that difference ought to be manifested in a different ethical outlook. We could go through the survey, looking at each item, but it would be more efficient—and more accurate—to create some additional indices. We'll start with an index of fairness and balance.

Index of Fairness and Balance

The procedure for creating this index is the same as that used in establishing the categories of publishers. Its individual items have already been discussed. They dealt with the Easter banner that read, "He Is Risen," the columnist who saluted his brother's new restaurant, and the problem of reacting to a competing medium's beat on a running story. Briefly, a news person gets one point for fairness in this index for wanting to do each of the following:

1. Get rid of that Easter banner.
2. Modify the treatment of the columnist's warm account of his brother's restaurant opening.
3. Acknowledge the competition's beat in print and cover the story according to its intrinsic news value.

To simplify the problem of comparing the four publisher types on this and other indices, we'll use index numbers, setting the average of the four groups at 100 and expressing each group's score as a ratio. Thus, a number above 100 indicates greater than average sensitivity, and a score below 100 represents less than average.

If our Statesmen, the publishers who do not try to obtain favored treatment for individuals or groups but who do interfere to improve the editorial product, are as good as they seem, they should show more sensitivity on this index than the others. And they do. However, it would be wrong to conclude that the Statesmen's exposure to newsroom concerns is the source of this sensitivity, because the Absentees, the publishers who stay out of the newsroom altogether, are nearly as sensitive. Moreover, this greater sensitivity on the part of the Statesmen is not consistent across all classifications of ethical problems. Here's how the four publisher types stack up on the fairness and balance index, using index numbers that compare with an average of 100.

	Politician	Statesman	Fixer	Absentee
Sensitive to fairness and balance	74	125	77	119

This table is reassuring because, of all the clusters of ethical values found in this survey, concern for fairness and balance is perhaps the closest match to traditional and generally accepted newsroom values. But let's try another cluster. The same factor analysis that points to fairness and balance as an underlying influence also yields an index of concern for financial conflict of interest.

Index of Concern for Financial Conflict

The financial conflict items were also discussed earlier: the business manager who junkets at the expense of newsprint suppliers, the photographer who peddles influence while shooting weddings on the side, and the reporter who suppresses information that would harm his own finances. Points are awarded those publishers who would fire the business manager, fire the photographer, and require the reporter to leave the damaging information in the story.

Here we find the Politician ranking high, while the Statesman ranks low. Only the Absentee is consistent, with another high rating:

	Politician	*Statesman*	*Fixer*	*Absentee*
Sensitive to financial conflict	120	83	69	129

Why should publishers who are highly active on the news side and publishers who are not active at all score higher than those with limited activity? Before trying to arrive at a simple theory to explain everything—which may or may not be possible—let us look at some other indices.

Index of Sensitivity to Closeness to Sources

The next index is a simple one, dealing with closeness to sources. The survey offered two cases, one dealing with a city hall reporter and one with a Washington correspondent who become part-time policy advisers after close friends reach the highest levels of power on their beats. A news person was classed as sensitive to the problem of closeness to sources if he or she would fire or transfer a reporter in at least one of those situations. Among the publisher groups, Statesmen and Absentees revealed the most sensitivity on this issue:

	Politician	*Statesman*	*Fixer*	*Absentee*
Sensitive to closeness to sources	100	108	85	108

Indices of Business Aversion and Self-Restraint

The remaining indices show hardly any differences among the publisher types. When business-office aversion is measured, we might expect Fixers to score lower than the others, and they do, although the difference is not great:

	Politician	Statesman	Fixer	Absentee
Business aversion	100	108	85	108

When the issue is self-restraint in publication, the four groups are again about the same except for the Absentees, who evince a stronger bias in favor of publishing. The index numbers in this table indicate readers whose publishers show a high degree of self-restraint.

	Politician	Statesman	Fixer	Absentee
High in restraint	111	106	111	72

Explaining the Differences

A full explanation for this pattern of differences in values must await further investigation, but pieces of the explanation make some sense. The Absentees score the most consistently according to traditional values, and that may be because their absence from the newsroom shelters them from any challenges to those traditional values. If the Politicians are low in traditional values, that may be due not so much to a lack of concern for ethical problems as to a tendency to appreciate the subtleties of those problems, an understanding gained from everyday contact with them and a habit of evaluating them on a case-by-case basis. It is important to remember that as these indices are constructed, the high score is not necessarily the most ethical score. A high scorer might be someone whose knee-jerk reactions or hypersensitivity to ethical problems removes him or her as far from logical and thoughtful consideration of the problems as someone at the opposite end of the scale who is totally insensitive. High scores, as we saw in Chapter 6, may demonstrate a readiness to push traditional newsroom standards to an adversarial extreme. An Absentee publisher, these data suggest, is more ready than others to tolerate such an outcome.

Viewed in this light, a certain amount of inconsistency might be socially and professionally desirable. Less consistent responses could mean that the codes, to the extent that they exist, are not being blindly and thoughtlessly applied.

Which Publisher Types Favor Formal Ethical Codes?

If this hypothesis has merit, if it is true that newsroom involvement makes codes seem less practical, then the Politicians among the publishers in our sample should be the least inclined to favor formal ethical codes and the Absentee should be the most committed to code ethics. Fortunately, the survey was able to measure this. The question was asked in several ways, including the following:

> Some newspaper people believe that every newspaper should have a written code of ethics or set of guidelines that its staff could consult when ethical problems came up. Others say that every situation is different, and each ethical problem needs to be considered on its own merits. Which comes closest to your belief?

The hypothesis works. Absentees are significantly more likely than Politicians to be code ethicists. With this breakdown, we return to absolute percentages instead of index numbers because they refer to a single item in the survey. The breakdown (in terms of readership):

	Politician	Statesman	Fixer	Absentee
Support for code ethics	40%	56%	69%	73%

The pattern persists when the question is put more generally:

> These are two statements about ethics. Please tell me which one of them comes closest to your view:
> 1. In deciding ethical questions, one should refer to certain universal truths about right and wrong which never change.
> 2. There are few, if any, universal truths, and each question should be decided according to what benefits the community in the long run.

Again, Absentee publishers were far more likely to favor code ethics (the first choice above) over situation ethics than were Politician publishers. The distribution:

	Politician	Statesman	Fixer	Absentee
Code ethics	62%	60%	65%	83%

It therefore appears that the idea of codifying ethical principles, while popular overall, is most accepted among publishers who are least likely to get their hands dirty with real-life application of those codes.

Measuring the Ethical Efficiency of Publisher Styles

The connection we have just made is more profound than it may appear at first glance. We have found a link between an attitude (what the publisher thinks of code ethics) and a behavior (the publisher's management style). This linkage is especially credible because the two measurements come from different sources. We have the publisher's self-report on code ethics and the editor's report on the publisher's management style. Too often in attitude research, what appears to be a connection between attitude and behavior turns out to be two redundant statements of the same attitude. A person's self-report of a behavior may be colored by the attitude with which it is correlated. By getting an external measure of the behavior, we have avoided that problem. We have also shown that there is substance behind our classification of publisher types.

Ratings of Publisher Impact on Newsroom Morale
This should bestir us to look for other effects (or perhaps causes) of publisher style. One variable that should interest us is newsroom morale. Generally, an organization that is goal-directed and unified by common aims and values will be a happier unit than one that is at odds with itself, uncertain, and lacking in leadership. While true of any organization, this generalization is particularly true of news organizations. News people work for psychic income as much as any other kind. An astute publisher realizes this and creates an organization that supplies psychic reward in the form of shared values and support for high ideals. It is an efficient way to attract and keep the most talented people. What kind of publishing style yields a management capable of maintaining a happy newsroom? If the traditional model of separation of business and editorial functions is the most efficient, the paper with an Absentee for a publisher should be happiest. Its newsroom is free to pursue news-side values untainted by the profit motive and led by an editor who is left alone by the publisher. That, at least, is what newsroom folklore tells us.

What we find, however, is just the reverse. The newsroom of a paper with an Absentee for a publisher is among the least happy. The happiest newsroom is found at the paper whose publisher takes an active role in producing and enhancing the editorial product—the Statesman. Here is the distribution where morale in the newsroom is estimated by the publishers themselves. They used a scale of one to ten, and in this breakdown a happy newsroom is defined as one rated at eight or better.

	Politician	Statesman	Fixer	Absentee
Readers served by happy newsrooms (publisher evaluation)	46%	58%	40%	30%

Here again, the two related phenomena are being measured by different observers. It is the editor who provides the data by which we classify the publishers, and it is the publisher who estimates newsroom morale. But is the publisher the best judge of morale in the newsroom? For a check, let us see how the same table looks when the editor is the judge of morale.

	Politician	*Statesman*	*Fixer*	*Absentee*
Happy newsrooms (editor evaluation)	36%	54%	37%	37%

So the Statesman has the highest newsroom morale, regardless of whether it is the editor or the publisher making the judgment.

Ratings of Publishers and Editors on Ethical Matters

Another measure of the relative ethical efficiency of the various publisher styles can be taken by examining how editors rate publishers according to their ability to deal with ethical matters. We can also see how publishers rate editors. If publisher and editor give each other high marks, we can be more confident that ethical issues are being well handled than if the marks are low. Ratings were made on a scale of A to F.

Here's how the "A" ratings of editors were distributed among different kinds of publishers:

	Politician	*Statesman*	*Fixer*	*Absentee*
A-rated editors	53%	80%	46%	71%

Statesmen have the highest regard for their editors, but Absentees are close behind. Fixers and Politicians have the least respect for their editors.

These feelings were reciprocated only in part. Editors like Statesmen the most and Absentees second. But the regard that Politicians profess for their editors is not returned in kind at all. Even the lowly Fixer—who intervenes for selfish purposes—is better regarded by editors than is the Politician. Here is the distribution:

	Politician	*Statesman*	*Fixer*	*Absentee*
A rated publishers	20%	72%	34%	61%

Surprisingly, editors' evaluations of their publishers were, for the most part, independent of publishers' views on substantive ethical issues. The most visible exception was publishers' standing on the issue of a reporter's closeness to sources. This characteristic, you will recall, was measured by stated willingness to take strong action to discourage a Washington reporter or a city hall reporter from getting too friendly with sources. Publishers who take the hard line on traditional separation of reporters and sources were significantly more likely to be respected by their editor. The circulation-adjusted breakdown:

	Publisher Support for Separation of Reporters and Sources	
	Weak	Strong
A-rated publishers	36%	64%

For the other ethical clusters, the publisher's belief had little or nothing to do with what the editor thought of him. The editor's evaluation depended more on procedural or background variables—age, for example. Older publishers got higher marks:

	Age of Publisher		
	23–46	47–55	56–82
A-rated publishers	40%	46%	53%

Editors evidently like direction even if they don't like a publisher's visible presence very much. The highest-rated publishers were those whose papers had formal, written codes of ethics. But the rating was even higher if the publisher admitted that he didn't know where to put his hands on that code right at that moment.

Conventional wisdom holds that editors prefer publishers who have been on the editorial side themselves, and this would lead us to expect those publishers with news-side experience to get higher ethical marks from their editors than those without. It was not so, however. In fact, there was a slight difference in the other direction, with the publishers who do not have such experience somewhat more likely to get the better evaluation from editors.

Other factors contributing to a high rating for publishers: education beyond the bachelor's degree; a large, competitive market; residence in the area of publication; and, to a modest degree, presence of an ombudsman column in the newspaper.

Finally, a basic psychological characteristic made a difference. Everyone in the survey was asked two questions that measure a general trust in other people. They are based on a scale first developed by Morris

Rosenberg in the 1950s and later modified by the Survey Research Center at the University of Michigan. They ask:

> Do you think most people would try to take advantage of you if they got a chance, or would they try to be fair?

> Generally speaking, would you say that most people can be trusted or that you can't be too careful in dealing with most people?

Publishers who gave the cynical answer to either question were far less likely to be well regarded by their editors for ethical abilities. A reader with such a cynical publisher has only a 24 percent chance of having that publisher judged ethically able by his editor. A reader with a trusting publisher has more than double the chance: 49 percent.

When publishers rate their editors on ability to deal with ethical concerns, the pattern is quite different. The substantive positions of the editors have a great deal to do with how their publishers rate them. For each of the five dimensions used in this study, editors who give the traditional responses get the highest marks. It is true even for business-office aversion, with the aversive editors considered by their publishers to be more ethically able. The effect is stronger with some scales than others, and the two scales with the most direct measures of traditional values—for fairness and balance and against financial conflict of interest—show the strongest relationship.

	Sensitivity to Financial Conflict	
	Low	High
A-rated editors	56%	75%
	Sensitivity to Fairness and Balance	
	Low	High
A-rated editors	57%	78%

The editor who expresses the traditional bias in favor of publishing in cases where there is some doubt was also more likely to be well regarded by the publisher than one who shows some self-restraint. The difference here was modest, however. A reader whose editor is low in self-restraint has a 68 percent chance of having that editor rated "A" in ethical ability by the publisher. For the high-self-restraint editor, the probability is 56 percent.

Defining the Ethically Efficient Newspaper

We have covered much ground here, and a brief summation is in order. We are getting close to a definition of the ethically efficient newspaper. By speaking of ethical efficiency, I hope to bypass debate over what is good and bad and to look at the manner in which an organization resolves its ethical dilemmas. One thing to look for is evidence of moral balance: a decision system that relies neither entirely on the heart, with intuitive responses from deeply held feelings, nor totally on the head, with coldly rational calculation of the net utility of each questionable act. Evidence of ethical efficiency and moral balance is not revealed directly, but some outcroppings exist that are subject to measurement. Considering only those characteristics that were measured in this project, the ethically efficient newspaper might show the following:

1. Some degree of freedom from knee-jerk responses. People who always follow the conventional rule may think they are being ethical, when in fact they are merely being thoughtless.
2. Mutual respect between editor and publisher. If the newspaper is ethically efficient, the editor and the publisher will know it, and they will like each other for it.
3. High staff morale. News people are in this business for psychic income as much as any other kind. Nothing can destroy morale as quickly as a perception that the place is being run without regard for moral values.

On each of these counts, as this chapter has shown, the newspaper whose publisher takes an active (and nonmalign) role on the news side comes out measurably ahead. This does not mean that such a publisher has a monopoly on ethical efficiency, only that it happens more often when he or she is in charge.

Such a finding clearly runs counter to the traditional belief that business and news operations ought to be kept widely separated. But this separation may be another example of a means to a good end that has outlived its usefulness. In its extreme form, journalistic ethics are the sole responsibility of what Norman Isaacs has called the "tribal-craft culture" of the newsroom, with outsiders—and the publisher is considered an outsider—excluded from the process of setting values.[3]

Those of us who inhabited newsrooms where the doctrine of separation prevailed believed that we were in charge of ethics and the business side was in charge of just about everything else. We were the good and altruistic guys; they were greedy and wore black hats. They had the grubby job of pursuing the company's economic self-interest; ours was the nobler task of looking out for the community's welfare. The adversarial model, by which so many activities in American life have been defined, fit even the activities within a single economic unit, the daily newspaper.

In that model, one side's activities seemed to justify the other's. The editorial side was free and unfettered in its pursuit of truth and justice because it didn't have to dirty its hands with economic matters. Conversely, the business side could be uninhibited in its quest for profit because serving the public interest was somebody else's department. The adversarial model has an appealing symmetry to it, and it may have made life easier for both sides, but some newspaper people eventually began to notice that the news side wasn't winning many close decisions. In the crunch, power rested with the side that controlled the purse strings. And the editors who did the most for their papers were those who learned the business side of newspapering well enough to get some control of that purse.

In recent years economic pressures on newspapers have forced many of them to begin to reject internal adversarial activity for a more efficient, cooperative mode. In this mode, the business side recognizes that it cannot sell advertising without readers and that it cannot get and keep readers without a high-quality editorial product. Some newspaper people still snort at the notion of calling a newspaper a product. Yet, like any product, a newspaper, in order to exist, requires capital investment, a manufacturing process, a sales and delivery system, and willing customers. But the most effective editors have always known that readers are customers who vote with their quarters and provide a healthy check on a power center that has fewer checks than most.

Some editors still fear that participating in business decisions will make them so profit-conscious that they will cease to be advocates for the public good. "An editor has to know where the money comes from, and it is currently fashionable to talk about 'the total newspaper,' " former *Minneapolis Tribune* editor Charles W. Bailey, has written, "but speaking from personal experience, I don't think most editors are especially qualified in matters of business and finance. And even if they were, I do not think they should spend much of their time and energy on such matters. They have more important things to do."[4] Some editors even take pride in their ignorance of financial matters. "I was never particularly concerned with the budget. I never knew how much there was in the budget," said a New England editor quoted in a study of the effects of different kinds of newspaper ownership.[5] But the model of a publisher who is so generous that the editor is allowed to write checks without limit while the publisher assumes all the burden of covering them requires a state of dreamy self-deception on the part of the editor. Resources are always limited. An editor who does not know the limits cannot do a good job of allocating those resources. More realistic editors believe that participation in financial decisions will enable them to play a more effective role in directing the newspaper's resources toward public benefit. The ASNE survey indicates that the latter is becoming the prevailing view. Its logic says that editing a newspaper is an economic activity, and editors who ignore the economic aspect risk sacrificing their ability to harness the full power of the organization on behalf of their readers and their community.

If the adversarial model is inefficient for newspaper economics, can it work efficiently for newspaper ethics? Should ethical outputs be a resultant force created by the clash of opposing interests? The concept is more traditional than it is logical. If there is one ethical code for the business side and a conflicting code for the news side, the net ethical output is likely to be unpredictable at best, and a system without consistency and predictability can hardly be called a system at all. We should consider the possibility that a newspaper's ethical responsibility ought to apply to the organization as a whole and is not something to be divided among competing elements. As newspaper managers come to understand the need for economic integrity, the time may be ripe for an appreciation of the need for ethical wholeness.

The model for such an organization is the newspaper whose publisher fits the category we have labeled "Statesman." This is the publisher who is an active participant on the news side for the sole purpose of making it better. Such publishers' ethical standards are respected by their editors, their news staffs are happy, and their responses to specific situations are just difficult enough to pigeonhole to convince us that they approach ethical problems with thought and logic rather than reflex.

Some editors will cringe at this suggestion, and rightly so, for it can be taken as an invitation for publishers who do not meddle in the news side now to get directly involved. The outcome of such a change would depend very much on the kinds of people they are. Perhaps Statesmen are born and not made, and perhaps the publisher who tries to change his or her behavior to become one will only make matters worse. Perhaps the kind of luck a newspaper has when its publisher is selected is the only important variable. Perhaps.

It is worth remembering, however, that the Statesman, like the other three oversimplified publisher types, is a construct invented for analytical convenience. Real-life publishers do not so much fall into discrete categories as reside on a series of continuous scales. Even the lowliest Fixer has some qualities of the Statesman, and the line between the two can be thin and arbitrary. Any publisher can move in any direction on any scale, and everyone has the potential to become more statesmanlike than he or she already is.

The key goal is to put the entire weight and majesty of the newspaper behind its ethical decisions and not to dilute those decisions by partitioning them off to different segments. A newspaper can never be the centrally directed monolith that the public often perceives, but the public is right in holding the newspaper as a whole responsible for what appears or fails to appear on the printed page. "That's not my department" is not an ethical response.

116 / *ETHICS AND THE ORGANIZATION*

NOTES

1. Kenneth Goodpaster, remarks to New England newspaper editors and publishers, Danvers, Mass., February 3, 1984.

2. Murray Kempton, *America Comes of Middle Age: Columns 1950–1962* (Boston: Little, Brown, 1963).

3. Norman Isaacs, "It's Up to Editors to Close the Credibility Gap," *Presstime,* February 1983.

4. Charles Bailey, "Exit Lines from a Minnesota Editor," *Washington Journalism Review,* January/February 1983.

5. Quoted in Loren Ghiglione, ed., *The Buying and Selling of America's Newspapers* (Indianapolis: R. J. Berg, 1984).

CHAPTER 8

Size and Ownership

If ethical performance by newspapers could be defined by a set of absolute rules, then newspapers of all descriptions and all kinds of locations could be held accountable to a single yardstick. But it is not clear that such absolutes exist. The variety of environments in which newspapers operate is too great.

How a newspaper serves its readers in a marketing sense often depends on the size of the city, the age of the population, the mobility of the population, and other aspects of community structure. The newspaper's internal structure sometimes makes a difference, too. We should not be too surprised to find that ethical outcomes also sometimes depend on these structural variables.

Trends in Newspaper Ownership

A main structural issue that has fascinated journalism researchers is the distinction between independent and group ownership. As more and more newspapers are gobbled up by chains, researchers have fretted over the effects of chain ownership. The results of their studies have been mixed.

Family Ownership

Traditionally, newspapers have been family operations, with the owning family having long and close association with the town where the newspaper is published. Such an arrangement gives the owners high visibility in their communities and, for some, at least, a reason to take personal pride in their product. This personal pride, more than economic considerations, motivated the owners toward professionalism and editorial excellence. There are economic consequences to poor quality, but they operate only in the very long term. Newspapers can improve or degrade their products without any immediate gain or loss of circulation or advertising because the advertisers and the readers will stay with them out of habit. All the paper has to do to retain short-term loyalty is to keep reaching the right doorsteps on time.

Therefore, whether the paper is good or mediocre depends on how long a time-horizon the owners use in their planning and how public-spirited they are. Family ownership, as Ben Bagdikian has noted, can produce very good or very bad results, depending on the kinds of people in that family. "The tradition of the personally involved owner is strong," he wrote in 1971, "and while it produces numerous cases of entrenched morbidity, it also is the most important single factor in papers of excellence."[1]

Group Ownership

When a newspaper is acquired by a group with headquarters in another city, some new values may be imposed on the people who put out the paper. Gerald Grotta reported in 1971 that editorial quality, or at least those aspects of it that could be measured, tended to stay the same or decline when a paper was acquired by a group. The only unambiguous effect he found was that prices went up.[2] However, there are a number of examples of newspapers that have undergone dramatic improvement under the stimulus of new ownership—such as the *Philadelphia Inquirer,* which became a consistent prizewinner after being overhauled by Knight-Ridder editors John McMullan and Eugene L. Roberts, Jr.

Some newspaper groups are centrally directed, while others preserve local editorial autonomy. One team of Minnesota researchers found that group papers are more likely to endorse presidential candidates but that, even within those groups that profess to encourage local autonomy, there is a good deal of uniformity.[3] Ralph R. Thrift, Jr., comparing group and independent papers on the West Coast, figured out a way to measure editorial vigor by counting the times a paper editorialized on local issues, chose controversial topics, approached them in an argumentative (rather than merely explanatory) way, and provided mobilizing information (that is, advice on what the reader could do about the situation). He found that, by these measures, after newspapers were acquired by groups, their vigor declined.[4]

Provocative as these studies are, the bottom line on group ownership appears to be that group ownership in and of itself is neither bad nor good. The outcome depends mainly on the nature of the group, just as it does with individual owners. Corporate culture substitutes for family tradition and determines the values that will govern the content of the paper. Some corporate cultures emphasize long-term improvement through attention to public service and reader concerns. Others care more about short-term profits. But no researcher has convincingly identified anything intrinsic to group ownership that pushes a newspaper in one direction or the other.

Corporate Ownership

There is another structural change that may have greater long-term effect, and that is the trading of shares in newspaper companies on public stock exchanges. A public company is under more intense pressure to produce short-term results than one that is held by an individual, family, or small group of private investors. By 1985, shares were being publicly traded in 15 corporations owning newspapers that accounted for more than a quarter of total daily U.S. circulation.

This trend began in the early 1960s. Dow Jones, publisher of the *Wall Street Journal,* went public in 1963. Times Mirror Co., which had been a closely held family corporation with stock traded over the counter, was listed on the New York Stock Exchange in 1964. Gannett Co. and Media General went public in 1967. Knight-Ridder's predecessors, Ridder Publications and Knight Newspapers, became public companies in 1969. The *New York Times* and Lee Enterprises made the move in that same year. Companies going public in the 1970s included the *Washington Post,* Harte-Hanks (whose management changed its mind and engineered a return to private status in the 1980s), and Affiliated Publications (*Boston Globe*).

In the 1980s A.H. Belo Corp. (*Dallas Morning News*), the Tribune Co. (*Chicago Tribune* and *New York Daily News*), and Park Communications went public. And Capital Cities Communications, a broadcasting company that had been publicly held since 1957, became a major newspaper publisher by acquiring the *Fort Worth Star-Telegram* and the *Kansas City Star.*

Why the urge to go public? The tax code has a good deal to do with it. A company whose shares have a market value that is set by public trading can be kept intact after its original owner dies while its portions are fairly distributed to the heirs and the Internal Revenue Service. But there are other conveniences. The money raised from the sale of shares can be used for investment in new technology or expansion. Mergers are easier. And the liquidity of the shares provides a means of rewarding employees by giving them part ownership through discounted stock purchase plans or stock options.

This development introduces a new source of influence on newspaper management and, potentially, on its ethical decisions. The investors who buy a company's shares have little direct voice, but their interests are looked after by the investment analysts, who work for large institutional investors and for brokerage houses. These analysts evaluate public companies and make buy-or-sell recommendations to investors. Their attitudes toward a company therefore directly affect the price of its stock.

Do the managers of a newspaper company care about the price of its stock? They do, for several reasons. A high valuation confers prestige. It makes the managers' own holdings and stock options more valuable. It makes the company less vulnerable to a hostile takeover. It strengthens the company's hand in making acquisitions, which are often accomplished by swapping shares rather than with cash transactions.

This desire for higher share prices makes corporation managers sensitive to the desires of stock analysts, and those desires have a short-term orientation because the market system encourages frequent trading, with the rewards based on near-term results. These analysts, then, tend to evaluate a newspaper company by its near-term earnings prospects and by its predictability. John Morton, who, like a number of other analysts, is a former journalist, says that this factor inevitably affects the attitudes of newspaper managers:

> If I were to put my finger on the thing that probably has the biggest impact on the newspaper companies, it is the sensitivity that being a public company develops in the company's managers toward its earnings performance. Rightly or wrongly, Wall Street tends to judge companies on their earnings performance, on its predictability, on its steadiness. . . . Institutional investors . . . like not to be surprised. . . . They like investments that they don't have to worry about. . . . And so . . . the system tends to reward companies that have fairly predictable earnings performance.[5]

Predictability in earnings has not been a strong point in the newspaper business. Depending as it does on local advertising for most of its revenue, it tends to be subject to the business cycle. It does very well overall, but there are some relatively bad years. Wall Street observers give credit to Allen H. Neuharth, chairman of Gannett Co., for demonstrating to the financial community that a newspaper company could overcome its vulnerability to cyclical downturns. Gannett did it by specializing in medium-size monopoly markets, which are less subject to cyclical variation, and by practicing earnings management. The curves were smoothed out by targeting major expenses and improvements in good years and using economy moves and rate increases to take the sting out of bad years. Gannett became known as the company with "never a down quarter" as it posted steady earnings gains through periods of business expansion and recession. The market responded by bidding up the price of its shares, and that made other publicly held companies want to follow suit.

This becomes an ethical problem if the distortions caused by earnings-oriented management get in the way of a newspaper's public service responsibilities. These responsibilities are much more important to news people than they are to the analysts who evaluate their work.

The Impact of Public Ownership on Newspaper Values

In the ASNE survey, news people representing about 40 percent of total U.S. circulation said that public ownership makes a difference in the way a newspaper serves its community. Among those who see a difference, two-thirds report that the pressures of public ownership hinder a newspaper's ability to serve the local community, at least part of the time.

This concern, however, did not come primarily from the editors and publishers in the publicly held companies. The view that type of ownership makes a difference was held by 43 percent of those in private companies and only 30 percent of those in public companies. And among those who said it did make a difference, the people who thought public ownership was a hindrance were concentrated in the private companies. In other words, people in both camps tend to believe the grass is greener on their own side of the fence.

Editors' and Stock Analysts' Values: A Comparison

Does public ownership change the basic value system of a news organization? To find out, we must first measure the relevant values.

The ASNE survey asked a question that had earlier been put to a sample of security analysts specializing in newspaper companies:

> Several possible "yardsticks" for evaluating newspaper companies are listed below. On a scale of 1 to 10, how important is each of these indicators to you? A score of 1 means the indicator is not important; a score of 10 means the indicator is extremely important.

The following list shows the rank ordering of the different yardsticks by securities analysts and by newspaper editors:

Analysts	*Editors*
1. Management quality	1. Editorial quality
2. Financial health	2. Product quality
3. Earnings consistency	3. Management quality
4. Readiness to introduce new products	4. Financial health
5. Readiness to adopt new production technology	5. Company image
6. Product quality	6. Readiness to adopt new production technology
7. Involvement with new electronic information systems	7. Community service
8. Company image	8. Readiness to introduce new products
9. Editorial quality	9. Earnings consistency
10. Community service	10. Involvement with new electronic information systems

There are many discrepancies, but the greatest involve editorial quality, which the editors ranked eight places higher than the analysts, and earnings consistency, which the analysts ranked six places higher than the editors.

It takes time to turn a corporate culture around, and the impact of the financial community's values on the editorial product may be obscure and hard to measure. There are some horror stories. The business manager of a paper acquired by Gannett in Salem, Oregon, reacted in a panic when he saw the profit standards of his new parent company and raised rates so sharply that advertisers rebelled and encouraged a competing newspaper to enter the market. But the more subtle responses are difficult to detect and possibly more dangerous. Concern for next quarter's bottom line might prevent a newspaper from making product improvements that would serve its community—and benefit the newspaper—over the long haul. Investments in new technologies might be forgone. Risky investigations might be passed up.

Attitude Change as a Measure of Stock Analysts' Influence

The easiest way to look for change is by measuring attitudes. For a baseline, we might take the scorn that John S. Knight expressed publicly toward the financial community. Knight was chairman of Knight Newspapers when the company went public in 1969, and he was invited to address the analysts. He later recalled:

> I made the first talk at the security analysts—the last talk I ever made—I was never invited again. My opening line was, "Ladies and gentlemen, I do not intend to become your prisoner."
> I told them why. I said that as long as I have anything to do with it, we are going to run the papers, we are going to spend money sometimes that they wouldn't understand why we were spending it, for future gains, and we did not intend to be regulated or directed by them in any respect. That's pretty challenging, isn't it? It was the right thing to say, too.[6]

At the other extreme are companies (although no newspaper companies that I know about) where hardly a move is made without considering how the analysts will react. John Morton expressed the belief that the ethical traditions of journalism offer some protection:

> I've heard of some industries where there's one analyst who practically runs some company because they're so afraid of what he's going to say. There isn't really that kind of relationship in the newspaper industry. For one thing, I think most newspaper companies, more so than any other industry I can think of, are sensitive to the ethical questions that are raised by that kind of relationship . . . I don't think you'll find any publishing executives who are that close with any analysts.[7]

Even Al Neuharth, the Gannett Co. chairman who awed Wall Street by racking up regular 15 percent or greater earnings gains year after year, was willing to risk a break in that pattern for the risky venture into the national market with *USA Today*. In 1983 the losses on *USA Today* held Gannett to a 3 percent gain in earnings per share. But the company regained its normal pattern of earnings growth in 1984, and by 1985 Gannett Co. was in a no-lose position. It could keep *USA Today* if it seemed on the way to making money or fold it if it looked like a loser. Either way would signal an earnings improvement, and the analysts would be happy.

If the analysts' attitudes are intruding into the culture of journalism, there ought to be some measurable attitude change. But how to find it? The above lists of priorities show how analysts and editors differ. But if the analysts' views are creeping into the decision-making structure of public newspaper companies, news people should be affected. Stanley T. Wearden and I, with these data in hand, tried to think of some ways that it might show.

The obvious approach is to determine whether the attitudes of the managers of publicly owned newspaper companies are more like those of the analysts than are the attitudes of people who run the privately held companies. A less obvious approach is to follow the suspected diffusion process: Analysts affect publishers, and publishers transmit the attitudes to their editors, while the editorial staffs are the last to become affected. At any given point in the process, then, publishers of publicly held companies would be most in agreement with the analysts, editors would be next, and the staffs would show the least agreement.

So we cranked those hypotheses through the computer and found that the news people in all five groups (formed by two categories of newspapers: public and private; and by three categories of news people: publishers, editors, and staff members) were in very close agreement and quite uniformly distant from the analysts. There was no sign at all that the news people in the public companies are picking up the analysts' values and making them their own.

There was some indication that group publishers, regardless of private or public ownership, were in somewhat more sympathy with the analysts' financial concerns than were publishers in individual-ownership situations. This lends some support to the fear expressed by Bagdikian, that group ownership makes newspapers less socially conscious, but it is weak support. The differences between the two kinds of publishers were modest, and the gulf was wide between both groups and the analysts.

Attitude measurement may not, however, be the best way to detect any changes that are in the making. Commitment to editorial quality is so firmly ingrained in the journalistic culture that news people could continue to give it lip service long after their quality-seeking performance had seriously deteriorated. Some objective measure of performance is needed, one that is unobtrusive and can't be thrown off by the emotional responses of the people being measured. There are ways to do that, and the final chapter of this book will suggest some. Such a measurement system could show how ethical outcomes vary with a number of structural characteristics and show it much more clearly than attitude measurement can.

The Impact of Size on Newspaper Values

If the effects of kind of ownership are both fascinating and obscure to researchers, the effects of another structural variable, size, are just the opposite: fairly obvious and not much researched.

In general, the bigger the newspaper and its community, the greater the commitment to the traditional journalistic ethic of independence. This does not necessarily mean that big newspapers are more ethical. It may mean only that being ethical is easier if you are big and operating in a big town.

For example, sensitivity to financial conflict of interest is much greater on the larger papers. You will recall from the analysis of the ASNE survey in Chapter 5 that a news person was classed as sensitive in this area if he or she supported two out of three of the following extreme actions: firing a business manager who violates company policy by taking trips paid for by newsprint suppliers; firing a photographer who uses his position to get wedding business; compelling an investigative reporter to disclose information that would increase his tax bill. At papers of 100,000 circulation or more, editors representing a majority of circulation, 52 percent, fall into this hard-nosed group. For the smaller papers, those with less than 30,000 circulation, the sensitivity rate is much lower: only 34 percent. And editors at papers in the middle come out, as one might expect, in the middle; their sensitivity rate on this issue is 48 percent.

Similar differences are found in other ethical areas. In the general classification of fairness and balance, the sensitivity rate for large-paper editors was 62 percent; at the smaller papers, it was 22 percent.

Editors at the smaller papers, as noted in Chapter 2, show considerably more restraint in publishing. Small-town readers are nearly twice as likely to have editors who score high on the restraint measure as those in the larger cities. Even the unwritten ethic of business aversion is measurably stronger in the larger towns, although the difference is not great.

Why these differences? Are small-town news people less ethical? I think not.

Isolation at Large Papers

At least part of the explanation, perhaps most of it, lies in the simple structural difference. Larger organizations are more highly specialized and can separate conflicting functions more definitively. Each specialist can execute his or her narrow task without feeling the conflicts that are felt by less specialized people who have multiple tasks. If compromises are made by the organization as a whole, the specialists are less likely to be aware of them or, if they are aware of them, are less likely to be affected by them, have less reason to appreciate any benefits of the compromise. Given this isolation, it is much easier for members of large organizations to give lip service to formal ethical standards. They are comfortable in the heavenly choir, because the ethical words and music cost them little in their isolated, insulated functional cells.

Consider the starkest case, advertiser pressure. A big-city paper has greater diversity of income sources and is therefore less susceptible to advertiser pressure in the first place. When the owner of the leading department store tries to interfere in news policy, the publisher can tell him to take a hike and get away with it. The fact that the attempt was made need never be communicated to the editors whose policies are being challenged. In a small town, where people are highly visible to one another in their daily comings and goings, the diversity is less and the social pressure correspondingly greater. And economic dependence on a few advertisers is much more likely. If an advertiser is offended, everybody knows about it, including the reporters who write about that advertiser.

The ASNE survey shows that the small-town people are much less absolutist, and this is probably because they, as generalists, are more likely to wrestle with ethical conflicts at firsthand. An editor-publisher I met once in the Midwest provided an extreme example. A banker was offended by something he read in the paper and cancelled the bank's advertising. Some time later, the bank was embarrassed by a lawsuit brought by a borrower in good standing whose car had been mistakenly repossessed. The editor-publisher sensed a good story here, but he also sensed an opportunity. He scheduled a visit with the banker, interviewed him about the erroneous repossession, and, in the course of the same visit, sold him a new advertising contract.

An immoral conflict of interest? Of course, at least on the level where obvious rule violations are considered. But at another, more utilitarian level, where ultimate results are prized more highly than formal rules, the case deserves a second look. This small-town newsman had an advantage not shared by his big-city colleagues, namely that a single mind could perform the task of reconciling the conflicting needs for honest treatment of the news and maintaining the newspaper's financial health. The owner of that mind had two moral duties: to keep his newspaper financially healthy and to report the news fairly and accurately. When there is conflict, when there is a situation where fulfillment of the two separate tasks is not possible without some temporizing on one side or the other, the small-town person is at least in a better position than his or her big-city counterpart to make the most efficient temporization. If some evil has to be traded for some good, the involvement is so personal and so direct that he or she is in the best position to trade the most good for the least evil. He doesn't have to sell out altogether. (Some do, of course. There are still small-town publishers whose main ethic is "taking care of our friends," and friends are defined as those who can do them some good—and that includes advertisers. Every profession has its wimps.)

In a larger organization, when compromises are made—and they do get made—the structure of the organization is likely to make fine-tuning quite difficult. Responses may be erratic and spasmodic. And the compromises may be concealed from the key players because one part of the organization does not know what the other is doing. Absolutist positions are taken, not because they are more moral, but because they are simpler and therefore more practical to administer.

The large newspaper's ethical awkwardness is partly inherent in the nature of large organizations. Subtleties can be lost when rules are made by top management, interpreted by middle management, and executed by staff. John S. Knight once ruefully recalled how he made an inadvertent contribution to the unwritten code of the *Miami Herald*. When the circus came to town, the elephants were walked across the causeway from the train station on the mainland to the performance arena at Miami Beach. After the *Herald* ran a picture of the elephants' parade on page one, Knight complained because it seemed to him that the picture represented free advertising for the circus. Years later, he learned that this incident had persisted in the newspaper's tribal memory as an unexpected aphorism: "The boss doesn't like animal pictures."

The other source of awkwardness stems from the isolation imposed by the journalist's role as watchdog and record keeper. In the absolutist vision of this role, the journalist is as pure and detached as the proverbial man from Mars. He or she belongs to no civic organizations or social clubs and has no friends outside the newspaper organization. Thus uncorrupted, he or she can pass lonely judgment on the actions and motives of everyone else. On a large paper, this can be very close to a literal description of the way news people think and try to behave. It is the way I thought as a young reporter in the 1950s until an older colleague snapped me out of it with an even more extreme statement. "Isn't it odd," she said, quite seriously, "how the only interesting people are newspaper people. Why is everyone else so dull?" After thinking it over, I could put my finger on the problem, and it was not dullness at all. It was just that the social barriers that made this perception of dullness possible were so powerful. They stemmed from these sources:

1. At large papers, young journalists are usually from out of town. Because the pool of talented people willing to work for newspaper wages is limited, large, quality newspapers recruit nationally. As these young people advance in their careers, they tend to pursue opportunities in a variety of cities and to live relatively rootless lives, never becoming well integrated into the social structure of the

communities where they report and edit. At the *Philadelphia Inquirer,* this problem became so obvious that the paper hired specialists in Philadelphia history, economics, and sociology from local universities to conduct yearly two-day seminars for the newcomers on the news staff.

2. The interesting people a news person meets tend to be socially unavailable. Usually, they are news sources. Some of them are rich and powerful, and both factors create disincentives for socializing with them: the reporters are of lower status, by virtue of being less affluent. And reporters are uncomfortable establishing close personal relationships with people about whom they might have to write negative or embarrassing stories.

3. The working hours tend to militate against off-the-job socializing. If you can't get to the party until 2 A.M., it had better be a newspaper party.

For editors, the social barriers are not so great, but the taboo against direct involvement in newsworthy organizations and activities is just as powerful. Some editors welcome the taboo, because it is an excuse for not participating in some tiresome activities. Others find it frustrating. The taboo is generally ignored by publishers. Thus the average newspaper reader is served by a publisher who belongs to 7 local voluntary organizations. For editors, the average is 2.3, and for staff members, it is 1.2. But these differences diminish as city size decreases.

Small-Town Involvement

In a small town the isolating forces are not nearly so germane. Isolation is neither socially nor physically feasible. The newspaper people are often among the most energetic and best educated in town, and the pressure on them to participate directly in projects for civil betterment can be intense. Thus readers of papers with less than 40,000 circulation are served by editors who belong to three local voluntary organizations, on the average. At papers of more than 200,000 circulation, the average is one. For staff members, these averages are 1.4 for the smaller papers and less than one at the larger papers (see Table 8.1).

TABLE 8.1

MEAN NUMBER OF CIVIC-ORGANIZATION MEMBERSHIPS, BY CIRCULATION

	1-39,999	*40,000-199,999*	*200,000 and up*
Publishers	6.5	7.3	7.2
Editors	3.0	2.7	1.0
Staff	1.4	1.3	1.0

This greater tendency of small-city news people to participate directly in local affairs affects one of the fundamental processes in the resolution of ethical conflict. Every journalist, in the formation and execution of ethical standards, is subject to two opposing forces, one internal and one external. The internal force consists of the body of journalistic lore and tradition whose primary values are honesty and independence. It provides the proverbial touch of starch in the backbone of the young reporter who goes out to question the high and mighty. It places accuracy at the top of the list of objectives and demands that journalists stand far enough away from what they observe so that their view remains untainted by special interest or subjective judgment. The inner-directed journalist learns the standards so thoroughly that he or she can act on them instantly and intuitively, without conscious analytical effort. The standards are learned from role models in the newsroom, from journalism teachers, and even from textbooks. If there is rigidity in the standards and in their application, it is at least partly because the pressures of daily journalism are so great that only a rigid and automatic response can deal with them efficiently.

The external force comes from the community that the newspaper serves, and its power is roughly inversely proportional to the size of the newspaper. The community has standards and values of its own, and it is interested more in substantive outcomes than in processes. Cooperation for civic betterment is high on its list of objectives, and it expects the newspaper to be part of the cooperative effort and not a perpetual or reflexive antagonist. It is not unusual for these civic values to clash with journalistic values. Those bent on civic improvement are likely to have short-run goals in mind and to give them more weight than the long-run benefits of an open and fairly reported political system. The risk of a serious clash is especially high when the journalistic values are applied rigidly and unthinkingly. One advantage of the smaller town is that the social situation forces the journalist to reflect more carefully on his or her values. Small-town journalists thus tend to be more flexible.

This flexibility can force small-town journalists into far more of the classic ethical problems than their more insulated brethren in the cities are likely to face. But the small-town environment carries a natural remedy in its customary openness. If everybody knows everybody else's business, then the conflicts are at least on the table.

The *Lewiston* (Idaho) *Morning Tribune* capitalized on this small-town quality in 1978 when it published a lengthy self-examination of its staff members and their ongoing conflicts. The paper has a circulation of 25,000 and is based in a town of 31,000. Some of the younger staff members were careful to avoid outside activities that related to their news jobs. Older staffers were more likely to plunge into community activity and to balance their conflicting responsibilities as best they could. Cassandra Tate, author of the *Tribune*'s report,[8] cited the case of a veteran reporter who was chairman of the local Historic Preservation Commission, a member of the board of the Civic Theater, and a Democratic precinct committeeman. The paper's editors try to keep from assigning a reporter to a story involving a group to which the reporter belongs, but, with a small staff, that is not always possible. And a story about historic preservation was written by the reporter who chaired the commission. He did not see a problem. "Historical preservation?" he said. "For God's sake, everybody's in favor of that."

A night managing editor, himself a member of a number of state and local bodies, including the state legislature, said, "I do not like cloistered, celibate people writing stories about people who are neither cloistered nor celibate. This town's too small. A metropolitan area is a different story, but that kind of divorcement is monastic here."

Another editor agreed. As quoted by Tate:

> I have found that truly sterile reporters are devoid of emotion, feeling, understanding and a sense of fairness. Every good reporter's got friendships. A reporter without friends, I don't want.
>
> Above all, you should attempt to be fair with your friends and your enemies. You can't say reporters can't know and be friends with people. I think that's more dangerous than apparent conflicts. You have to be part of the community. Otherwise, you're just a journalistic android.

The "journalistic android" is another version of the mythical man from Mars and a pretty fair description of just what the traditional model of journalistic detachment calls for. However, before being too critical of small-town standards, we might do well to distinguish between the means and the ends of ethical behavior.

The end is fairness. Traditional standards of separation and remoteness from sources are means to that end. But no one, as we saw in our discussion of conflict of interest in Chapter 5, is completely remote from the world about which he or she writes. There are always ties that require one to make some internal effort to submerge one's prejudices and personal convictions. The practice of formal separation serves two functions: it reduces the workload for that internal monitor, and it maintains a public relations function by keeping up appearances for the community's sake.

The appearances are less important in a small town, because the community welcomes involvement, knows the surface conflicts, and can discount or otherwise allow for the reporter's biases. The business need to maintain credibility through formal separation is much less. However, the internal monitoring task is more demanding. Submerging one's own leanings may take more of a conscious effort. The high visibility of a small-town reporter's position, enhanced by such self-disclosure efforts as that of the *Lewiston Morning Tribune,* can be helpful in reminding the reporter to continue to make that effort. This is a prime example of the healing power of information, a phenomenon well known to journalists but perhaps insufficiently applied to the profession's own problems. Other publishers have considered the Lewiston effort interesting, and the paper's editor-publisher, A. L. Alford, has been a popular speaker at meetings of publishers. But none that he knows about has copied that move or his other innovation, which is to keep his income tax returns and those of his editorial page editor on file for public inspection. Alford finds this puzzling because it seems to him that it should be natural for publishers to want to make things public. He has a point.[9]

In the contrasting standards of small and large papers, we have what might appear at first glance to be a case of ethical relativism. The relativist view holds that moral principles are fundamentally different in different cultural settings. If there is no way to reconcile these differences, then people have to settle for living as best they can according to their own principles. But applying that view to the case of large and small newspapers makes the dilemma too easy. The underlying principles are the same in both large and small settings. Only the manner of application is different. So, too, is the nature of the compromises.

And one purifying strategy, the strategy of openness, applies to both. Because this strategy is so beautifully consistent with the First Amendment ideology that underlies the way news people relate to the rest of the world, you would expect the news business to be much readier to embrace openness-enhancing solutions than it is. Perhaps in time it will be, but some maturation may need to occur first. News people may have to grow out of their narrow, parochial perspective and begin to gain a fuller view of themselves as part of a world system. Even First Amendment fundamentalism contains the seeds for such a morally mature view.[10] For a look at that possibility, we should examine the ways that news people see themselves in relation to other groups. The ASNE survey opens a small window on that outlook, which is the subject of the next chapter. Attempts to institutionalize a policy of openness will be examined in Chapter 11.

NOTES

1. Ben Bagdikian, *The Information Machines: Their Impact on Men and the Media* (New York: Harper & Row, 1971).

2. Gerald L. Grotta, "Consolidation of Newspapers: What Happens to the Consumer?" *Journalism Quarterly* 48 (Spring 1971): 245–250.

3. Daniel B. Wackman, Donald M. Gillmor, Cecilie Gaziano, and Everette E. Dennis, "Chain Newspaper Autonomy as Reflected in Presidential Endorsements," *Journalism Quarterly* 25 (Autumn 1975): 411–420.

4. Ralph R. Thrift, Jr., "How Chain Ownership Affects Editorial Vigor of Newspapers," *Journalism Quarterly* 54 (Summer 1977): 327–331.

5. John Morton, quoted in Philip Meyer and Stanley T. Wearden, "The Effects of Public Ownership on Newspaper Companies: A Preliminary Inquiry," *Public Opinion Quarterly* 48 (Fall 1984) 564–577.

6. John S. Knight, quoted in ibid.

7. John Morton, quoted in ibid.

8. Cassandra Tate, "Conflict of Interest: a Newspaper's Report on Itself," *Columbia Journalism Review,* July/August 1978.

9. Telephone conversation with A. L. Alford, June 1985.

10. The concepts of ethical relativism and moral maturity are discussed in Lawrence Kohlberg, *The Philosophy of Moral Development* (New York: Harper & Row, 1981).

CHAPTER 9

Reference Groups

The reader is king. Practically all news people, regardless of position or ideological persuasion, will agree to that proposition. Whether the news person is motivated by devotion to the First Amendment or by the basest marketing considerations, the reader is the person he or she most wants to serve. But there is another audience that is acknowledged to be of nearly as much concern: the audience of fellow news professionals working for the same newspaper. Beyond these two groups are some other, more specialized audiences, and concern for them varies considerably, depending on the values of the individual news person. Both the unanimity of concerns for readers and colleagues and the divergence of concerns for the more specialized groups help define some underlying ethical matters.

Identifying News People's Reference Groups

Knowing who news people's reference groups are—that is, whose approval they care about—is a basic element in understanding their ethical behavior. Values exist not in isolation but as part of a social system, and the system can be defined by the nature of its other members. To discover whom news people include in their relevant social system, the ASNE survey asked this question:

> Suppose that your paper's performance was being graded by different groups. Each year, each group would send you a report card. For each group listed, please indicate whether you would be extremely interested, very interested, somewhat interested, or not interested at all in that group's report card on your paper.

Readers, as expected, were at the top of the list of reference groups: 93 percent of the publishers and 87 percent of the editors said they would be "extremely" interested in their paper's report card from readers.

The second most important reference group was the paper's own editorial staff: fully 78 percent of the publishers and 81 percent of the editors expressed extreme interest in the opinions of that group. And here we find some documentation for one source of ethical tension in the news business. News people want to please their readers, but they also very much want to please their colleagues.

Unfortunately, while news people are exquisitely attuned to the finest nuances of one another's tastes, they lack reliable means of finding out what their readers like. As a result, when the interests of the two groups diverge, as they inevitably do at times, the divergence may not be noticed. Even if it is noticed, the need to attend to it may be rationalized away. Much self-indulgence on the part of news people is rationalized by the belief that it is good for the readers, whether the readers are smart enough to know it or not. Two common examples:

1. Reporters care much more than readers about the minutiae of government procedure. I fell into this trap often as a Washington correspondent. Hanging around Capitol Hill, I became so preoccupied with the tortuous paths taken by legislation that the process became more important to me than the legislative product. The shifting alliances, the subtle bargains, the parliamentary maneuvers seemed endlessly fascinating. I wanted to write about every twist and turn, and I rationalized this interest with a rather weird mental picture of the U.S. Congress as a sort of New England town meeting where the entire population participated, at least vicariously. By carrying the details to the masses, I was giving them their democratic birthright. The problem with that image, of course, is that the readers care much more about outcomes and the near-term effects on their own lives than they do about such procedural niceties as discharge petitions or live pairs in roll call votes. Good editors protected me—and our readers—from some of my worst excesses, but not all.

2. Newspaper reporters are frustrated magazine writers. A newspaper gets a reputation as a reporter's paper if it runs long, long articles on obscure topics. A more reader-oriented paper imposes stricter discipline on its reporters, forcing them to solve the problem of getting the information into the reader's head in an efficient and palatable manner. Reporters tend to overestimate the amount of effort that readers will expend to learn about a topic that may be of only marginal interest to them. At the same time, journalists tend to be quite uninterested in any empirical evidence about what gets read and what really concerns readers.

Insularity in the Newsroom

Herbert J. Gans has offered several reasons for this inattentiveness on the part of journalists in general. One is that, coming primarily from liberal arts backgrounds, they are suspicious of any kind of quantitative evidence. If they cared about things that could be counted or measured, they would be accountants or engineers instead of journalists. Another problem is that many journalists have noticed that much audience research only documents the obvious and is performed by people with little understanding of the nuances of news-gathering procedure or of journalistic responsibility. A third problem is that journalists are quite protective of their autonomy, which can be threatened from a variety of sources, such as advertiser pressure, a publisher's malign interests, or community pressure. To a beleaguered journalist, an audience study can look like just one more attempt at manipulation of the news product. And, perhaps worst of all, audience research is generally performed by the business side, of which news people have a long-standing suspicion.[1]

The gap between newspaper people and their audiences is not a new problem. William Breed, a sociologist, examined the newsroom as a self-contained social system and reported that the newsroom environment promotes conformity and insularity.[2] A newsroom is a busy, noisy, even profane place, and the task of generating the daily product, filling all the pages on deadline, requires short reaction times and fast judgments. In order to function at all, news people in that environment need to internalize their values so thoroughly that they can act on them automatically, without spending a lot of time thinking about them. These values include the independent, man-from-Mars stance, and a bias toward reformism. After all, nothing demonstrates the utility of the news more than community response, and the greatest utility is in responses that make things better. This bias is certainly a wholesome one, and it tends to make the insularity problem self-limiting. If your goal is reform, you have to get the public's attention; to do that, you have to maintain some sort of two-way communication. The marketplace has its own long-term corrective for journalists who harp on themes that no one wants to hear about: people stop buying the paper. That corrective however, often acts painfully slowly, and in the meantime journalists who talk only to one another, who only reinforce the values of the news-gathering system, can endanger their effectiveness. Journalists in big cities, as we saw in Chapter 8, experience the problem most intensely. One of them, Dave Mimmer of the *Minneapolis Star*, has expressed the problem with this complaint: "We become so withdrawn that we're not in touch with anyone. We're becoming more elite and withdrawn than cops. I'd rather have to worry about a guy who's getting too close to sources than a guy who's not in touch with anyone."[3]

Other-directed Journalists

When values are totally internalized, they can become self-reinforcing, no longer needing the sustenance of the group. The advantage of this arrangement is predictability and an unconscious ease of implementing the values. The disadvantage is slow adaptation to changing situations. David Riesman, Reuel Denny, and Nathan Glazer noted a basic change in the American character from a rigid, inner-directed style to a more flexible other-directedness capable of picking up cues from others to facilitate adaptation to social change.[4] Fascinated by this typology, other researchers have looked for the inner-/other-directed dimension in different fields, including journalism. Stuart Schwartz, in a small-sample study, equated inner-directedness among journalists with professionalism and independence. The inner-directed journalists, he wrote, "appear to have a value structure anchored by selfhood [and] integrity." The other-directed news people in contrast, were low on professionalism and more concerned about an orderly society and being helpful to others.[5] Chris Argyris, in a behind-the-scenes look at a newspaper, which he did not name but which bears a strong resemblance to the *New York Times*, blamed other-directedness for some of the management problems in the newsroom. The other-directed executives were so absorbed in the emotional responses of others that they failed to recognize symptoms of some of the same emotional problems in themselves, even when these problems were blocking creativity and fresh ideas.[6]

This notion of other-directedness as a variable that can help explain newsroom behavior is an interesting one, and the ASNE data make it possible to explore it further. Besides asking about interest in the hypothetical report card from readers and other newspaper people, the survey asked about some other groups that could conceivably issue reports that news people would care about. Table 9.1 presents the complete list of groups and the percentage of circulation represented by editors and publishers expressing extreme interest in each group. Dianne Lynne Cherry analyzed these responses, using a statistical method called factor analysis—the same method, described in Chapter 2, used to find the hidden codes that incline news people toward unrestrained publishing and business aversion. Factor analysis was originally developed by psychologists to help in the interpretation of psychological tests based on a large number of multiple-choice

TABLE 9.1

	Editors	Publishers
Readers	87%	89%
Your own editorial staff	81	78
People who put out other newspapers	45	41
Retail advertisers	36	47
Politicians	34	25
Classified advertisers	33	42
National advertisers	31	35
Journalism school faculties	30	24
Potential investors in your company	29	29
Journalism students	26	21
Security analysts	22	18

questions. The procedure reduces the large number of questions to a few interrelated clusters, and the idea is that these clusters represent some underlying factors that are a lot more useful for explaining what is going on than the battery of individual question items.

Sometimes the results seem fairly obvious, and that turned out to be the case when Cherry factor-analyzed the items listed above.[7] One factor proved to be concern (or lack of it) for financial interests. Thus retail advertisers, national advertisers, classified advertisers, and potential investors all tended to command the attentive interest of the same people. So it makes sense to lump them together as a single reference group, which we'll call the Financial Group.

Security analysts had some association in this group, but it was not an exclusive one. Because of this ambiguity, the security analysts were dropped from this analysis, which depends on clean-cut categories.

The second interesting cluster brought together the journalism school faculties, the students, people who put out other newspapers, and politicians. These are all groups with some professional interest in newspaper quality. The fact that they are associated with the same factor is a sign that a news person who cares about one of these critics with a professional perspective also cares about the others. We might as well label them the Critical Group.

The third factor in Cherry's analysis was equally obvious, but not as useful. Readers and "your own editorial staff" were generally concerns of the same news people. But this is already a given, since nearly all the news people cared strongly about both groups. There is no point in looking for factors that promote this attitude when it varies so little.

Classifying News People's Concern
for Financial and Critical Reference Groups

At this point, if you followed the logic used for developing publisher types in Chapter 7, you probably sense another classification scheme coming. And you will not be disappointed. The news people in the ASNE sample can be classified as either high or low in concern for the opinions of the financial group as a whole and as either high or low in their concern for the opinions of the critical group. And that naturally leads to four categories. Figure 9.1 makes the categories easier to visualize. (Rounding makes the percentages shown in the figure add up to 101.) That the groups are of nearly equal size is a by-product of the method and not the result of some natural law. Factor analysis forces the factor definitions into uncorrelated dimensions that come out that way. So there is some arbitrariness here, but one has to draw a line somewhere, and the point that produces approximately equal-size categories seems as good as any other. Now let us reflect on the four categories thus created.

FIGURE 9.1
REFERENCE GROUP TYPES

Concern for financial group

		High	Low
	High	Promoter 27%	Champion 24%
Concern for critical group			
	Low	Merchant 24%	Loner 26%

The news person who wants to please both groups is evidently the sort of person who wants to make everybody happy, so "Promoter," the label coined by Cherry, is indeed a good one. The news person who cares about the professional critics but not about the financial groups is clearly a person for whom editorial quality is an overriding consideration. The label "Champion" is also a good one.

Then there is the news person who cares for the opinions of the financial group but not for the professional critics. In Cherry's words, they are "business people whose business just happens to be news." This is the classic countinghouse journalist so roundly denounced long ago by such publishers as William Allen White and C. L. Knight.[8] It was Knight, the publisher of the *Akron Beacon Journal* and the father of the legendary John S. Knight, who once said, "Better to set fire to your plant, leave town by its light, and take to raising speckled peas on a windy hillside with a bob-tailed bull than remain a human cash-register editor.[9] The term "human cash-register editor" has a nice ring, but for the sake of brevity, we'll use Cherry's label, "Merchant."

Now comes an interesting category, the source for much that is both good and bad in newspaper journalism today: the "Loner." This is the news person who does not care very much about anyone's opinion. The Loner fits the classic First Amendment fundamentalist model: totally aloof, inner-directed, doing what he or she thinks best regardless of whatever slings and arrows may be encountered. Some of the news people in this category are guided only by their internal professional standards. Others may just be drones who put out the paper without much thought to standards of any kind and then go home.

If we followed the stereotypes of folklore, we would expect publishers to be mainly Merchants and Promoters, while editors and staff are mostly Champions or Loners. And, indeed, there is some truth in the stereotypes.

Two-thirds of the newspaper audience is served by publishers who fall into either the Promoter or Merchant category, with Merchants slightly ahead, 36 percent to 32 percent. The few publishers who were Champions, those who cared about professional critics but not about the financial community, were more likely to be older than the average publisher. They were also found more frequently on larger papers. Perhaps these are publishers who have achieved financial success and have reached a stage in life where they are more concerned about their places in the history of their communities. Some of them may also be corporate officials in large groups where jobs are so specialized that somebody else worries about the bottom line.

The Merchant publisher, the businessperson whose business just happens to be newspapers, is more of a small-town phenomenon. Forty-three percent of small-town newspaper audiences have Merchant publishers, while 30 percent in the small towns have Promoters. At medium and large papers, the chance of getting a Promoter or a Merchant is about fifty-fifty.

Editors were fairly evenly distributed across the four categories except for a bulge, 32 percent, in the Loner group. This was primarily a phenomenon confined to the small and medium cities. In large cities, editors developed reference-group preferences that were surprisingly similar to those of small-town publishers: big-city editors, too, were disdainful of what politicians and professors might say, but were concerned about the financial community. These Merchant editors were older than average. What is going on here?

It does not take a very complicated theory to explain both the aging finance-minded editors and the mellowing publishers who become less concerned about financial interests as they age. It is simply this: As editors and publishers age, they learn more about one another's fields and gain more respect and sympathy for them. These are not extreme changes. The editors and publishers don't reverse positions and carry on the same old arguments in their switched roles. They just move closer together. And this appears to be mostly a large-paper phenomenon. Specialization is more intense there, and the organizational structure has been a stronger factor in keeping the editors and publishers apart. But time seems to heal that breach.

Where does the news staff figure in this process? As Table 9.2 shows, members of the staff are found least often in the Merchant category (14 percent) and most often in the Champion category (35 percent). No surprise there. The Champions tend to be young, and they perceive newsroom morale to be low. They are unlikely to be involved in community organizations. You will recognize the stereotype: the young, cynical, insular journalist who considers the business side of the organization an adversary. These are the people we can picture sitting in Murray Kempton's "dirty lofts" and cursing the man who owns the place, particularly if the owner is a Merchant. [10] We can also recognize the publisher stereotype here, the fat cat who cares more for the bottom line than for professional standards. And the editor who must mediate between these conflicting forces gets frustrated, withdraws, and becomes the solitary figure, alone with his or conscience, referring only to internal standards to adjudicate the conflicts.

TABLE 9.2

	Promoter	Merchant	Champion	Loner
Publishers	32%	36%	15%	18%
Editors	24	22	22	32
Staff	25	14	35	25

These stereotypes, are, however, only weakly supported. Most publishers are not Merchants, most editors are not Loners, and most staff members are not Champions. Every position is represented in each of the reference group categories. So there is a core of mutual understanding that holds these diverse news people together.

And the diversity that exists among them may be viewed as healthy and necessary. A newspaper is both an organ of community service and a business run for profit. The two functions are interdependent. In the long run, either will fail if the other does not succeed. If different people at the newspaper care about different reference groups, they may be serving as parts of an informal system of checks and balances. It could be unhealthy for either the professional critics or the financial interests to have too much influence. What the reader needs is a newspaper that has the financial clout to perform public service, including bold and risky service on occasion, and that can maintain the respect of both financial and professional critics over the long haul.

The desirability of such an outcome is obvious. Good ways to tell when a newspaper is attaining it, or on the way to attaining it, are not so obvious. The reader needs to know how close the newspaper comes to fulfilling its potential for public service. And editors, publishers, and staff members need more precise methods than are currently used for scoring themselves on community service. The chapters in Part IV will address both those issues.

NOTES

1. Herbert J. Gans, *Deciding What's News* (New York: Vintage Books, 1980), pp. 231–234.

2. Warren Breed, "Sociology in the Newsroom," *Social Forces* 33 (May 1955): 326–335.

3. Dave Mimmer, quoted in Bruce M. Swain, *Reporters Ethics* (Ames, Iowa: Iowa State University Press, 1978), p. 96.

4. David Riesman, Reuel Denny, and Nathan Glazer, *The Lonely Crowd: A Study of the Changing American Character* (New Haven: Yale University Press, 1950).

5. Stuart Schwartz, "Inner-Directed and Other-Directed Values of Professional Journalists," *Journalism Quarterly* 5, no. 4 (Winter 1978).

6. Chris Argyris, *Behind the Front Page* (San Francisco: Jossey-Bass, 1974).

7. Dianne Lynne Cherry, "Newspaper People's 'Significant Others': Ethics as a Function of Reference Groups," *Newspaper Research Journal* 6, no. 3 (Spring 1985): 33–46.

8. William Allen White, 1925 obituary of publisher Frank Munsey, quoted in White's *Autobiography* (New York: Macmillan, 1946), p. 629.

9. C.L. Knight, quoted from memory. Published source unknown.

10. Murray Kempton, *America Comes of Middle Age: Columns 1950–1962* (Boston: Little, Brown, 1963).

PART FOUR

Toward a Moral Foundation

CHAPTER 10

The Reader as Watchdog

Newspapers are the watchdogs of society, but who will watch the watchdogs? You might as well nominate yourself, in your role as reader, for this chore. If news people are sincere in their assertions that readers constitute their most important reference group, then readers should be in a good position to use their influence to effect some improvement. And it can be done, despite a couple of obvious problems.

Problem No. 1: Newspapers do not have any very good ways of getting feedback from their readers. We saw in the previous chapter how news people tend to be disdainful of audience research as a form of feedback. But that is a problem only if you rely on the newspaper to take the initiative. When readers take the initiative, news people listen. Complaints are heard. Sometimes they are even heard systematically. For example, one method that editors have for deciding on how to allocate the limited space for comic strips is test dropping. They drop a strip that is suspected to have low popularity, then see who complains. If there are few or no complaints, the strip stays out. If there are a lot of complaints, it is put back. I call this measure the "squeal index." Squeals are attended to, so don't be afraid to make some noise.

Problem No. 2: Many newspaper transgressions take place behind the scenes. Bad things are done to you, the reader, that you never know about. Improvements to the paper that should be made are not made, and you never notice because it never occurs to you that a newspaper could do these things for you. Or news that you ought to have is withheld because somebody considers it too expensive to get or underestimates your intellectual capacity for dealing with it.

This problem, by its very nature, defies any final solution. But this chapter can at least alert you to some of the common sins of ommission and suggest ways of spotting them. Those that remain unspottable will have to be handled by newspapers willing and able to act as their own watchdogs, and the final chapter of this book will be about that. This chapter is about the things that readers can watch for. We'll start with an easy one.

Does Your Newspaper Put Readers or Advertisers First?

Readers come before advertisers. The ASNE survey is clear on that score. The most valued advertisers are retailers, and news people representing 37 percent of circulation said that they are extremely interested in what retailers think about their paper's performance. This compares to the 89 percent whose news people are extremely interested in what readers think. Do readers come first at your paper? Individual newspapers are not identifiable in the ASNE survey, but you can find out on your own by looking at today's paper. There is no need to rely on what the people who put it out say. Just look at what they do.

Retail Display Advertisements

Start with the first section. You will notice that the front page is free of ads, which in itself shows that some priority is given to readers. That wasn't always the case. Front-page display ads were common in the nineteenth century, and the *Boston Globe* had them until Tom Winship became editor and tossed them out in 1966. So now we take for granted that news is a newspaper's first priority and should be the only thing on page 1.

But what about the other up-front pages? There is wide variation here, and you can get a quick sense of how much precedence readers are really given over advertisers by looking at the first few inside pages. Somewhere before you get to the editorial page or the local news or some other department, usually by page 7, there should be one or two additional ad-free pages devoted to current spot news. Where concern for readers is maximized, this treatment—what editors call "open pages"—will be found on pages 2 and 3. If concern for readers is strong, but less than maximal, you will find a few ads on pages 2 and 3 and some open pages a bit farther on. The *New York Times* was using this format in the mid-1980s. By 1985, the *Los Angeles Times* and the *Boston Globe* had adopted a consistent policy of keeping the second and third pages open. In contrast, the *Miami Herald* liked to pack ads close to page 1, often placing a full-page ad on 3, the critical right-hand page that is the first to be seen when you peel back page 1. The *Herald* did have a habit of opening inside pages for spot news, but these pages were generally farther back in the front section.

The papers with the least concern for their readers are those that barely manage to find space for the news at all, once they get past page 1. News crawls down the gutters at the center of the spread-out paper, or it creeps along the top margins, held up by ads that dominate the pages. At the least caring papers, you will find that ads occupy the upper outside corners, leaving the news in an inverted pyramid that straddles the interior portions of the two facing pages. Because the outside corners are where your eye is naturally drawn when you page through the paper, that can make the news especially hard to find. If you bought the newspaper primarily for news, you get the uncomfortable feeling that you are not getting your money's worth, and you have to work for the little you do get.

The issue is not entirely how much of the total newsprint available should be devoted to news and how much to advertising. That is a complicated economic issue, and ads typically take up from 50 to 70 percent of the available space. The issue that determines whether a paper is reader-oriented is how it uses those precious, highly visible pages at the front. The question is determined in only one way: by a power struggle between the news side and the business aide. The advertising people like those visible pages, because they are easier to sell. They might even claim that they can't sell as many ads if they don't have those pages. This is not a credible argument. Advertisers need a well-read, respected, reader-oriented paper, and pandering to their short-term desires only cheapens the product as an advertising medium. Now that you know about this, you can pick up your local paper and see who is winning this power struggle in your town.

This war between the editors and the ad salespeople has some more subtle aspects. There is a growing belief that the backs of section pages, traditionally awarded to advertisers who can pay for full-page displays, should belong to the reader. The editors at the *Chicago Tribune* won this battle in 1922 when Colonel Robert McCormick established a picture page on the back of the paper. Half a century later, his successors still used that back page for news, although the picture format was gone. And in 1976 they added another open page, this one at the back of the front section, to provide a sprightly daily "briefing" on the previous day's events. This pro-reader effort has not been widely copied, perhaps because most newspapers don't face the competition the *Tribune* had to contend with in the 1970s.

Sometimes you can get a glimpse of a newspaper's basic character when a major story breaks and you can observe directly how far it will go to inconvenience advertisers for the sake of bringing you the full story. In 1898, the *Charlotte* (N.C.) *Observer* cancelled advertising contracts to make way for news of the outbreak of the Spanish-American War. In contrast, in 1963 the *Miami Herald* failed to open up its up-front pages for the details of the assassination of President John F. Kennedy, deciding to leave the advertising in those critical pages undisturbed. Page 3A of the November 23 issue was dominated by a Burdines ad, and not because Burdines insisted on advertising that day. The department store pulled its copy and left only a black border surrounding its paid space and the legend, "A nation mourns the loss of a great American, John F. Kennedy." Of course, the paper did find some open space to report the assassination, adding eight open pages. But they were far back in the section, pages 16 through 23, where the reader had to hunt for them. By the 1980s, editors were being given leeway to display their efforts more prominently when a big and complicated story broke on short notice. The *Miami Herald*'s open pages for the 1986 space shuttle crash were at the front of the paper. And this is a way for you as a reader to estimate a newspaper's willingness to serve you when the chips are down. When the big story breaks, compare that day's paper with the one for the day before and see how the layout—

the relative positioning of news and advertising—at the front of the paper has been adjusted to accommodate the news.

Such accommodation of big stories does not happen often enough, perhaps because the short-term benefits of giving the advertisers their way are easy to see, while the long-range benefit of putting the reader first is less obvious. There is such a benefit, and the best publishers know it. Historians of three world-class papers, the *New York Times,* the *Los Angeles Times* and the *Miami Herald,* have traced their success in the second half of the twentieth century to decisions made during critical times of newsprint shortage in World War II. At each of these papers, the publisher decided to reject advertising in order to preserve news space. Their rivals cut the news hole and kept the ads. When the great postwar shakeout came, with a single paper ending up dominant in most markets, those papers were the ones that had kept faith with their readers. The *Miami Herald*'s James L. Knight recalled many years afterward, "We had shown that there was a vast difference in the publishing philosophy of the *Herald* organization and that of the [Miami] *News*—as a matter of record—that was the beginning of the decline of the *News.*"[1]

Classified Advertisements

Retail advertising is not the only category that reveals where the publisher's heart really lies. Classified advertising is regarded almost as fondly, and, if the newspaper you read most often is a large one with multiple sections you can see how the basic policy dilemma has been resolved. If the advertising department dominates, the classified ads will always be together in a single section of the paper. Because the size of the section varies by season and day of the week but is usually large, it limits the options for sectioning the rest of the paper. Sometimes the only way a paper can be organized into the sections it needs—separate sections for sports, business, and local news, for example—is to split the classified section among two or more other sections.

On a paper where the editor really has clout, that will happen from time to time. So if you sometimes see the automobile ads in the sports section while the rest of the classifieds are someplace else, you should feel good about it because it indicates that readers are being given first priority. But if the classified section is always self-contained while pages that look like they are supposed to be section fronts are hidden in the middle of sections, then you know that the advertising department is dominant and you ought to complain about it.

Putting Readers First: A Checklist

That readers should come before advertisers is commonly accepted and not controversial in the folkways of journalism, at least in abstract principle. A related principle, not so clearly accepted, holds that readers are more important than the editorial staff itself. The data described in Chapter 9 show that news people representing 78 percent of circulation say they are "extremely interested" in the judgments of their own editorial staffs, which is less, although not a lot less, than the 89 percent with the same level of concern for readers. But do they act on that concern?

The degree to which a newspaper puts its editorial staff concerns ahead of reader concerns can also be measured, but it is not so obvious as advertiser dominance. You have to look closely. The checklist of criteria is a long one, however.

Overall Tone

For a start, consider the general tone of the newspaper. If its newsroom is well managed, it will have a consistent voice: shrill or sober, respectful or smart-alecky. This voice can vary depending on the market, or the section of the market, at which the paper is aiming. From your perspective, you should get the feeling that you are hearing from an old friend who has something to tell you about which you know nothing. That friend would first need to arouse your interest in this new subject and then give you the information in a way that makes you want to keep listening—or reading.

The point is perhaps best made by a contrary example. I once lived in an affluent suburb of a major city. One day, we suburbanites awakened to find our trees afflicted with a peculiar infestation: Gossamer strands of webbing ran from the tops of the trees to the lower branches and shimmered in the sunlight. The effect was mildly alarming, as though whatever had spun those webs had dropped in suddenly from another planet. Naturally, we wanted to know what the creature was and whether the trees would be harmed, and if we should do anything about it. Eagerly, we waited for the next day's newspaper.

There was a story, all right. But it didn't say a thing about the nature of the creature or its long-term effect on trees or what, if any, repellent measures we ought to take. Instead, the story was about the panicky reactions of the homeowners, and it was written in a gleeful tone that poked fun at our situation, contrasting our normal complacency with the distress caused by this heaven-sent phenomenon. You could almost hear the writer chortling. You could also get the idea that this was a paper whose reporters did not like its readers very much. The mysterious webbing went away of its own accord. The trees survived. The only casualty was the homeowners' trust in that local paper.

Self-Aggrandizement

Some manifestations of a newspaper's attitude toward itself and its readers are subtle. Watch out for signs of self-aggrandizement. If the newspaper is trying to con you with a phony mystique, it will have lots of stories with vague or nonexistent indications of where the information comes from. A good giveaway is a story that opens with some fairly startling information that is treated as an announcement by the newspaper, such as: "A $50,000 shortage has been discovered in the city's tree-trimming account, the *Daily Bugle* learned today." A newspaper that acts as its own source is a pompous newspaper and is trying too hard to impress you. Just as bad are stories that attribute their information to "sources" without any qualifying information to let you know what sort of sources they are. There are legitimate situations where the newspaper cannot reveal its sources, but it should always let you know why and give you some information to help you judge the credibility of the source. Thus, "a source in the city auditor's office" or "sources close to the mayor's staff" is better than the simplistic and uninformative "sources said." This last formulation adds no information to the report and yet is used compulsively by some writers as a nervous habit, something like the repetitive "you know" that some people use constantly in conversation.

The worst kind of self-aggrandizement occurs when reporters adopt the mysterious-source pose gratuitously to give themselves an air of importance. Leonard Downie has ruefully recalled how young reporters at the *Washington Post* developed this bad habit after Watergate. He recalled a situation

> where a reporter in Prince Georges County . . . went to a fire and said that a reliable source said that the fire started in the kitchen. In fact, the fire marshal would have gladly been on the record, but the reporter thought this was the way to do it. And we tried to stamp that out. And often we're lax about it.[2]

Interaction between Reader and Newspaper

Contempt for the reader can surface in less subtle ways. Columns where there is interaction between the reader and the newspaper are a place where the newspaper staff's true feelings about its readers will surface. Some newspapers still run Action Line columns that display this sort of interaction. The Action Line originated in Houston, but the first one I ever saw began in the 1960s under the direction of Kurt Luedtke at the *Detroit Free Press,* and its tone was beautiful: crisp, efficient, respectful, and always helpful. A reader who had a problem with a government agency, a business, or a neighbor—or, for that matter, even with an inanimate object like a stuck bureau drawer—could write to Action Line. And when Action Line intervened—at least in those instances that were published in the column—the results were magical. Previously stubborn auto dealers fixed transmissions, local bureaucrats cut their own red tape, doctors even made house calls. The column was an immediate success, and other papers quickly copied it. But in my travels, I soon saw that some of those other papers either didn't get the point or were produced by news people who harbored deep hostility to their readers. If a reader wrote in with a dumb question, the Action Line writer would use the occasion to point out what stupid readers the paper had. Or the columnist would quarrel in print with the poor reader, saying that the problem was the reader's own fault, so get lost and don't bother us with it.

The pace set by Luedtke in Detroit was difficult to maintain, and Action Line columns began to move to the back of the paper or to disappear when editors got tired of them in the 1970s. But there is another place where you can witness reader–editor interaction, and that is the letters-to-the-editor column on the editorial page. Check to see if the paper lets the readers who contribute to that column have the last word or whether the letters are followed by quarrelsome, italicized editor's notes designed to contrast the editor's right thinking with that of the wrong-headed reader. A reader-oriented newspaper, with only rare exceptions, bites its tongue and leaves the letters column to its readers. At the other extreme are newspapers that use the might of the editorial columns to strike down hapless readers who disagree with them in the letters column. In one case I know about, a reader wrote to disagree with an editorial and, in the course of defending his disagreement, made a minor error of fact. The editor seized on this error of fact and published a lengthy editorial criticizing the reader, even going so far as to enumerate some of the reader's educational attainments and wondering how such a learned person could make such a dumb mistake.

Receptiveness to Opposing Viewpoints

Such an attitude on the part of the editor indicates the paper's general tone and the level of respect that it has toward its readers. It is also related to another issue that is easy to check, and that is the paper's openness to viewpoints other than its own. The first means of checking is simplicity itself. Turn to the editorial page, in most papers a left-hand or even-numbered page. Now look at the facing page. It should be an open page, free or mostly free of ads, and it should be devoted to opinion columns, guest editorials, cartoons, and other matter selected to give you, not the newspaper's view, but a diversity of views, including those that contrast most sharply with the newspaper's own. If the paper endorses Democratic candidates for office, a Republican view should be prominently and regularly displayed on this page. If the paper hates government regulation, you should find proregulation views here. This is the op-ed page, and it is especially important that it be present in a newspaper that dominates its market. If there is no such page, your newspaper does not respect you.

Coverage of "Micronews"

Here is yet another yardstick of a newspaper's respect for its readers. All news can be divided into two categories: the few items that interest many people and the many items that interest a few people. The former is clearly the most cost-efficient and the most interesting to the reporting staff. Salaries being what they are, news people work more for glory than for money, and the glory is to be obtained by writing the page-one stories, the few that have the broadest interest.

But if you examine your newspaper closely, you should be able to find the other kind of news: brief listings or snippets that are very important to only a small number of people: neighborhood crime reports, real estate sales, marriage licenses, Little League box scores, information about what local schools are doing. Some of the information appears in the little bitty type that printers call agate. A newspaper that respects its readers will look out for individual concerns as well as the major collective concerns, and one sign that it cares is a large amount of agate type. There should also be neighborhood news in regular type, and you should expect to find it whether your paper's circulation is 3,000 or 300,000. The larger paper does it by publishing different sections for different neighborhoods, a practice called "zoning."

James K. Batten promoted this concept as president of Knight-Ridder in the 1980s. He called it "micronews." In selling the concept to the staff of the *Charlotte* (N.C.) *Observer,* he offered this example: A public school is having budget problems, and it decides to lay off the saxophone teacher. A youth whose life has been given meaning and direction at a critical time by this teacher will be adversely affected. For the youth and his family, information about that one aspect of a large and complicated educational resources issue is the most important thing in the newspaper that day. It is a hard point to sell to a newspaper staff. For some time after Batten's departure, reporters in Charlotte disdainfully spoke of such intense local coverage as "saxophone journalism." But the newspaper that provides it is one that cares about its readers, and its absence is a good sign that you are being served by a self-indulgent news staff.

Coverage of Television

My next suggestion for evaluating the reader-service orientation of your favorite newspaper will offend a lot of news people. It represents one of the most serious and long-standing blind spots in the newspaper business, and it is an excellent way to sort the papers that care about you from those that don't. It has to do with the paper's coverage of television.

Newspaper people do not like television, which is a perfectly rational, even intelligent, point of view. What is not rational is their means of dealing with it. In the early years of television the attitude was that newspapers should say as little as possible about TV because mentioning it would only encourage it. Newspapers thought their mission in life was to get news that had not been on television. A TV monitor at the city desk would be used to log the stories on the evening news. Anything the newspaper had working that was not on television that night would get bigger play. If TV had it, the story would be downplayed. That seems idiotic, but it's so.

Today, a younger generation of editors has learned that TV does a lot to shape the interests of newspaper readers and that a well-edited paper will recognize those interests and adjust to them in a positive way. One such adjustment is the increased foreign coverage implemented by some newspapers in response to the way TV brings events overseas into viewers' homes. But that is difficult to measure. Here is a simpler test: As you clear the dishes from the supper table and are trying to decide whether to spend the rest of the evening taking a walk, reading Proust, or watching television, will your newspaper help you make that decision? Can you pick up that day's paper, easily locate the TV listings, and find enough information about that evening's television choices to make a good decision?

Television had been around for a long time before most newspaper editors decided that they did have a duty to help you plan your viewing time. By the middle 1970s, comprehensive daily TV guides with additional information about major events were the norm. Then cable came along, complicating the newspapers' task enormously. Cable did more than add channels that needed to be reported on. It Balkanized the media market, covering a newspaper's circulation area with a variety of local systems that offered different things on different channels to different sets of viewers. Newspapers were slow to pick up this additional challenge of helping the reader with a problem that had grown so much more complicated.

Here is a test to apply to your newspaper. Pick up your most recent weekday copy and see how many of the following situations it can solve:

1. You are an old-movie buff. Is there a corner of the page where you can find all the old movies to be shown on TV that day listed together? If not, is there a distinctive symbol or type face in the regular listings that enables you to scan those listings and pick out the movies? Failing that, are the listings at least complete enough so that by picking your way through the list you can find them all?

2. You like most country music, but certain performers are particular favorites. There is a channel on your cable system dedicated to country music. Does your newspaper tell you who is performing on that channel on that day?

3. Your cable system has a local-origination channel where local officials and civic leaders are interviewed about current issues. Your neighborhood school principal is going to be interviewed about teacher-recruitment problems. Does your newspaper tell you, or do you have to find out by word-of-mouth or dial flipping?

Coverage of Other Leisure Activities

A comprehensive TV log is just one item in a large body of information in the category of news that you can use to make your life fuller and more efficient. A good newspaper will give you consistent, easy-to-find listings on a great variety of leisure activities. Try this simple test:

You are thinking of going to a movie tonight. You turn to the newspaper to see what's available. After scanning the ads, you look for a comprehensive, compact listing that provides, in one place, the following information: name and address of the theater; name of the movie; show time.

Sounds ridiculously simple, doesn't it? Yet not all papers provide that material, at least not as editorial matter. According to a study by Leo Bogart of the Newspaper Advertising Bureau, only about half the nation's newspapers print any regular movie timetable at all (although those that do account for 70 percent of circulation).[3] Some do run such columns as editorial matter, but limit the listings to movie houses that advertise in the newspaper on that particular day. Some provide such listings for a limited number of theaters, but not to all within or near their circulation area. I once lived in a town on the fringe of a large metropolitan area, and I had a choice of four daily newspapers that were home-delivered to my block. Only one of these newspapers provided comprehensive movie listings for my town, and it was based in a large city 30 miles away. The others did not care that much about their readers.

Getting such information, the kind that winds up in agate listings, is a chore, and people who consider themselves journalists don't like to do it. When I was in Topeka in the 1950s, the *Daily Capital* had an agate column called "Breakfast Table Chats." It was a listing of club meetings, and it was used mainly by church groups and sewing circles in the poorer sections of town. We took their notices by telephone, and it was slightly maddening to have the phone ring with what we hoped would be a call from a key source for a hot story but turned out to be only a clubwoman with an item for "Breakfast Table Chats." My resentment of that column was wrongly placed. Perhaps it could have been assembled more efficiently, but the service it provided demonstrated more concern for those readers than many of the stories that interested young reporters.

Coverage of Local Public Bodies

The next item on the checklist may seem at first to contradict this emphasis on the trivial, but on reflection you will see the consistency. This one concerns the coverage of local public bodies: city councils, school boards, boards of zoning appeals, and the like. These agencies and organizations exist in profusion, and covering them is the easiest and cheapest way to fill the paper with news. One reporter at one meeting can bring back columns of minutiae that are of great interest to the people who serve on such boards and councils. It is not so interesting to people whose lives are not touched by all the meetings and maneuvers that eventually lead to action.

What the reader needs and deserves for this kind of local news is interpretation. The reporter should spot and track the trends, the competing power blocs, the likely effects of all these small struggles. To do this, the reporter has to get behind the surface agendas of the meetings and find out what is really going on. It is not easy. A news staff that is organized to do it well learns to think in broad contexts. An individual city council meeting is not so much a story topic as just one source of information about the underlying currents, trends, and controversies in the community. The meeting is one piece of a bigger and more complicated story, and the details are useful only to the extent that they add to the understanding of that story. A newspaper that cares only about filling the news hole as cheaply as possible will take the minutiae for their own sake as space fillers.

An extreme example: In 1965 the Melan Bridge across the Kaw River between downtown Topeka and North Topeka collapsed, killing a motorist. On the advice of its attorney, the city council decided not to investigate possible causes of the bridge collapse, amid hints that the investigation might turn up evidence that the relatives of the dead man could use to sue the city. These bare facts were duly reported, but no editorial questions were raised about the city's responsibility toward its citizens, about flaws in the inspection system that might have allowed the bridge to collapse, about the reluctance to compensate the dead man's family. Nor was there any detailed reporting on the topic, no interpretive pieces on whose specific interests were being protected, no sign of any curiosity about the underlying problems that could have allowed the use of an unsafe bridge. The council's decision not to investigate was just one of many actions duly reported in a routine account.

When such lapses occur, it may seem to the reader that malice must be involved. But, most often, the cause is simply a lack of vigor, which can in turn be traced to a management decision, conscious or accidental, not to support a vigorous news effort. And the extent to which you get interpretation and analysis is a good indication of vigor in news coverage. You have a right to expect it.

Vigor of the Editorial Page

Readers also have a right to expect vigor on the editorial page. How do you detect it? Ralph R. Thrift, Jr., figured out a way while he was a graduate student at the University of Oregon, and it is so simple that almost anyone can apply it.[4] A vigorous editorial page will have a healthy proportion of editorials that meet one or more of the following tests:

1. They are argumentative. They build a case for a specific side of an issue and let you know where they stand.

2. They deal with local matters. It takes very little vigor to argue against the morality of an attack on an American embassy in some faraway place. It does take vigor to be argumentative on local matters that have some direct effect on readers and that local leaders can do something about.

3. Vigorous editorials will express these argumentative, local opinions in a context of controversy. In other words, they will not limit themselves to citing the importance of hometown pride or traffic safety or motherhood. They will select topics on which people in the circulation area disagree.

4. They will give you information on which you can act. Such "mobilizing information" tells you whom to write to, where to call, when to show up, what to do to improve the local, controversial situation about which the newspaper is being argumentative.

How often should such you expect such editorials to appear? Thrift surveyed a limited number of West Coast papers and found that the rate of argumentative editorials on local matters in controversial contexts ranged from 8 to 18 percent of all editorials, which doesn't seem awfully vigorous. Unless you live in the world's only perfect town, your newspaper ought to have at least one such editorial almost daily. If you don't find any in the course of a week, your newspaper may be suffering from terminal ennui, and you should complain.

Continuity in News Coverage
The next test deals with the continuity of the news product. Is each day's paper edited as if one day's events were unconnected with another's, or is the content planned to give you the continuous threads of related events that develop from day to day? If you save a week's worth of papers and go back and check, you might be surprised.

If about 1960, the *Miami Herald* started an experimental weekend news summary aimed at high school students. It consisted of four pages, each a quarter of the regular newspaper page, and I was assigned to write it. The task seemed simple enough: just save the week's *Herald*s, clip the main stories, and summarize them. But it turned out that it couldn't be done, at least not with the *Miami Herald* as the sole source. On local news, the *Herald*'s follow-through was always beautiful. But a running national story that had new developments every day would be fully covered on some days and not at all on others. To get enough detail to summarize these continuing news events, I had to dig up other sources, including other newspapers, such as the *New York Times*. Finally, in desperation, I took to saving the spiked wire copy and searching it to fill the gaps.

The problem faced by the *Herald* and many other newspapers, then and now, was that it cared much more for news written by its own staff than for material coming from outside sources. As a result, local news was carefully followed and checked to see that there were no gaps. There were well-staffed city and state desks to ensure this continuity. National and international news, in contrast, was handled by a lone wire editor with a great amount of space to fill and not much time to sort through the volume of material that crossed his desk and to reflect on how best to use it.

The *Herald* eventually corrected that problem by creating a national desk equivalent in importance to the city and state desks. Other large papers of high quality have done the same, and the job of national editor has become a prestigious one, often a key rung on a career ladder. But your test as a reader is simply to see whether you can follow the main elements of a running story—one with new events every day—with your newspaper as the only source. IF you can't—if you have to rely on broadcast news or other newspapers to fill the gaps—you should complain.

Coverage of Health and Safety Issues

Ingrained in the newspaper culture is the notion that readers should be given what's good for them, whether they are interested in it or not. Often this belief is used as a rationalization for giving readers what the editor is interested in. To avoid any example tainted by argument over what is really good for the reader, let's take a clear-cut case: knowledge that people need for their own health and safety. The ASNE survey put this question to editors, publishers, and staff people:

> Suppose that there were an issue that really meant a lot to the health and safety of people in your community, but people weren't very interested in it. Should the paper try to get people interested, or should it wait until their interest is aroused in some other way?

There was no controversy here. Everybody in the survey, with the exception of three editors representing about 1 percent of the nation's readership, thought that the paper had a duty to get those people interested. This is as close to unanimity as any group of newspaper people will ever get. But what happens in real life? The reality is that newspapers and other media have done a rotten job of educating you and me about the real risks that we face in everyday life.

For example, lots of newspaper readers are afraid to fly in airplanes or to live near nuclear power plants. Most of these same readers are not afraid to ride in a car without a buckled seat belt. Nationally, in the early 1980s, only about 11 percent of Americans wore seat belts. Very few people realize that one of the easiest and most cost-efficient things you can do to extend your life is to develop the habit of fastening your seat belt every time you ride in an automobile. By "cost-efficient," I mean that the increased life expectancy that you get in return for the effort expended is greater than just about anything else you can do. Is there a reason you don't know this intuitively?

Life-preserving and life-enhancing habits do eventually become ingrained in a culture. Religious restrictions on eating certain foods, for example, probably originated as life-enhancing strategies. The day will almost certainly come when the social pressure to fasten your seat belt will be quite irresistible. But creating rules as powerful as that takes time; first there has to be an intuitive appreciation of the link between the practice and the effect. If your newspaper really cared about your health and safety, it would look for ways to help you develop a gut-level appreciation for the various risks and benefits of behaviors that you can control. What newspapers and media in general do, however, is quite the reverse. By emphasizing the outlandish and the dramatic, they paint distorted pictures of the risks of everyday life.

This distortion has been ingeniously documented. Barbara Combs and Paul Slovic advertised for volunteers in the student newspaper at the University of Oregon and asked the 74 subjects they recruited to estimate the actual death rates in the United States from a variety of causes. They also analyzed the content of two medium-size newspapers to see what kinds of causes of death are most often written about. They learned two disturbing things. One was that a personal picture of real-world risks drawn from what was reported in the newspaper is bound to be grossly distorted and unrealistic. The second was that the pictures inside the heads of the people they talked to were more like the spooky, violent world of newspaper content than they were like the real world. For example, the average person in this study thought that homicide was twice as frequent as emphysema as a cause of death. In fact, emphysema causes more deaths. In general, the relative importance of diseases such as stroke, cancer, diabetes, and tuberculosis was underestimated, while violent causes of death were overestimated. This is the same bias found in newspaper coverage.[5]

A newspaper may not be able to solve this problem completely, because the violent deaths are usually the most interesting and therefore the most marketable as news. But when editors can plainly see that the distorted emphasis in reporting is leading to life-endangering behavior on the part of their readers, wouldn't you expect them to do something about it? For the most part, they don't. Two examples will illustrate this negligence.

For decades, public safety authorities knew of the strong connection between alcohol and accidents of all kinds, especially highway traffic fatalities. However, because the public winked at drinking and driving, little was done with this knowledge. The public simply did not develop an intuitive appreciation for the connection between drunken driving and death. By the mi-1980s that was starting to change as society in general became more conservative and more health-conscious. Some newspapers have helped by tracking the change in attitudes and doing trend stories that reinforced the basic attitude change that has been taking place. But few if any have built the goal of enlightening their readers about alcohol as a cause of death into their routine coverage of traffic accidents. How can they do this?

It is very simple. All newspapers have to do is take advantage of the same morbid curiosity they exploit when dealing with multiple-fatality disasters like airplane crashes: report the cause. Whenever alcohol consumption contributes to a traffic fatality, report that. Does your newspaper do that? Check. If it does not, you have grounds for complaint. Editors can't plead lack of reader interest here. The biological basis for morbid curiosity may be related to the fundamental need to monitor the world's perils and learn how to avoid them.[6] A report on a death should include all the relevant causes, not just the immediate cause, namely, a car crash. And it should especially include the avoidable causes, the clues that will help you modify your own behavior to avert a similar fate.

This need for reporting, of course, also applies to the use of seat belts. More people would have an intuitive appreciation for the benefits of seat belts if newspapers routinely reported whether or not accident victims had been wearing them. The *Chapel Hill* (N.C.) *Newspaper* began doing this for all accidents covered by its city police in the early 1980s. Most newspapers don't care that much. Some editors give the excuse that it would embarrass the surviving relatives if the paper were to report that the dead person had not been wearing a seat belt or had been drinking—hardly a convincing argument, in light of editors' normal readiness to use all sorts of embarrassing information about live people. It is easy enough to find out what your paper does. If seat belt use is not routinely reported in stories of automobile deaths, your paper is missing a chance to help its readers cope with a risky world.

For a newspaper to intervene deliberately in the reader's relationship with the world is a fairly audacious act and contrary to the obsessively objective, man-from-Mars stance taken by some First Amendment fundamentalists. It requires making some judgments about the nature of the world and the needs of the reader. This contradiction does not hinder the fundamentalists in their belief that it is their constitutional duty to save the public from itself. The passive model of editing—wait until an issue or problem surfaces as a reportable event before devoting news space to it—is not subscribed to on a conscious level. Nevertheless, many newspapers do follow it unconsciously, and you can catch them at it. Here are some more suggestions for ways to do it.

Skepticism About Paranormal Phenomena

Take, for example, one of the basic values of Western civilization, the belief in the efficacy of rational investigation. Scientific method, with its modern paradigm of data collection, hypothesis testing, experimentation, and statistical analysis, has elevated our civilization from thousands of years of darkness. We do not burn witches, make human sacrifices, or plan the day's activity by looking for messages in the patterns of cracked animal bones. Well, not quite. There is still a residue of superstition in most of us, and there are modern-day struggles between these dark impulses and our urge for rational inquiry. And where do newspapers come down in this struggle? If you haven't been paying attention, you may be surprised to learn that newspapers like to put down science and encourage our simple-minded attraction to the paranormal.

If someone claims there is a haunted house in your town, if a child is said to be gifted with telekinesis (the ability to move objects without touching them), if a local psychic helps the police find missing persons, if some syndicated astrologer claims to know the future, the chances are fairly good that your newspaper will report these claims uncritically. By uncritically, I mean that not even the objective model—getting both sides of the story—will be followed. It is not unusual for a newspaper to simply announce some paranormal event and let it go at that, as if there were no reason to question it.

Curtis D. MacDougall, whose reporting textbooks inspired several generations of news people, including mine, capped his writing career with a straightforward documentation of the way newspapers deal with superstition.[7] Mainly, they wallow in it, even encourage belief in it. MacDougall listed case after case. Considering the historical difficulty that science has had in overcoming superstition, and considering that history's pendulum could well swing back to another dark age of necromancy, this failure of skepticism is foolish at best and downright dangerous at worst. Some concerned scientists and science writers have formed an organization to combat this tendency on the part of newspapers and other media. Their Committee for the Scientific Investigation of Claims of the Paranormal publishes its own journal, the *Skeptical Inquirer*, and tries to get at least equal time for the scientific view.[8] Such efforts should not be needed, but they are. Watch to see how your newspaper handles tales of reincarnation, poltergeists, and mystic prophets, and then judge for yourself what kind of a job it is doing.

Coverage of Emerging Social Problems

Giving readers what's good for them is a sound idea, but it is poorly applied. Newspapers are strangely passive when new social problems arise. One proof is their reaction to the way in which public attention to certain kinds of problems blows hot and cold. When a social problem gets a highly visible position on the agenda of public concerns, is it because newspapers put it there, or did something else happen? Usually, it is something else.

Take the problem of missing children, for example. In 1983 a government report estimated that 1.5 million children are missing in any given year. That figure has since been subject to some revision and questions of definition, but there is general agreement that the problem of missing children is real, large, and heartbreaking. Some voluntary organizations began efforts to locate missing children by getting their pictures reproduced on television, on milk cartons, on turnpike tickets, on supermarket bags, on billboards, and in other unexpected places—that is, other than newspapers. Where were the newspapers in this effort? Child snatching is a real problem, and if the newspaper business has a strong public-service component, shouldn't newspapers donate some space for pictures of missing children? If your newspaper did—and still does from time to time—score it some points. If it never did, you should wonder why. It is not because helping out in the search for missing children is particularly troublesome or expensive. Starting in 1985, the Associated Press began supplying pictures and profiles of two missing children each weekday to each of its newspaper clients. The *Valley News* of West Lebanon, New Hampshire, began a monthly page of pictures of missing children, and some other papers followed suit. "I just got sick and tired of seeing everybody else being public spirited and not the newspapers," the *Valley News* publisher, Willmott Lewis, Jr., explained.[9]

The slowness of newspapers to join this cause may be in part a manifestation of the "not invented here" syndrome. Newspaper people sincerely believe that their still-vast power of information dissemination should be used in the public good. But their parochial interests and failures of imagination can limit their performance. If you, as the reader, never complain, you must take some of the blame, too.

Factual Accuracy

The next series of tests involves accuracy. All the formal codes and almost every news person's informal codes hold accuracy to be the greatest good. Without it, a newspaper has no reason to exist. And yet, as we have seen, there are situations where news people value other things more than accuracy. Some will sacrifice it to improve the structure of a story or to hype a lead. Others will settle for diminished accuracy to avoid controversial news-gathering methods, such as hidden recorders and participant observation. And some will sacrifice it for their own convenience; to them, the checking and double-checking needed for accuracy just don't seem worth the trouble. How does your newspaper tackle the accuracy problem?

One test for accuracy is not very systematic, but the chances are good that you have had or will have the opportunity to apply it at one time or another. Think about the last time your newspaper covered an event about which you had some personal knowledge. Did the writer get the facts right?

According to a survey by MORI Research of Minneapolis for the American Society of Newspaper Editors, nearly three-quarters of all adults have had the opportunity to compare their personal knowledge of an event with the newspaper coverage. A majority found that coverage accurate, but a disturbingly sizable minority was highly critical. Those with personal knowledge of a news event were asked to rate the accuracy of its coverage on a scale of 1 to 5, with the 5 standing for "very accurate." Most in the national sample gave high or at least neutral ratings. But 14 percent scored the paper's coverage at 1 or 2:

Not at all accurate			Very accurate	
1	*2*	*3*	*4*	*5*
5%	9%	27%	36%	23%

The people who gave their papers scores of 1, 2, or even the neutral 3 on this test had significantly lower opinions of their newspaper's ability to tell the truth in general. They were also less sure that the newspaper had a genuine concern for the community's well-being. These views were so strong that, even though they were held by a minority, they offset the positive views of the majority who found that the newspaper performed well on their personal accuracy tests. The net result is that even a small number of errors can inflict serious damage on a newspaper's reputation.[10]

A newspaper's accuracy is directly related to the resources its management devotes to making it accurate. Speed, accuracy, and clarity are to newspapering what blocking and tackling are to football. Without these basics, flashy embellishments do not do you, the reader, a lot of good. A flea flicker or a triple reverse can be fun to watch, but without the basics neither is very effective.

Signs of Openness

When a newspaper has the basics down, it will usually be a confident newspaper. Confidence is expressed not by bravado and strutting, but by an instinctive openness. A news staff knows when it is doing its job well and does not fear criticism or open discussion of its method or its errors.

Where can you spot the outward signs of this openness? The corrections policy is a good place to start. Look for a daily corrections column, appearing in the same place in the paper every day so that readers can find it easily, with a frank listing and correcting of factual errors that the paper has made. A confident and open newspaper will not pass blame, as in: "The John Jones arrested for drunken driving last Saturday was John R. Jones of North Bleek St., not John J. Jones of Leek Ave. as reported to this newspaper by city police." If the corrections column habitually blames others for the errors, the news staff is not as confident as it should be. And the implication that the newspaper is not ultimately responsible for the truth or falsity of the information in its columns is incorrect. It takes a sloppy reporter to use a sloppy source. Good newspaper people, legend has it, wear both belt and suspenders: check and double-check. They are not going to be caught with their pants falling down.

An open newspaper will have corrections to report almost every day. It is simply not possible to produce the volume of printed information contained in a daily paper without a few errors. Some newspapers limit their corrections to those errors which the editors deem serious by some subjective and not easily defined standard. Others will correct even the most trivial errors. The *New York Times,* a confident newspaper if there ever was one, reported on the Coca-Cola Company's 1985 marketing misfire (when the traditional Coke formula was temporarily discarded) with a chart showing changes in market share of the major soft-drink brands. Coke went from 24.8 percent of market share to 21.7 percent, a loss of 3.1 percent of market share. The table in the *Times* called the 3.1 figure the "% change." Well, it is a change and it is a percent (of market share), but percent change by the usual definition would describe the amount of change as a percentage of the earlier market share—that is, 3.1 divided by 24.8, or 12.5 percent. This is a minor, technical point and one that an editor would be justified in letting pass. But not the *Times.* The next day's paper carried this notice on a section front:

Correction

A table on the front page of Business Day yesterday with an article about Coca-Cola carried an incorrect label for the final column of figures. The figures represented the change, in percentage points, in the market share of the major soft drink brands from 1983 to 1984.[11]

It is very difficult not to trust a newspaper that will bring to your attention errors that trivial.

According to the ASNE survey of news people, the most frequent policy, affecting 55 percent of newspaper readers, is to have corrections appear under the same kind of headline in the same part of the paper, in order to make them easy to find. Another 21 percent of readers are served by editors who say they keep the headline constant for easier identification but let the column float from one part of the paper to another as space for it is available. For the remaining 24 percent, corrections are more of an ad hoc affair. Neither the headline nor the location is standardized.

Despite all these good intentions, if you pick up a newspaper on any given day, you may not find any corrections at all. The number of errors that are given the corrections treatment compared to the number that occur is quite small. The rate of purely objective errors—those errors that are not matters of judgment about emphasis or interpretation—has been estimated at about one for every three news stories. This means that for a day to go by without any errors at all is extremely improbable. Many errors may, of course, go unnoticed by the editors because the people who spot them don't bother to call them to his or her attention. As a reader, you should take some responsibility for catching errors. If you spot one, do your newspaper a favor and drop the editor a note pointing it out.

One sure sign of an open attitude on the part of a newspaper's management is the presence of a full-time reader representative or ombudsman. The next chapter will describe the ombudsman function in more detail. Some ombudsmen write columns describing particularly interesting ethical problems the newspaper has encountered. Editors also sometimes write such columns, taking you behind the scenes for a look at some of the tough calls they have made on the handling of certain stories and inviting you to compare your own judgment with theirs.

One other sign of openness involves the lengths to which the paper will go to point out conflicts of interest that its staff or outside contributers might have. Unfortunately, newspapers have not figured out any good way to make such disclosures routine. The widely praised exercise in disclosure by the *Lewiston Morning Tribune* discussed in Chapter 8 was a one-shot effort that, seven years later, had not been repeated. Perhaps some sort of annual report, published in the newspaper to detail the various outside connections and interests of the staff, would be an effective way to handle the problem.

In the long run, openness may be the best single indicator of a newspaper's sense of responsibility. Any ethic based on the First Amendment must embrace openness, and news people who have thought clearly about their values must apply it to their own actions as well as to the actions of others. Lou Gelfand, the reader representative for the *Minneapolis Star and Tribune,* has said that the number of newspapers with such positions would more than double "if only half of those newspapers who editorialize for citizen review boards of police were to establish ombudsmen."[12]

Newspapers have experimented fitfully with ways to institutionalize openness. The two most promising experiments have been ombudsmen and news councils. Neither concept has gotten very far. Now it is time to explore that hesitancy and its causes.

NOTES

1. Letter from James L. Knight to Lee Hills commemorating Hills's thirtieth anniversary with Knight Newspapers, September 26, 1972. From Hills's files.

2. Leonard Downie, remarks at seminar held by the Wisconsin Newspaper Association, Madison, Wisconsin, March 15, 1984.

3. Leo Bogart, "How U.S. Newspaper Content Is Changing," *Journal of Communication* (Spring 1985): 82–87.

4. Ralph R. Thrift, Jr., "How Chain Ownership Affects Editorial Vigor of Newspapers," *Journalism Quarterly,* Summer 1977, pp. 327–321.

5. Barbara Combs and Paul Slovic, "Newspaper Coverage of Causes of Death," *Journalism Quarterly,* Winter 1979, pp. 837–849. For a broader context, see "Health Risk Reporting: Roundtable Workshop on the Media and Reporting of Risks to Health," Institute for Health Policy Analysis, Georgetown University Medical Center, 1985.

6. "Morbid Curiosity and the Mass Media: Proceedings of a Symposium," School of Journalism, University of Tennessee, Knoxville, 1984.

7. Curtis Daniel MacDougall, *Superstition and the Press* (Buffalo, N.Y.: Prometheus Books, 1983).

8. Alan L. Otten, "People Will Believe Anything, Which Is Why *Csicops* Exist," *Wall Street Journal,* 19 July 1985, p. 1.

9. Marcia Ruth, "Missing Children," *Presstime,* June 1985, pp. 6–8.

10. *Newspaper Credibility: Building Public Trust* (Reston, Va.: American Society of Newspaper Editors, 1985).

11. The *New York Times*'s Coca-Cola correction appeared on 13 July 1985, p. 23.

12. Lou Gelfand, quoted in Mark Fitzgerald, "Struggling for Recognition," *Editor & Publisher,* July 13, 1985, p. 7.

CHAPTER 11

The Healing Light

Newspaper people believe with particular intensity in the healing power of information. This faith is justified. It is the practical underpinning of the First Amendment. "The good sense of the people," said Thomas Jefferson in 1787, "will always be the best army." And for that good sense to assert itself, complete information would have to "penetrate the whole mass of people."[1]

Every major journalistic code of ethics refers, at least implicitly, to information as a good in itself. This belief is expressed starkly in the opening words of that early and now superseded code adopted by the American Society of Newspaper Editors in 1923: "The primary function of newspapers is to communicate to the human race what its members do, feel and think."

So strong is this belief that a modern corollary of sorts has arisen. It holds that information is, in and of itself, so powerful that for a newspaper to exercise other forms of power concurrently is excessive and a breach of ethics. In 1983 the *Miami Herald* won a Pulitzer Prize for its successful editorial campaign to improve the government's treatment of Haitian refugees who drifted to Florida shores. Prize juries are impressed by successful campaigns, but the *Herald* later drew some criticism when it was disclosed that its success was based on more than just the power of the printed word—much more. The reforms were the result of direct lobbying efforts by newspaper personnel who were not content to put their views in print and let it go at that. Editor Jim Hampton, noticing that the paper's editorials on the subject were not having much effect, joined a committee of community leaders to put direct pressure on government officials. He was not sneaky about it. The Pulitzer nomination described his active efforts. The *Herald* won the prize, but then it drew a frown from journalism ethicist Gilbert Cranberg, who said that Hampton had "broken one of the most generally accepted rules of big-city newspapers: you don't become involved with the news you are covering."[2]

The same belief, that power to inform is so basic that newspapers should abstain from other kinds of power, was behind the controversy in an earlier case involving the *Miami Herald.* It and some other Florida news-papers took a licking from their out-of-state peers when they contributed company funds to oppose a statewide referendum that would have legalized gambling in south Florida. The power of the printed word is enough, their critics said. Let it go at that. In the ASNE survey, publishers representing 67 percent of the nation's newspaper circulation and editors representing 87 percent said that it was wrong for a newspaper to contribute cash to such a campaign.

The history of journalism bears out the notion that light, by itself, is power. That history is rich with examples of public policy turning 180 degrees in response to information made public. As a young reporter in Miami, I wrote that the school board was paying far more for insurance on its buildings than was paid by other local jurisdictions and that political cronies of board members were reaping the commissions. The board changed its ways, cut premiums in half, and diverted the money to better purposes, including a pay raise for teachers. It accomplished this in a few months, although its members had resisted for years vigorous internal and unpublicized efforts by school administrators to reform the sytem.[3] Even the best minds see old problems in a new light when the glare of publicity is focused on them.

Newspaper people know this both intellectually and intuitively. It is the basic rationale for what they do. It gives them power, often at an early age, and it can compensate for long hours and low pay. Without it, they would just as soon sell insurance or write advertising copy.

Given this belief that information is light and that it has healing power, we might justifiably think that the obvious solution to the newspaper industry's own internal moral problems would be the same sort of healing light. Knowing of the gut-level appreciation of this power among news people, we would expect them to turn to it instinctively, even reflexively, without stopping to quibble over whether it is just or appropriate.

Unfortunately, they don't, at least not on a routine basis. When a newspaper does something questionable or stupid, the quite human tenden-cy of the editor and the staff is to forget about it as quickly as possible. There are, however, some impressive examples of newspapers responding to an internal crisis by turning their own spotlights on themselves with particular intensity. Three cases stand out:

In 1967 a reporter for the *Philadelphia Inquirer,* Harry Karafin, was caught using his access to the news columns to extort money from local businesses. Joseph C. Goulden, a respected *Inquirer* reporter, was assigned to investigate his colleague. Karafin was convicted of blackmail. He died in prison.

Ten years later, by which time ownership of the *Inquirer* had passed from Walter Annenberg to the Knight-Ridder group, prize-winning writers Donald L. Barlett and James B. Steele used their investigative talents to explore the relationship of a former political reporter, Laura Foreman, with Henry J. Cianfrani, the state senator who eventually spent 27 months in Allenwood Federal Prison Camp for racketeering and mail fraud.

In 1981 the *Miami Herald* sent for its Washington correspondent, Tom Fiedler, to shed some light on a different sort of case, one for which wrongdoing on the part of the paper or its staff was not so clear. A former reporter, Robert Hardin, had circulated a voluminous critique of the paper's coverage of the Miami Police Department in which he blamed the newspaper for provoking that city's May 1980 riots. At first the *Herald* ignored Hardin, but finally decided to treat him as news. Fiedler was brought in partly because his out-of-town posting could make him more objective but also because local staff writers were reluctant to tackle a job that might result in criticism of their friends and colleagues.

The writers in each of these examples followed an objective, just-the-facts approach to reporting in which each fact was authenticated and attributed. When the chips are down, a good newspaper wants to hold ambiguity to a minimum and demonstrate to its readers that they are getting the straight story. And a reporter who draws such a touchy assignment knows that a lot of colleagues are looking over his or her shoulder at every keystroke. These stories provided the desired catharsis. (Indeed, some news people think such efforts risk going too far and focus too much on the deviance of individual reporters while underplaying institutional failings.) But they were exceptional cases, with action taken on an ad hoc basis in response to a transitory problem. They were not triggered by a routine oversight function, and resistance to making such efforts routine remains high.

The Jeffersonian liberalism with which news people view the external political system turns to something quite different when their gaze shifts to their internal problems. The few newspapers that have experimented with ways to keep that internal light burning have not been widely copied. The problem is one of figuring out who should control the spotlight.

Remember that the newspaper's power stems from its status as an independent source of information, one not beholden to those whom it illuminates. If the newspaper itself is to be placed in a spotlight, the hand controlling that light should be similarly independent. Devising an independent mechanism for self-analysis has not been easy. Two still very tentative forms that have been tried in this country are the ombudsman and the news council.

The Ombudsman

In Scandinavia, where the concept originated, an ombudsman is a public official who helps citizens redress grievances against government agencies or officials and pick their way through that country's mammoth bureaucracy. It is roughly the same function performed in the U.S. national government by congressional case workers. The ombudsman is basically an independent source of information, and the position's power stems from information in two different ways: knowing where to go to get something done and being able to call attention to specific cases of injustice.

The first newspaper to adopt the ombudsman idea was the *Louisville Courier-Journal,* then a prestigious family-owned newspaper whose liberal standards applied both inside and outside the organization. Norman Isaacs was the editor, and he got the idea in 1967 from a prophetic *New York Times Magazine* article by A. H. Raskin, who suggested that newspapers create

> . . . their own Departments of Internal Criticism to check on the fairness and adequacy of their coverage and comment. The department head ought to be given enough independence in the paper to serve as an ombudsman for the readers, armed with authority to get something done about valid complaints and to propose methods for more effective performance of all the paper's services to the community.[4]

Louisville's pioneer ombudsman was John Herchenroeder, the former city editor, and he served from 1967 to 1979. Unlike many later ombudsmen, he did not write a regular column, although he did contribute occasional pieces related to his work. His main task was to respond directly to readers with complaints and to formalize internal standards and procedures. By 1985 some 35 ombudsmen were at work nationwide, and most of them wrote columns in addition to their internal responsibilities.

The key to the ombudsman's function is independence. In its most formal version, the office of ombudsman is kept structurally separate from the news and editorial operations so that it is more than a complaint desk. It is an independent source of information about the internal operations of the newspaper.

Among the national elite papers, only the *Washington Post* was quick to establish a pure ombudsman. The holder of the job serves for a limited term, a policy that promotes both independence and a fresh, unjaundiced view. He (as of this writing, all of the ombudsmen have been males) is usually hired from outside the company and does not stay with the newspaper after his term expires. It can be a prestigious and highly visible position, as it was for Bill Green, who took leave as director of university relations for Duke University in 1980 and was the *Post* ombudsman when the Janet Cooke case erupted. Green's lengthy report on the *Post*'s shortcomings helped to restore the prestige the paper had lost after it had returned its Pulitzer prize.

In the ASNE survey, editors representing 14 percent of daily circulation reported that they carry columns by independent ombudsmen—that is, ombudsmen whose reports are not subject to approval by the editor before publication. The ombudsmen are concentrated among the larger papers, however. In 1985 the Organization of Newspaper Ombudsmen had an active roster of 30, and the median circulation of the papers for which they worked was about 130,000. Their work was given visibility by a column launched in 1984 in *Quill* by Richard P. Cunningham, the former associate director of the National News Council.

The advantage of an ombudsman column is its informality. The ombudsman may air reader complaints, comment on them, tell what he or she would have done, and even pronounce some general rules. The more vigorous among them will even denounce the newspaper's own general policies. Sam Zagoria, ombudsman of the *Washington Post* in the mid-1980s, didn't think his paper's correction policy was aggressive enough. In 1985 he published a list of errors made in 1984 that the *Post* had known about but had not corrected. He said the need for corrections had been

> dismissed by defensive writers or editors as being unimportant or forgiven in the haste of putting out a daily paper. The logic escapes me. When readers note that an error goes uncorrected, confidence in the reporters, editors and the *Post* in general declines.[5]

Often, there is enough "on the one hand this, on the other hand that" in an ombudsman column to keep it from being too threatening to the newspaper's staff and management. Social pressures within the journalism fraternity are heavy, and when an ombudsman is outspoken, the backlash can be strong. David Shaw never had the title of ombudsman, but when he became press critic of the *Los Angeles Times* in 1974, he fulfilled many of the same functions by turning his journalistic analytical power on the profession itself, including his own newspaper. One editor stopped speaking to him for a year. Another threw one of his stories into the trash basket. A third wrote him a letter "terminating our personal relationship." The last, recalled Shaw, had been a good friend.[6]

When ombudsmen are rotated frequently and when they come from outside the newspaper, as is the case at the *Washington Post,* the effect of this pressure is minimized. A short-timer is more immune to social pressure. And a rotating ombudsman position cannot develop into an ongoing power center in its own right. This structure makes the situation more palatable to the objects of the criticism, who know they will outlast the critic. Rotation has another interesting effect. It can keep the ombudsman's findings from developing into a consistent body of thought and precedent, which might form the basis for a detailed code of ethics. This is a mixed blessing.

The thought of being pinned down to a detailed set of rules is anathema to many news people, particularly the First Amendment fundamentalists. In the view of these journalistic anarchists, the existence of any rule, even if it is a self-imposed one for the sake of consistency, is a potential infringement of their First Amendment freedom to publish whatever they want, whenever and however they want to publish it. "The simplest and most innocuous form of press regulation," said Michael Gartner, formerly president of the *Des Moines Register,* "is an ethics code." Speaking at a Duke University seminar in 1984, Gartner noted that codes can be used as "fodder for the foes of the free press."[7]

Few news people are as absolutist or as outspoken as Gartner, but variations on his viewpoint are widely held. Many news people see themselves as beleaguered by forces that would extinguish the light-giving power of the press by finding ways to regulate it. The reflexive defense is to resist all rules and rule-making institutions. Freedom, these journalists seem to be saying, means total caprice and unpredictability, the freedom of the proverbial hog on ice. This antipathy toward definable rules and standards is a minor source of resistance to the concept of the ombudsman, but a major source of objection to the other major institutional method for casting the healing light of information on newspapers' own problems. That institution is, of course, the independent news council.

The News Council

News councils organized in this country have taken as their model the British Press Council, which assumed its present form in 1964. An earlier version began operating sporadically in England in 1953, then collapsed from lack of direction. The successful version operates under this key rule: Anyone who asks it to investigate a complaint must agree not to bring any civil action against the newspaper that is the object of the complaint. This rule appeals to newspapers and complainants alike. The number of libel actions in England fell after the council got rolling, sparing both newspapers and potential plaintiffs the trouble and cost of litigating complaints.

Attempts to create news councils in this country have started from that same premise. You might think that the chance to develop a substitute for libel action in this country, where newspapers are complaining loudly about the cost and the chilling effect of megabucks verdicts, would cause the professional and trade associations of journalism to fall all over themselves trying to establish news councils. No such luck. The problem is that the most ambitious effort to start a news council, pumped into life by foundation money in 1973, was a spectacular failure. The National News Council had its financial underpinning cut off by those same foundations in 1984, and it survives only as a ghostly archive at the University of Minnesota. The apparent moral of its 11-year existence: news councils won't work in this country.

But there is evidence to the contrary. The Minnesota News Council started two years before the National News Council, and it is still going strong. The 1983 ASNE survey shows substantial minorities of news people who believe that a news council at least at the state level is worth a try. Publishers representing 21 percent of daily circulation and editors representing 29 percent agreed with the statement, "A state news council, modeled after the National News Council, would be a good idea." And, perhaps most significantly, staff members accounting for 49 percent of circulation agreed. This greater agreement among the staff is partly a function of age. The average age in the survey was 51 for publishers, 49 for editors, and 37 for staff members. Younger editors and staff members regarded the news council idea most favorably. At age 30 and below, the statement was supported by a majority of both editors and publishers. Past the age of 40, the balance tips the other way, with majorities of both editors and staffers opposing a state news council. A widely supported news council may be the kind of fundamental innovation that requires a generational change before it can receive adequate support.

The people who have torpedoed recent efforts to launch news councils in such states as Kentucky and Wisconsin have been older editors and publishers who are less able to appreciate the demand for openness that modern society places on its media. The idea is bound to be tested anew among a newer generation of leaders.

Whether it works or not will depend a lot on the kinds of people who try to make it work. Minnesota was lucky. Its news council was founded by venturesome news people willing to take risks for an audacious experiment operating on a shoestring. The National News Council operated in more timid fashion, kept secure from short-term disaster by its foundation grants. In its early years, the National News Council spent more on office rent than the Minnesota Council had for its entire operating budget. National council members wasted valuable time nitpicking the bylaws. Its cases were limited at first to the "principal national suppliers of news"—and then only when a citizen originated a complaint. The council would not originate an investigation on its own. The problem with this limitation is that the most grievous sins of the press are committed in out-of-the-way places. A serious effort to improve the standards of journalism cannot be limited to the *New York Times* and the *Washington Post.*

Despite these problems, there were six rousing years, 1976 to 1982, during which the National News Council looked as if it might make it. That was when Norman Isaacs, the curmudgeonly former editor of the *Louisville Courier Journal,* was in charge. Operating more by gut instinct than by the book, he shook the council out of its passivity and went charging after controversy. The whole point of a news council, after all, is to attract attention. Isaacs realized that shedding light is useless if no one is interested enough to look your way. When the council went after John McGoff, the publisher of Panax Newspapers, who directed a vendetta against Edward M. Kennedy in his news columns, some media companies began to see the value of the council and even contributed financially for the first time.

Support from the media it watches is a news council's essential requirement for survival. The Minnesota News Council has that. The *Minneapolis Star and Tribune* backed the council from the start. John Finnegan, editor of the *St. Paul Pioneer Press,* served on the council for three years, has seen his own paper have its wrist slapped, yet still backs the council. "This is an open society in Minnesota," he says. "We've always had an open society. We feel we can discuss our problems openly and come to a decision."[8]

The National News Council and the Fear of Regulation

When the big, prestigious papers back a plan for self-improvement in the industry, the others follow. That works in reverse, too. Norman Isaacs didn't realize it at the time, but he witnessed the death blow to the National News Council three years before it was born. This not-so-spontaneous abortion came in 1970 at a fateful meeting called by Lester Markel, the retired Sunday editor of the *New York Times.* Markel was brilliant, crusty, and somewhat embittered because the *Times* had retired him before he was ready. He worked with the Twentieth Century Fund to design the master plan for the National News Council. And then he called a meeting of the people whose cooperation would be needed if the council was to succeed. It was a new notion that was being sprung on these people, and they thought they were there to give advice and guidance.

Abe Rosenthal of the *New York Times* went to that meeting. "For him to come to that kind of a meeting was a good sign," Norman Isaacs later recalled. But when the plan was unfolded by Markel and a representative of the Twentieth Century Fund, Rosenthal exploded. It seemed to him that he was being presented with a *fait accompli* to endorse, he wanted no part of it, and he left in anger.

When the National News Council finally got started early in 1973, it had the backing of the *Washington Post,* the *Wall Street Journal,* the *Christian Science Monitor,* CBS, the Associated Press, and United Press International. It did not have the backing of the *New York Times.* What came from the *Times* instead was a memorandum to the news and editing staffs signed by publisher Arthur Ochs Sulzberger (Patrick Brogan has reported that it was drafted by Abe Rosenthal) declaring the *Times*'s nonparticipation: "We will not be a party to Council investigations. We will not furnish information or explanations to the Council. In our coverage, we will treat the Council as we treat any other organization: we will report their activities when they are newsworthy."[9]

In justifying that stand, Sulzberger took a position common to news people of the fundamentalist persuasion, the view that sees the virtuous press beset by evildoers and special pleaders seeking to start the news people moving down some slippery slope to a loss of independence. "We do not think that the real threat to a free press in the United States arises from a failing of the press to be fair and accurate," said the Sulzberger memo. "The real threat to a free press comes from people who are attempting to intimidate or use the press for their own ends."[10]

One reason that this view is so stubbornly held is that a great deal of truth underlies it. Information is power, controlling its flow is important to special interests, and they do try to intimidate the press. But the First Amendment fundamentalists adopt a sort of domino theory, which holds that they have to fight to get their way every time for fear that even the slightest compromise could topple them into complete and irreversible surrender. The National News Council, in Sulzberger's view, was "a form of voluntary regulation." The implied argument is that a little bit of voluntary regulation can be the first step down the slippery slope to a lot of government regulation.

If that were true, newspapers in Minnesota ought to be on their way to being pretty firmly regulated by now. There are news people in that state who do not like its news council, but they cannot claim that it has led to government regulation or hampered their management of the media. And those who support the council argue that in the long run it will have just the opposite effect: it immunizes against the regulatory virus rather than sensitizes to it.

"That's the theory that I buy into," says John Finnegan, editor of the *St. Paul Pioneer Press and Dispatch.* "If you go in for a certain amount of self-regulation, then you have a way to head off government regulation."[11]

The absolutists' fears are not vague. They offer a scenario. Every time a news council judges a newspaper's action as right or wrong, a record is made. Eventually, a body of precedent could be built from these case-by-case decisions. Certain uniformities would begin to emerge, and then some scholar or jurist would sit down, identify the uniformities, and organize them into a code. When that happens, warns Creed Black, publisher of the *Lexington* (KY) *Herald-Leader,* "there is the likelihood somebody will pick that up and try to enact them into a law or throw these things back into your face in a courtroom or use News Council decisions in libel cases."[12]

Indeed, some of these things have happened. Robert Schafer, while a graduate student at the University of Minnesota, examined the first 10 years of decisions by the Minnesota News Council and found that some uniformities were beginning to emerge. For example, the council, while stating reluctance to interfere with an editor's gate-keeping role, has generally favored a right of reply through letters to the editor for aggrieved parties.[13] In contrast, the U.S. Supreme Court has held that there is no legal right of reply that can be used to compel a newspaper to publish a letter it does not want to publish.[14]

To a nervous publisher, it might seem as if the news council is plunging ahead to abridge press freedom where the Supreme Court fears to tread. But that view misses the distinction between a moral right and a legal right. To say that someone whose controversy has been aired in the news columns or who has been criticized on the editorial page should have the chance to tell his or her side of the story is not such a radical notion. And the whole points of the news council's intervention is to keep the principle on the moral plane, where it belongs, and out of the civil or criminal codes, where it decidedly does not belong.

Some news people have trouble keeping the legal–moral distinction clear. Newspaper lawyers have sometimes advised their clients against maintaining any kind of written ethical standards. A libel plaintiff seeking to prove malice might use a departure from the written code as evidence of malicious intent. A capricious newspaper, one with no identifiable standards, is evidently less likely to be malicious under the law. Those who follow that advice are sacrificing a major moral advantage for a minor tactical benefit.

The News Council's Advantage over the Ombudsman Plan

The two self-illuminating devices, news councils and ombudsmen, have different strengths and weaknesses. A newspaper can initiate an ombudsman program unilaterally. A news council takes an unusual amount of cooperation, and enlisting that cooperation can be a tremendous effort. A disadvantage of the ombudsman is that its cost makes it basically a large-paper solution to the illumination problem. For the bigger papers, the extra staff position does not represent a significant portion of payroll. On the smaller one, it does have an impact on the budget, and for an editor who has to choose between an ombudsman and a courthouse reporter, the ombudsman is an obvious frill. Papers large enough to support an ombudsman financially and confident enough to support the position emotionally are likely to be pretty good newspapers to begin with. Their ombudsmen probably help the long-run cause of credibility (although research has so far failed to show short-term results), and they demonstrate good faith with the readers. But their scope is necessarily limited.

A news council, in contrast, can go anywhere. It does not depend on the financial resources of any one paper. And the Minnesota experience has shown that the built-in obstacles to getting started can be overcome.

The Minnesota News Council: A Success Story

The Minnesota News Council was largely the creation of one man, Robert M. Shaw, who was serving as manager of the Minnesota Newspaper Association at the time. A bold and creative manager, he arrived at that post from a varied background, including study in philosophy at the University of Minnesota, an advanced degree in journalism, some time at the University of Heidelberg, and service at *Stars and Stripes*. J. Edward Gerald of the University of Minnesota School of Journalism called him "an adventurous spirit." The plan for a state news council grew out of a conversation in the spring of 1970 among Shaw and publishers Gordon Spielman of Trimount and Philip S. Duff, Jr., of Red Wing. They decided that it would be a good idea to provide a place for people to lodge complaints against newspapers and that the association's Goals and Ethics Committee would be a logical place. The idea of adding public members to the committee was raised. From there, it was a logical step to a council independent of the association. Once that decision was made, it was implemented quickly, before substantial opposition could be mounted, in September 1971. "It came about very rapidly because of his [Shaw's] style of operation," recalled Gerald more than a decade later. "If it had been a long, drawn-out discussion, it would have failed."[15]

A state supreme court justice, C. Donald Peterson, was the first chairman. The organization began as the Minnesota Press Council but changed its name after an evaluation committee in 1981 urged it to expand and include broadcasting in its area of concern.

The Minnesota News Council's goals were set forth in its constitution:

To preserve the freedom of the press;

To maintain the character of the press in accordance with the highest professional standards;

To review, on a continuing basis, the performance of the Minnesota press regarding matters of general public interest;

To urge and assist the Minnesota press in the fulfillment of its unique responsibility to perform in the public interest.

When a complaint is made, the council logs it and assigns a case number. The complainant is then advised that he or she must make an effort to settle the problem directly with the management of the news organization. If that fails, the council will accept a formal, written complaint documented with clippings. At that point, the complainant signs the waiver of future legal or administrative action on the same complaint. The enforceability of that waiver has never been tested in court in Minnesota, but the council's attorneys say they think it will stick. Once the waiver and documented complaint are in hand, the council asks for a written response from the news organization. This request goes to management, not to the individual employee whose action or inaction drew the complaint. If, after the response is received, the complainant is still unhappy, the matter can go to a hearing. Both sides can present their cases informally; legal counsel is allowed but not encouraged. If the news organization's representative does not show up, the hearing is held anyway.

Compared to the National News Council, the Minnesota group has been a modest undertaking. Its annual budget for 1985 was $65,000, which supported the work of a director and two part-time staff people. The policy has been to seek diverse financial support, and in 1985 the distribution was roughly one-fourth each from newspapers, corporations, and foundations, with the balance coming from individuals, associations, and earnings on investments. The council's growing workload consisted of about 80 cases a year, of which only 10 percent resulted in hearings and written determinations. Most cases were dropped by complainants who cooled off or didn't want the bother of pursuing them, or were resolved through conciliation.

All the Minnesota News Council's cases originate with the public. Unlike the National News Council, the Minnesota council has not reached out on its own to get interesting and important cases. Tom Patterson, the executive director, and some of the editors who back him, believe that this restraint contributes to the support that the council gets from the state's media companies. Minnesota news people know that the complaints being investigated are real ones and that the council is not trying to carve out a position as an independent power center. It has not even published a collection of its decisions. This is due in part to financial constraints, but it also reassures editors who fear that such a collection could be codified and become the basis for some form of regulation. This fear may be academic. The council keeps permanent records which form such an interesting body of lore and precedent that volunteer codifiers, probably scholars backed by foundation grants, will eventually do the job. It is only a matter of time.

One moral that may be drawn from the contrasting fates of the Minnesota and national news councils is that small is better. But there are some drawbacks to smallness. In 1985 Tom Patterson was working out of an obscure office in the University of Minnesota's Audio-Visual Services building. He would rather have been in a storefront, where people could walk in and learn more about the council. He would have liked to have funds to develop an outreach program that would generate more business elsewhere in the state. A disproportionate number of complaints originate in the Minneapolis–St. Paul area and involve only the Twin Cities media. A group of independent evaluators who studied the first nine years of the council's operation found that the council had "yet to achieve genuine statewide recognition."[16] A person with a complaint against a newspaper out in the state may not want to go to the trouble and expense of traveling to a hearing in Minneapolis, although a few do. A procedure for conducting traveling hearings would help, but the money for travel has never been available.

And after a dozen years, stable funding remained a continuing problem. "I've been going around with a tin cup all my life trying to get money for worthy causes," said Robert Shaw, "and it's a tough, tough row to hoe for a news council."[17] The good news is that the amount of money needed to get a news council started is not great. In the first six and a half years of its life, the Minnesota News Council operated with no paid help and a budget of only $10,000 a year. Other states could start out at the same level, according to Patterson, so long as they have "a strong volunteer organization and people committed to doing the work on a volunteer basis."[18]

Support for State News Councils

If volunteers are to do it, then there have to be people who believe in it. And there are. Support for the news council idea is strongest precisely where the ombudsman is the least feasible, among the smaller papers. The ASNE survey found that editors, publishers, and staff members are all more likely to support the state news council concept if they come

TABLE 11.1
SUPPORT FOR STATE NEWS COUNCIL, BY NEWSPAPER SIZE

	Small	Medium	Large
Publishers	33%	25%	14%
Editors	49	24	22
Staff	61	56	37

from small papers, those with circulations of less than 40,000. And those at papers in the medium range, up to 200,000 circulation, are more supportive than those in the very largest newspapers. Table 11.1 shows how this support varies. The percentages indicate the circulation represented by those in each group who agree that a state news council would be a good idea:

This relative strength at the grass roots is not enough, of course. The National News Council failed without support from enough larger papers. The Minnesota News Council succeeded with that kind of support. But these data are encouraging because they show that once the barriers to large-paper cooperation are overcome, a workable reservoir of grass-roots support is already in place.

There will be more news councils, and news people will embrace them cooperatively, if not always enthusiastically. They will do so because their belief in the healing power of information is deeply held, and its logic must inevitably take them to an attitude of openness about their own affairs.

NOTES

1. Letter to Edward Carrington, January 16, 1787, in *The Portable Thomas Jefferson,* ed. Merrill D. Peterson (New York: Viking Press, 1975).

2. Gilbert Cranberg and Elizabeth Bird, "A Prize in Deed: The *Miami Herald*'s 1983 Pulizer," *Washington Journalism Review* (April 1984): 47.

3. The *Herald* articles appeared on the local-news page, September 1959.

4. A. H. Raskin "What's Wrong with American Newspapers," *New York Times Magazine,* 11 June 1967, p. 28.

5. Edward Gerald, personal interview, Minneapolis, Minnesota, October 18, 1984.

6. David Shaw, Introduction, *Press Watch* (New York: Macmillan, 1984), pp. 20–21.

7. Michael Gartner, remarks to a panel on media ethics at Duke University's British-American Festival, June 8, 1984.

8. Interview in St. Paul, Minnesota, October 19, 1984.

9. Quoted in Patrick Brogan, *Spiked: The Short Life and Death of the National News Council* (New York: Twentieth Century Fund, 1985), p. 13.

10. Ibid.

11. Interview in St. Paul, Minnesota.

12. Creed Black, quoted in Marcia Ruth, "Does Anyone Miss the News Council?" *Presstime,* March 1985, p. 32.

13. Robert Schafer, "The Minnesota News Council: Developing Standards for Press Ethics," *Journalism Quarterly,* Autumn 1981, p. 356.

14. *Miami Herald Publishing Co.* v. *Tornillo,* 418 U.S. 241 (1974).

15. Edward Gerald, personal interview, Minneapolis, Minnesota, October 18, 1984.

16. "Report of the Committee to Evaluate the Minnesota Press Council," February 8, 1980, p. 7.

17. Robert Shaw, personal interview, Minneapolis, Minnesota, October 18, 1984.

18. Tom Patterson, personal interview, Minneapolis, Minnesota, October 18, 1984.

CHAPTER 12

The Marketplace

When individuals or groups start worrying about ethics, it often means they are in some kind of trouble. This does not mean that they lack sincerity. Jailhouse religious conversions can be most sincere. And getting into trouble can be a useful reminder that one is not alone in the world, that people do depend on one another, and that the opinions of others are of value.

Such responses demonstrate how market forces can be effective in bringing about reform, whether the impetus comes from the figurative market of public opinion or from a more literal market that depends on specific buyer choices. Whether the people on whom one depends are clients, constituents, or customers, it is always wise to pay attention to them.

Thus there was a surge of interest in business ethics at the start of the twentieth century, after the Progressive movement had arisen late in the nineteenth century to attack the abuses of business. The Social Darwinist model of every man looking out for himself and letting the buyer beware gave way to a new concept of service. Thus, the first Rotarians organized in 1905, intending to form a social club in which members could help one another maximize their business contacts and their profits; a few years later, they thought it over and decided to make service to the community their primary goal, an orientation they retain today.[1] Similarly, interest in medical ethics after World War II was a response to the revelations of experiments on humans by Nazi physicians. Concern for professionalism in police work followed what reformer August Vollmer called an "era of incivility, ignorance, brutality and graft" before the turn of the century.[2]

Newspapers' Response to Trouble

Newspaper people are not much different. Their periods of concern for ethics do, however, seem to coincide with the troubles of others as well as their own. The first code of ethics of the American Society of Newspaper Editors, as we saw in Chapter 2, came at a time when the national government was in trouble over the Teapot Dome scandal and its revelations of the conversion of publicly owned petroleum resources to private gain. The next major round of code writing was a half-century later, when the Watergate affair revealed another instance of corruption in the national government. If your business is to call attention to the sins of others, the thought that you may have a few of your own can be quite unsettling. Besides making you feel hypocritical, it can give your outraged targets the opportunity to distract attention from their own transgressions by attacking yours.

These flashes of interest in ethics have not produced much in the way of behavior change. The codes of ethics amount to lists of virtues that are of little help in solving the real problems that occur when the virtues conflict. And, as the ASNE study has demonstrated, ethics is treated as a public relations problem. When strong stances are taken, such as a prohibition against concealed recordings, it is done more to avert criticism than because of any thoughtful weighing of the consequences for basic values. And those values remain unclear. Even in such a basic area as conflict of interest (Chapter 5), ethical determinations appear to be based more on the business impact or the public relations value of the decisions than on any clear and logical allegiance to some basic set of values.

If so little is being done, you might suppose that newspapers are not in any kind of trouble these days. But your supposition would be wrong. By the mid-1980s it had become clear that the newspaper industry was in trouble on a number of fronts. And it was not doing very much about its problems. Perhaps it had been so successful for so long that it was too set and comfortable in its ways to change despite the signs of decay. Students of history have recorded numerous episodes when people knew that their civilization was dying and that their own behavior contained the seeds of that destruction and who nevertheless kept repeating the destructive behavior. This is the material of tragedy, and it has been suggested that tragedy is history's one reliable and recurrent theme.[3]

Nothing as esoteric as a Freudian death wish is needed to explain this pattern. Part of the problem is a simple inability to postpone gratification, to trade some pain now for some gain later. Some perceptive economists have found an additional dimension to the problem. Life has a way of presenting conflicts between what individuals want for themselves and what they want collectively for their groups. Thomas Schelling has written eloquently about the broad "class of situations in which some of the costs or damages of what people do occur beyond their purview, and they either don't know or don't care about them."[4]

Gridlock on city streets is an example. Traffic would flow much more smoothly if every car refrained from pulling into an intersection on the green light until the car ahead had cleared the intersection. But to the individual facing that choice, there is an immediate and visible cost, the risk that the light will change and he or she will have to sit through a red light before proceeding. So most of us pull into the intersection and accept the other risk, that the light will change while we are stuck in the intersection, leaving us blocking the lateral traffic. When this scenario is replicated at one intersection after another, gridlock results. Nothing moves, and everybody loses. Even those who abuse the system by blocking the inter- section would be better off if no one would abuse the system, but in the absence of any system of control or coordination, they are motivated to sacrifice their group interests for a lesser individual interest. Economists are challenged by such problems, and they try to find structural solutions that will change the incentives. Such a strategy may be more promising than a purely ethical approach, even though Kant's edict to follow that moral law which you would have apply to everyone certainly fits.

Evidence of the Current Trouble

Whether the problem is one of ethics or economics, the newspaper industry may now be in a bind of this sort, where only a moral awakening or a restructuring of incentives can provide an escape. A newspaper that is con- temptuous of its readers, careless with facts, closed to complaints, tolerant of arrogance among its staff, more concerned about values other than fast, fair, full, and accurate reporting incurs costs that may not be immediately visible or painful but that can lead to the decay of newspapers as an institu- tion. And by the mid-1980s, the signs of decay were clear for all to see.

Decline in Readership
The simplest indicator of newspaper health is circulation. At mid- century, total daily newspaper circulation in the United States was 53.8 million. By 1984 it had grown to 63.3 million, and that growth was fairly consistent, although there were some worrisome years in the 1970s and early 1980s when total newspaper circulation suffered a temporary decline. But growth, by itself, does not mean much in a country expanding as fast as the United States was in that period. Thus newspaper circulation grew only 17.6 percent in the years 1950–1984, while the nation's population grew by 55 percent.

Realizing that raw circulation is a poor indicator, the newspaper industry relied for years on the ratio of circulation to households in its pitches to advertisers. When there were more newspapers sold than there were households in the United States, this statistic, called "household penetration," had an impressive impact. In 1950 the figure was 124 percent, meaning that the newspaper circulation was equal to 124 percent of the number of households. But then the number of households began increas- ing even faster than the population as postwar affluence propelled more single people into their own homes. Newspaper household penetration fell below 100 percent in the late 1960s and was down to 73 percent by 1983. Table 12.1 tells the story.

TABLE 12.1

NEWSPAPER HOUSEHOLD PENETRATION, 1950-1984

Year	Population (millions)	Households (thousands)	Circulation (thousands)	Penetration (percent)
1950	152.3	43,554	53,829	124%
1960	180.7	52,779	58,882	112
1970	205.1	63,401	62,108	98
1980	227.7	80,776	62,202	77
1983	234.5	83,918	62,645	75
1984	236.7	85,407	63,082	74
1985	238.8	86,789	62,723	72

Sources: U.S. Bureau of the Census and American Newspaper Publishers Association

As newspapers have been forced to compete with other kinds of media, both broadcast and innovative forms of print, their emphasis to advertisers has been less on circulation and more on readership, particularly readership among desirable demographic groups. Readership is a less exact number than circulation, because it must be estimated from expensive sample surveys. Interviewers ask sampled members of the population if they had read a newspaper on a given day or, less precisely how often they read a newspaper. The decline has been clear, although it is not as steep as the decline in household penetration. In the 1960s average daily readership of newspapers was close to 80 percent.* By 1985 it was down to 64 percent. The audience was voting with its feet, and it was slowly walking away.

The number of hard-core newspaper fans, those who have to have a paper every day, was also down. The trend as measured by the National Opinion Research Center at the University of Chicago, is shown in Table 12.2. These numbers were especially disappointing to industry analysts in the 1980s because the demographic patterns of the population had pointed to an upturn. The underlying structures of society were stabilizing. Much of the decline in readership had been attributed to the baby boom. As its members became young adults, they increased the number of people in the age group where readership was light. As they aged, newspaper publishers,

---

*Average daily readership includes everyday readers plus those who read less frequently.

TABLE 12.2

EVERYDAY NEWSPAPER READERS

1967	1972	1975	1977	1978	1982	1983	1985
73%	69%	66%	62%	57%	54%	56%	53%

fervently hoped the baby boomers would adopt the readership habits of their elders.

They did not. Because the newspaper-reading habit gets its lifelong hold most often around the age of 30, the customer base for newspapers had a dramatic potential for growth starting in the late 1970s and peaking in the late 1980s, when the peak of the baby boom reached the critical age of 30. The effect should have appeared by 1985 but it didn't. The aging baby boomers still had the low readership patterns they had displayed as young adults. The average daily readership figure for newspapers in 1984 of 65 percent would have been even lower if it had not been for the inclusion of the *Wall Street Journal,* which had not been counted in earlier tabulations, and *USA Today,* which had not been around earlier.

It is true that the decline in readership slowed appreciably—and even paused briefly—when the demographics pushed this larger audience onto the scene. But the fact that none of that decline was reversed in this period of greatest opportunity should have been troubling to thoughtful managers of newspaper companies. The opportunity would be brief. Following the baby boom generation was a thin wave of people from lower birthrate years, which would reduce the potential market of young adults, the chief source of new customers, throughout the 1990s.

Shifts in Advertising Trends

The newspaper business was able to adapt somewhat to this change by making changes in its own structure. It encouraged the decline in the number of people who read two papers—considered an expensive redundancy by advertisers—by closing afternoon papers in markets where morning-afternoon combinations operated under the same ownership. The nationally circulated *Wall Street Journal* and *USA Today* filled the gap for the remnant that still needed two papers.

And advertisers still needed newspapers. The aging of the baby boomers created new markets for consumer goods and contributed to underlying strength in the economy, which benefited newspapers. Although the audience was declining, it was still an affluent, educated audience desirable to advertisers. Cheered by this demand, publishers as recently as 1984 were boosting the prices they charged for advertising well beyond the prevailing inflation rate. But there were clouds on their prosperous horizon. One was the increasing reliance on local advertisers, who represent a greater potential threat to editorial independence than the more remote national advertisers. In 1950 national advertising was 25 percent of the total for newspapers. By 1984 it was 12.6 percent and falling. This decline occurred despite trends in broadcasting—cable, videocassette recorders, and other competitors for viewer time—that made it more difficult for network broadcasters to deliver large audiences.

Another cloud was an increasing reluctance of advertisers to use what news people call the "run of the paper," or ROP, for their advertising. This is the part of the paper that carries the news and provides the credible context that gets the advertiser's message into the home. This ROP advertising, the bread and butter of the news business, was gradually being supplanted by preprint advertising, the slickly prepared color booklets that fall out of your newspaper when you open it up. Because they are printed separately, these preprints carry no news and editorial freight, and the newspaper is simply the delivery service for them. Worse, the newspaper competes for this business with the U.S. Postal Service, whose aggressive pricing forces the newspapers to charge less for preprints than they do for ROP advertising. As ads are sucked out of the run of the paper into preprints, the support for news and editorial services declines as well.

Why should advertisers prefer to have their preprinted messages arrive in the newspaper rather than the mail? Junk mail has a bad image. The newspaper context offers an aura of comparative credibility. So newspapers have two reasons to want to be believed. One is the obvious reason that a credible newspaper is (or should be) more likely to be read. The other is only slightly less obvious: advertisers prefer a credible environment for their messages. There are not many ads in the supermarket tabloids, despite their large circulations.

Loss of Confidence in Newspapers

An archive of historical data on newspaper credibility is available. Since 1966, the Harris Survey has asked this question in some of its national surveys: "As far as people in charge of running [name of institution] are concerned, would you say you have a great deal of confidence, only some confidence, or hardly any confidence in them?" In 1973 the National Opinion Research Center started asking the same question, annually through 1978 and then at one- or two-year intervals. Their results are usually similar, but not identical. Of the two series, the one from NORC is the more reliable because of its consistent format, context, and timing. NORC always uses personal, in-home interviews conducted in the spring. Its trend for confidence in the people who run "the press" can be summarized by subtracting the percent expressing "hardly any" confidence from the percent expressing "a great deal" of confidence. That makes the value positive if the high-confidence people outnumber those with hardly any confidence. The findings of recent years are not encouraging:[5]

1973	1974	1975	1976	1977	1978	1980	1982	1983	1984
8	8	6	11	10	0	5	−3	−10	−5

According to two political scientists who study public trust in institutions, Seymour Martin Lipset and William Schneider, not all of this decline is within the control of the people running the institutions asked about in the poll, including the press. Confidence rises and falls with events in the news, and the public has higher confidence in just about every institution when things are going well. The nation experienced a general decline in trust in its institutions from the 1960s until the early 1980s as one unhappy development followed another: the Kennedy and King assassinations, civil rights violence, war in Vietnam, Watergate, large-scale drug abuse, runaway inflation, and high unemployment. "The public is inclined to believe that the system works unless it receives compelling evidence to the contrary," wrote Lipset and Schneider. "Unfortunately, evidence of this sort has not been in short supply during the past 15 years."[6] Newspapers carried this bad news and bore some of the blame—perhaps justly, in view of the industry's self-professed role as the watchdog of our political leaders. If those leaders produce bad results despite being watched, it is not unfair for that watchdog to bear some of the blame.

Unfortunately for newspapers, there is more to their problem than that. Starting midway through President Ronald Reagan's first term, the economic situation got brighter, with both inflation and unemployment in check. The public started feeling better about some of its institutions—but not the press. From the Watergate period on, Lipset and Schneider have reported, attitudes toward the press stopped tracking so consistently with those toward other institutions, and begun to display an inverse relationship with attitudes toward the executive branch of the federal government. In other words, when the public likes the president it hates the press—and vice versa. That state of affairs might be okay for the press when there is a bad president, but the combination of external events needed to produce favorable public attitudes is peculiar, to say the least. The public likes the press· most, these data seem to say, when the nation is enjoying peace and prosperity and everybody is angry at the president! How did the press get into this trap? Evidently, the adversary model, which the press has vigorously promoted, has been swallowed by the public all too thoroughly. If the press and the president are always seen in conflict, then they both can't be doing a good job at the same time. When one is up in public esteem, the other is down.

This state of affairs was not solely the fault of newspapers. In 1985 MORI Research Inc. produced a study for the American Society of Newspaper Editors showing that people who answered the question about confidence in "the press" had broadcast media and magazines as well as newspapers in mind. When the question was rephrased to ask specifically about newspapers, ratings on the confidence scale went up. And even the original question, asked by MORI in a six-week period ending in January 1985, showed some signs of mellowing, with the press-confidence gap down to less than one percentage point. Nevertheless, the public in the mid-1980s retained a residual suspicion toward newspapers that the industry could ill afford to ignore.

Collectively, the industry did not ignore it. The American Society of Newspaper Editors commissioned the survey of its own industry on which this book is based. That project was followed up with the landmark MORI Research survey of the general public to assay newspaper credibility. Both ethics and credibility were the topics of numerous professional meetings and seminars. But individual newspaper managers, hard-pressed as always to keep up with the daily demands of their jobs, were slow to make basic changes.

Libel Suits

Meanwhile, trouble was brewing on another front. Although the 1964 Supreme Court ruling in *Times* v. *Sullivan* made it difficult for a public figure to win a libel action, the number of libel suits of all kinds, including those brought by public figures, began to grow. Juries, finding the complaints of defamation easier to understand than the subtleties of the First Amendment, began awarding large sums of money to those who sued and won. In 1984 the Libel Defense Resource Center, a media-financed research operation in New York City, reported that damage awards were beginning to exceed even the huge sums given in medical malpractice and product liability actions. In 80 libel cases between 1980 and 1983, the average award was $2.17 million. That compared to an average of $666,000 in medical malpractice cases and $786,000 in product liability cases during the same period. This was true despite the fact that people who sue a bad doctor or who are injured by a defective product have often suffered catastrophic physical consequences and a long-term loss of earnings. The damage to a person who has been libeled, hurt feelings and some presumed though not easily demonstrated loss of reputation, is intangible by comparison.

What made the difference was the practice of awarding punitive damages: sums designed to be big enough to punish the offending media and make them be more careful in the future. Take away the punitive damages, the LDRC reported, and the average libel award drops to $550,000, which is smaller than but still in the same ballpark as medical malpractice and product liability awards.

As of the mid-1980s, not one of these million-dollar libel awards had been collected or affirmed on appeal. The appeals judges do understand the First Amendment, and plaintiffs who win at the trial level often lose on appeal. In the period 1982 to 1984, people who sued newspapers in libel cases won 65 percent of the cases at the trial stage, but they held onto their victories in only half of the appeals. That meant an overall success rate of 33 percent (without allowing for cases that had been settled or were still pending at the time of the study). Among all cases, including those that never made it to a jury, the rate was lower, but it was still high enough to make plaintiffs and their lawyers want to keep trying for those giant awards, even though the awards that survived appeals and post-trial motions were relatively small.[7]

Another factor was motivating people to keep on litigating against newspapers and other media, and it was an unexpected consequence of

Times v. *Sullivan.* Before *Sullivan,* the surest and safest way for a newspaper to win a libel suit was to prove the truth of what it had reported. And truth is so powerful and so fearsome to errant officials that it serves as a highly effective deterrent. "Never sue a newspaper for libel," one politician was said to have advised another in the 1950s. "They might prove it on you."

The *Sullivan* case removed that burden of proving truth from the defending newspaper and placed a burden on the plaintiff to prove that the newspaper acted with malice or reckless disregard for the truth. A libel trial was no longer a forum for determining the truth but for deciding such technical matters as intent and privilege. This situation provided the plaintiff with a magnificent opportunity for a symbolic victory. Many libel plaintiffs, especially public figures, are less interested in the money than in a validation of their complaint. They want public recognition of their grievances, and they want it in the most dramatic way possible. A big-award jury decision does that for them, whether or not the judgment survives the appeal process and whether or not the award is ever paid. If the jury verdict is reversed on the *Sullivan* standard, the aggrieved person can claim that the malice test is a technicality and that the moral vindication of the jury verdict still stands. And, indeed, news of a multimillion-dollar judgement is likely to be remembered while the details and even the outcome of an appeal are forgotten. "The plaintiffs don't necessarily sue to win: but they win by suing," said University of Iowa law professor Randall P. Bezanson.[8]

If libel plaintiffs sue for ego satisfaction rather than money, shouldn't there be a cheaper method for all concerned? Is it really necessary to enrich lawyers and clog the court system for the sake of some hurt feelings?

Apparently it is. We have already seen in Chapter 11 how most news people are too threatened by the idea of news councils to allow that kind of a safety valve. (In Minnesota, the one exceptional state, the largest newspaper, the *Minneapolis Tribune,* reported in 1985 that it had negotiated a decrease in its libel insurance premium. Lawyers associated with the newspaper had different views on the reasons for that decrease, but at least one held that it was partly on the basis of the news council and its work.) And the ombudsman idea has been painfully slow to catch on, their number taking nearly two decades to grow to 30. In the absence of news councils and ombudsmen, is any other remedy left? Well, some simple courtesy might help. This novel suggestion came from Gilbert Cranberg after he retired as editorial-page editor of the *Des Moines Register,* signed on as a professor at the University of Iowa, and started investigating the circumstances behind libel actions. He found that newspapers were missing a golden opportunity to defuse complaints when they first came up.

A dispute makes its way to trial in four stages, Cranberg found: (1) publication; (2) a complaint to the offending medium; (3) a visit to a lawyer; (4) off to court. That second step, the complaint to the medium, constitutes a golden opportunity that most newspapers foolishly neglect to use. Instead, it is the lawyers who take advantage of the golden opportunity.

Newspaper newsrooms are busy, noisy, profane places where the task of getting another paper out each day takes full concentration and allows little time to dwell on yesterday's triumphs and mistakes. So when the victim of an erroneous report or insult, real or imagined, calls to complain, he or she is unlikely to find a sympathetic ear. In fact, such a person is likely to get insulted again. Newspapers simply do not have any systematic or well-thought-out procedure for handling complaints. And having an ombudsman, though it demonstrates good intentions, may be counterproductive. Cranberg discovered that the reporters at newspapers with ombudsmen who wrote columns and named erring staff members were much less likely to pass on complaints. And the reporter is usually not the best-equipped person to make the complainant feel better. Cranberg heard accounts of reporters insulting complainants and reporters sitting on complaints. Said Cranberg, "The first time the editors learned about these complaints was when libel suits were filed."

What makes news people so hostile toward complainants? The time pressure is only part of the problem. Another part, as Cranberg has noted, is that a newspaper, to meet its basic standards of truth and fairness, has to be conditioned to resist pressure. Information is such a precious good that organizations and individuals with special interests to promote are always trying to manipulate its flow to serve their own ends. News people encounter a great variety of pressures from a great variety of directions, so, observed Cranberg, "a siege mentality develops in which demands for retraction or other vindication can be regarded as forms of pressure, signals to circle the wagons." [9]

Resistance to Suggestions for Reform

So we return to the paradox that surfaced in the opening chapter of this book. In their daily struggle to bring light to the rest of the world, newspapers keep their own operations in darkness. Does this mean that the newspaper industry suffers from a kind of institutional neurosis that tragically impels it toward self-destructive behavior? Chris Argyris, in his case study of the inner workings of a newspaper, which he called *"The Daily Planet"* but which looked remarkably like the *New York Times,* was fascinated by what he called the "brittleness" of the news people. [10] Brittleness is literally an inability to bend without breaking. Brittle people overreact to problems, are easily upset, even hypersensitive. These characteristics may be fostered by a working environment that is internally competitive, with winners and losers decided every day as individuals and groups fight for the best stories and the best display in the limited space available. The organization of the *"Daily Planet"* newsroom was hierarchical, with little room for collegial give-and-take, little openness and confident exchange of divergent views. One psychological defense that Argyris saw often employed in this situation was projection, a tendency to see the hang-up of brittleness in others while denying it in oneself. And he found a parallel in the newspaper's relationship with the larger world.

That larger world (as seen by the newspaper) is full of self-serving, hypersensitive people who try to cover things up and who frustrate journalism's drive to make society open and full of light. But is this picture of the world as closed and resistant to exposure simply a projection of the journalists' own shortcomings? Argyris makes a case that it is and that the news people may be their own worst enemies:

> If this is the case, one could predict that newspapers will vigorously resist the behavior they would require of others. For example, newspapers may demand that institutions of government be open to the press, but they will nevertheless argue that they themselves should be closed to examination. They may insist upon being the artillery of the press, but they will see no reason why outsiders should take aim at their methods of operation. And newspaper officials will be quick to condemn their critics not only because they represent a threat to the freedom of the press, but because an investigation of the internal workings of the press, might reveal that newspapers are managed by a system whose characteristics are the very ones they so often denounce.[11]

Argyris's field is organizational behavior, and his prescription for newspaper management is to submit to examination by specialists of his persuasion, who would help the newspapers to rebuild their "living systems" and create an environment of openness and participatory management in which newly confident news people could shed their defensiveness in a spirit of self-renewal. In other words, he is for truly radical reform. However, the chances of achieving it seem quite remote. Argyris's book itself demonstrates the difficulty, because it ends up being an account of his failure to provoke change at *"The Daily Planet."* My own prescription is somewhat simpler, although it is also based on internal reform. The next chapter spells it out.

NOTES

1. Carl A. Zapffe, *Rotary* (Baltimore: Rotary Club of Baltimore, 1963).

2. August Vollmer, quoted in Samuel Walker, *A Critical History of Police Reform* (Lexington, Mass.: Lexington Books, 1977), p. 71.

3. Herbert Muller, *The Uses of the Past* (New York: Oxford University Press, 1952).

4. Readers intrigued with this idea should see Thomas C. Schelling, *Micromotives and Macrobehavior* (New York: Norton, 1978).

5. National Opinion Research Center, *General Social Surveys, 1972-1983: Cumulative Codebook* (Storrs, Conn.: The Roper Center, 1985).

6. Seymour Martin Lipset and William Schneider, *The Confidence Gap* (New York: Free Press, 1983), p. 159.

7. "Defamation Trials, Damage Awards and Appeals: Two-Year Update (1982-1984)," LDRC Bulletin No. 11 (New York: Libel Defense Resource Center, 1985).

8. Randall P. Benzanson, quoted in Dean Woodbeck, "Actual Malice Test Encourages Lawsuits," *Editor & Publisher,* July 13, 1985.

9. Gilbert Cranberg, the Silha Lecture, University of Minnesota, Minneapolis, May 1985.

10. Chris Argyris, *Behind the Front Page* (San Francisco: Jossey-Bass, 1974).

11. Ibid., p. 237.

CHAPTER 13

An Ethical Audit

Nothing makes a problem come alive like putting a number to it. Newspeople know this instinctively, and they use agate type to cram wide expanses of numbers into those parts of the paper where scores are easily quantified—the sports pages and the business pages.

Keeping score changes behavior. Walter Lippmann noted this when he wrote his classic book *Public Opinion* nearly 70 years ago. When statistics on infant mortality were first published, he observed, the rates of infant mortality almost immediately began to go down. "Municipal officials and voters did not have, before publication, a place in their picture of the environment for those babies. The statistics made them visible, as if the babies had elected an alderman to air their grievances."[1]

Well-managed companies know the value of keeping score, and they use our culture's preoccupation with numbers to exact top performances from their workers. Even newspaper companies do it. Some of the larger newspaper companies operate under "management by objective," or MBO, systems. An MBO system ties an executive's compensation to quantifiable aspects of his or her performance. When I was on the corporate staff at Knight-Ridder, I negotiated with my boss at the start of each year on my goals for the year and their respective weights on a scale that added to 100. When the year was over, we negotiated again on my degree of success with each goal and put a number on it. The total was then applied to my bonus for that year—which also depended on how successful the company as a whole had been—and the result was a satisfying bulge in my paycheck.

Therefore, the tools for improving some of the key aspects of newspaper ethical performance are already at hand. Not all the elements of ethical behavior can be quantified—or even agreed upon, for that matter—but some can be. And these quantifiable elements are basic enough and obvious enough that there is no good reason not to use them.

In the 1960s and 1970s, the antiwar and civil rights movements often vented their ire at American business as a conservative, change-resisting institution. Some businesses responded with searching self-examination, and

189

out of that introspection grew a movement for corporate social accounting. If a corporation could keep score on its business performance, for the tax people and the shareholders, the reasoning went, perhaps it could also measure its total impact, for good or for ill, on all of society. It was an ambitious concept.

One of the most far-reaching proposals envisioned isolating the impact of each of a business firm's activities, from its production to its new business development, on each of its many constituencies, including customers, workers, shareholders, suppliers, and the community. It was a "mind-boggling proposition to contemplate," in the words of Robert W. Ackerman and Raymond A. Bauer, two pioneers in the social-accounting movement.[2] One difficulty was that business firms were suddenly being held accountable for consequences of their actions that went well beyond their traditionally defined responsibilities. The effects of pollution, of women's and minority members' roles in the work force, of product quality, were all issues that might have long-term impact on a company —and on business in general—but be hard to quantify in terms of the money-measurement principle of traditional accounting.

The concept of the corporate social audit was designed to let businesses get a handle on such problems—by putting numbers on them—before they became too large to be managed. Some companies even formed "social responsibility committees." At first there was some thought that corporations should use their technical and financial clout to take on all sorts of social problems. By the late 1970s that wave of enthusiasm had waned, and efforts were concentrated on matters directly associated with a firm's specific activities and involving its long-term self-interest. Fortunately for newspapers, their main opportunities to audit their own behavior fall within that narrow range. The greatest of these opportunities is in the area of accuracy.

The Accuracy Audit as a Measure of Overall Ethical Concern

In focusing on accuracy as an indicator of overall ethical stance, a newspaper—or an outside observer, for that matter—would be engaging in what social scientists call "operationalization." To operationalize is to move from the large and the abstract to the specific and the measurable. The concept of "morality" is big, complicated, and incapable of being measured. Source-perceived accuracy is a small outcropping of that concept, but it is related to the concept and can be measured. Operationalization carries certain risks, the greatest of which is that you can become so fascinated and preoccupied with the aspects of a problem that are measurable that you begin to believe that they are the only important aspects.

The beauty of choosing accuracy as the target for measurement is that there is no question that it is central. A newspaper that tolerates no conflicts of interest, does not pander to advertisers, and follows all the other injunctions of the various journalistic codes is still unfit to meet its First Amendment responsibilities if it cannot get the facts right. For any list of ethical audit measures, an accuracy test clearly deserves first priority.

First Amendment theory and a pragmatic concern for the problems of journalism point to accuracy as a fundamental problem underlying the more specific ethical concerns of newspapers. Fairness, balance, and objectivity do not mean much if the facts are not right. As long as a newspaper avoids bending the truth, many lesser transgressions can be tolerated. But without accuracy in reporting, First Amendment claims to privilege are empty. Any attempt at improvement must start here, a point made by ASNE in its 1975 statement of principles:

> Good faith with the reader is the foundation of good journalism. Every effort must be made to assure that the news content is accurate, free from bias and in context, and that all sides are presented fairly. Editorials, analytical articles and commentary should be held to the same standards of accuracy with respect to facts as news reports.

The pioneer in newspaper accuracy measurement was Mitchell V. Charnley, longtime faculty member at the University of Minnesota. In 1936 he reported on his method of checking the accuracy of stories in the *Minnesota Daily,* the undergraduate newspaper.[3] Charnley and his student assistant clipped randomly selected stories, at the rate of about 25 a day, pasted them to questionnaires, and sent them to the sources named in the stories. The questionnaires asked respondents to list any errors and to provide corrections.

This procedure yielded an error rate of .77 per story, or about three errors for every four stories. The technique has since been widely copied, both in other academic studies and by newspapers developing information about their own staff performance. Error rates as high as 1.52 per story have been found.[4] But, as later academic refinements have shown, the method has some flaws, and these flaws have tended to keep newspapers from making more than anecdotal or casual use of the information developed. As usually applied, accuracy surveys are used to spotlight particular instances of error and as a goal to reporters to keep striving for improvement, but not to make comparisons among individuals, departments, or newspapers. As outlined by William B. Blankenburg of the University of Wisconsin in 1970 and amplified by William A. Tillinghast of San Jose State University in 1982, the problem is that the definition of an error can be subjective.[5] Another problem is that the sources who identify errors may not be disinterested judges. Accuracy checks face an even more basic problem than these.

Because news people deal primarily with words and with qualitative values, they tend to get nervous when numbers appear to be tainted by ambiguity or subjectivity. Such problems, however, can often be made manageable. An editor's tendency is to throw up his hands and say, "It's comparing apples and oranges." The fact is that apples and oranges can be compared, and it often makes perfect sense to do so. If you were managing the local soup kitchen and could order only one fruit, you would compare apples and oranges on price, transportation cost, nutritional value, shelf life, storage cost, availability, and other dimensions. And if different people evaluate newspaper accuracy in different ways, it makes sense to look at those ways and to try to decide which ways of measuring are relevant to the goal of improving the newspaper's performance.

Measuring Objective Versus Subjective Errors

Blankenburg, Tillinghast, and others who have thought about the problem make a distinction between subjective and objective errors.[6] Objective errors include misspelled names, wrong dates, incorrect numbers, erroneous addresses, and other points of fact about which there should be little dispute. Subjective errors include emphasis, distortion, and significant omissions. Tillinghast also classifies misleading headlines and misquotes as subjective errors, because there is often disagreement over what constitutes a misleading headline or a misquote.

When he surveyed news sources mentioned in stories in the *San Jose Mercury* and the *San Jose News* in the summer of 1980, Tillinghast found an error rate of .91 per story. Nearly two-thirds of the errors were in the subjective category, with omissions the most frequent. Tillinghast then did what other researchers had not tried before. He took the error complaints to the reporters who wrote the stories to see whether they agreed or not. What he found was startling. Where errors in the subjective category were concerned, the reporters agreed with the news sources only 5 percent of the time. Even when the errors involved objective facts, reporters acknowledged error less than half the time—in 46 percent of the cases.[7]

In some of the cases, the reporters were probably right, in that the information in their stories was accurate as of the time it was written. Sources who disagreed sometimes had the benefit of later information—for example, the victory margin in a close election before all the votes had been counted. In other cases, the reason for disagreement was not so understandable—a dispute with a source, for example, over whether the source's title was "judge" or "justice."

Where subjective error was claimed by the news sources, the reporters had a little more room for raising credible disputes. But even in these cases of disagreement, it is difficult to relieve the reporter of all liability for the error. For example, a reporter writing about a quarantine to combat plant disease said, "the quarantine prohibits moving any plants of the elm species into the quarantine area." According to the original source, however, the quarantine barred the movement of elm plants not only into the area, but out of the area and within the area—a significant difference. The reporter's response? It was a matter of "semantics. We're saying the same thing."

In another San Jose case, a reporter indirectly quoted a physician on why a baby should be restrained in a moving car: "Because a baby's head is so much larger than the rest of his body, the baby can become a human missile." This one is worth thinking about for a minute. Obviously, a baby's head is *not* larger than the rest of its body. What the physician was thinking of—and he so indicated in the accuracy survey—was the *relative weight* of the head. A baby's head is bigger in proportion to the rest of its body than an adult's head is. But for babies and adults alike, the head is heavier in proportion to its volume than the rest of the body. That's what the physician meant, and it is fairly obvious to anyone who thinks about it.

The reporter blamed the error on the physician because the statement "came directly from my notes." The physician acknowledged that he might have failed to qualify his statement sufficiently. But both this example and the preceding one show a peculiar reluctance on the part of the reporters to accept responsibility for getting things right. In the elm quarantine case, the reporter is accepting approximate accuracy as sufficient. And in the baby's head case, the reporter seems content to pass on erroneous information without feeling any responsibity to evaluate it to see whether it makes sense or not. It is almost as if the reporter were a mindless processer of words, with accuracy being somebody else's responsibility. It isn't.

Some of the same stonewalling by reporters was found where sources complained of inaccurate paraphrasing. A reporter quoted a source at a college newspaper as saying the staff had not decided whether to print liquor and tobacco ads. In fact, the source said later, the indecision concerned beer and wine ads, not liquor ads. The reporter claimed that was not an error: "He believes wine and beer are not liquor; I think they're all in the same alcoholic bag." But the dictionary definition of liquor is "an alcoholic beverage made by distillation rather than fermentation," so the reporter was wrong.

Problems with Source Evaluations

These examples of errors of omission or paraphrasing might suggest that the best index of a newspaper's overall error rate would be source evaluation without regard to what the reporters say. But there is another large category of error complaints where the views of sources are every bit as suspect as those of the reporters. These are cases where the sources' complaints are more nebulous, and the problem is not so much accuracy as the undesirable effects of the story.

For example, a judge granted an injunction forcing a city to rescind its ban on "safe and sane" fireworks. The judge complained about the newspaper report of his order. He said the article was factually correct and the quotes were accurate, but "the tenor is that I was insensitive to the fire hazard and the city's dilemma." How much of the judge's own words and behavior contributed to that impression and whether any inaccuracy at all could be attributed to the reporter would be extremely difficult to ascertain. In another case, a source complained that a story about overcharges to electricity users failed to describe several plans being considered to compensate the customers, even though "I carefully reviewed each with the reporter, who seemed to have a thorough understanding of them."

What the sources in such cases often fail to realize is that they are not the clients in the reporting process. The real client is the reader. And a version of a story that presents a source in the most favorable light or that is for some other reason the version he or she would most like to see may not be the one that serves the reader best. A city council, for example, might like to see all its actions listed and given equal weight. A reporter might pick one out of a dozen actions as worth reporting and ignore the rest. And the reporter is right in doing so if there is only one action that would interest enough readers to justify the allocation of space in the paper. Public officials are sometimes surprised to see how little importance is given their work in the competition for newspaper space.

This category of general dissatisfaction was more frequent when a story had more than one source. A source who was in full control of the story was less likely to make complaints that would be disputed by the reporter. In that one-on-one communication process, mutual expectations appear to be better reconciled.

The San Jose case demonstrates two ways to measure error and suggests a third:

1. Take the source's word that an error has occurred and leave it at that.
2. Check the source's finding of error with the reporter and count only those cases where source and reporter are in agreement.
3. Check both the source and the reporter and make an independent judgment.

The last strategy makes the most sense. Giving the reporter a chance to respond would not be a large administrative burden, and, in any event, each instance of reported error ought to be discussed with him or her. Exhaustive investigation of each complaint would not be necessary, and it is such feedback that makes improvement possible. As the examples cited here indicate, a purely factual error is fairly easy to distinguish from a case where the source is unhappy because of more extraneous matters.

However, even the raw rate of claimed error is worth tracking. Changes over time could alert management to problems that otherwise might surface in less benign fashion. And error rates are barometers of the way a newspaper is run, which suggests that accuracy is by no means an intractable problem. While William Blankenburg was measuring accuracy in the news columns of the *Bend* (OR) *Bulletin* in 1967 and 1968, the following things happened: an experienced reporter retired and was replaced by a novice; another reporter got into trouble with the law; the general manager left; the publisher, normally active on the editorial side, became ill; a controversial local election was held.

Blankenburg did not report the error rate before and after all these events, but he said there was a "striking deterioration" in the paper's accuracy between the early and late phases of the study. From that, he said, "we find that performance on accuracy is not necessarily stable, and that staff disruptions and environmental stresses appear to have deleterious effects."[8]

Who Should Conduct an Accuracy Audit?

The case for regular accuracy audits appears to be a strong one. The question remains: Should they be conducted by the newspaper's own staff or by an outside organization?

To perform an accuracy audit with the rigor that seems called for requires special skills. Editors have sufficient research skill to conduct casual checks on their own with the clipping-and-questionnaire technique if all they care about is anecdotal information. The market research departments of larger newspapers have the necessary quantitative skills for a more rigorous check, but they are usually under the control of the business side, and their findings might be viewed by the staff as unwelcome interference.

An outside agency has the advantage not only of being neutral but also of having the capacity to standardize across different newspaper markets. Belden Associates of Dallas often presents readership data to clients with comparative figures from a variety of other markets (labeled Market A, Market B, and so on, to avoid disclosing competitive data), which helps a newspaper see how normal or deviant its public image is.

Because accuracy research can be done with a mail survey, its cost should be far less than the usual market study. Proper safeguards would be needed to ensure that accuracy, not inoffensiveness to sources, was being measured. Otherwise, an audit program could backfire, leading reporters to try too hard to keep sources happy. But the visible, verifiable, objective errors are probably good indicators of the volume of overall error; and if the measurable ones can be reduced, other kinds of error will probably decline along with them.

Other Aspects of Ethical Accounting

After that, the next step is not so clear. An accuracy audit affects two general constituencies—readers and sources. It is probably not practical to try to develop measures of the impact of a newspaper's actions on all its other, more specific constituencies, as Ackerman and Bauer attempted. But it may be possible to push the notion of an audit just a little bit further and add some measures beyond an accuracy check.

One constituency that is often overlooked by newspaper managers and their staff is composed of the people who come in contact with the newspaper on an occasional basis—to place an ad, to inquire how to submit a picture or buy one that appeared in the paper, to complain about delivery or about an advertiser, to disagree with an editorial or suggest a news story, to seek further information about something that appeared in the paper or to buy a back issue, or to ask to use the library to track down a clipping. In each of these kinds of contacts, the caller may think of the newspaper, unless it is very small, as a formidable bureaucracy. And the first thing the caller wants to know is how to manage its bureaucratic procedures—whom and when to call to handle a specific problem.

I know of no systematic research that describes how successfully newspapers handle such contacts. The anecdotes I have accumulated from my own experience indicate that there is tremendous variation. At some newspapers, it is so hard to get anyone even to answer the phone that you wonder how they ever receive information. When your call is answered, you may not get the reception you expect. Once I tried to return a call from a reporter at the *Washington Post*. I reached instead a very irritated person on the city desk who let me know clearly that she did not know where the reporter was, did not care, and was in no mood to deliver a message that I had returned the call. Yet when I lived in Washington and had occasion to call the *Post* about the delivery service, I was always greeted with courtesy, quick understanding of the problem, and a genuine desire to solve it. As one who is familiar with the inner workings of newspapers, I did not find the contrast surprising. But to an outsider, such discrepancies can be jarring.

Angus Campbell, the pioneer public opinion researcher from the University of Michigan, became interested in social accounting in the last years of his life. He suggested a measure that he called the "index of official insolence."[9] The label comes from the soliloquy in Hamlet (Act III, scene 1) in which the prince bewails, among other slings and arrows, "the proud man's contumely, the pangs of despised love, the law's delay, the insolence of office."

Can the contumelies endured by ordinary people at the hands of bureaucrats be measured? Some of Campbell's colleagues eventually found a way.[10] They asked a national sample of adult Americans about encounters they had had with government agencies and what they thought about them. One of the questions was, "How much effort did the people at the office make to help you? Would you say it was more than they had to, about right, less than they should have, or no effort at all?" The agencies scored fairly high. Most of their clients, 57 percent, thought that the bureaucrats had shown a level of effort that was "about right," whereas only 12 percent said the effort had been less than it should have been and 8.5 percent reported "no effort at all." And 16 percent said the agency staff had actually done more than they needed to.

Survey research would be one way to get at the same sort of information for newspapers. A series of questions modeled after those used by the Michigan researchers could be added to a newspaper's routine market study at little additional cost. Such a study could be elaborated to a point where comparisons might be made across the different departments of the newspaper, documenting the relative "official insolence" of, say, the city desk and the circulation department.

The Michigan researchers suggested another type of project to complement the survey—a special organizational study in which the people interviewed would be the clients and the bureaucrats. Only in that way could one really reach an understanding of how and why an office functions as it does. The general survey provides a rough measure of the overall problem. The specific study gets at the reasons behind it and would be more helpful in finding a solution.

There is a third possibility—the field experiment. Anyone can do one, but it is best done systematically. Call up a newspaper and see how easy it is to get the answer to some innocuous question, such as the name of the person who edits the letters to the editor or the procedure for getting a meeting notice listed. Rate each call according to the ease of finding the person with the answer, and the politeness and helpfulness of the employees. Is it ethical to make calls with such a concealed purpose? Newspapers do it all the time. No one who deals with the public should object to having his or her performance in those dealings monitored by someone who has the public's interest at heart.

My remaining suggestions for ethical accounting deal with the readers as constituents and apply two well-tested social science tools—content analysis and the public opinion survey. In these applications, the survey gets at general feelings toward the newspaper, and we have to assume that ethical stance is one of the factors that influences these feelings. Content analysis, in contrast, is quite specific.

Here is the method you could use to rate the ways a newspaper meets its First Amendment responsibility by providing a comprehensive and coherent account of world and national news: Pick a trial week (or sample of weeks, for a really comprehensive study). Study the major national media for that week and create a "market basket" of items of information that a well-informed reader would need in order to understand the changing world. This market basket might contain two compartments, one for absolutely essential items and another for those that are not essential but that would be helpful. The target newspaper can then be evaluated simply by counting the number of these information needs that it met. The two-compartment system ensures that the most essential items are kept distinct.

One problem with this approach is that it makes the national media the standard for everyone else. They are good, but maybe not that good. It would be better if there were some higher, even hypothetical standard to which everyone, including the national media, could be held accountable.

That ideal could be approached by studying the market basket for anything omitted by the national media—stories with holes or stories that included hints that were never pursued. And a sample of regional papers could also be studied to augment the market basket for worthy items that were passed up by the *New York Times* and the *Washington Post.*

Other suggestions for evaluating your own newspaper made in Chapter 10 could be applied more systematically by using formal content analysis. The index of editorial vigor first mentioned in Chapter 8 has promise. The percentage of vigorous editorials—that is, those that take stands on controversial local matters—could be monitored, and declines or improvements in editorial vigor could be noted over time. Openness and willingness to admit mistakes are also qualities that can be monitored and quantified. The frequency and display of corrections would be logical indicators.

Survey research of a general nature—as opposed to the quite specific task of asking about bureaucratic encounters—is more problematical. The 1985 national survey conducted for the American Society of Newspaper Editors by MORI Research Inc. provides a good model for the general approach. It included a wide variety of questions about attitudes toward newspapers in general and some questions on specific matters related to ethics that were phrased in terms of the newspaper the respondent read most often. Those interviewed were asked to evaluate their newspaper on a series of five-point scales defined by words and phrases of opposite meaning, such as fair–unfair. A response of 1 meant "extremely fair," while a 5 signified "extremely unfair."

This series covered a wide range of dimensions, some quite general—like the fairness question—and some very specific—such as whether reporters are well trained or whether the newspaper watches out for the community's interests. One unexpected result was that the questions asked did not make a lot of difference. People who gave a newspaper high or low marks on one question were likely to judge it the same way on the others. This suggests that readers do not think about their newspapers in great depth or detail but have a fuzzy feeling toward them that can generally be described as favorable or unfavorable. While a newspaper's ethical positions probably have something to do with this feeling, lots of other matters can affect it, too. As Seymour Martin Lipset and William Schneider have shown, in the work described in Chapter 12, public evaluation of institutions depends very much on how things have been going lately.[11] If your town is undergoing a crisis, all its institutions, including the newspaper, are likely to be rated less favorably than when life is relatively calm. In one unpublished market study in which I participated, a newspaper's confidence ratings dropped sharply after it undertook an investigation that revealed a hazard to consumers from the products of a leading local industry. Eventually, its ratings climbed back to normal.

Your newspaper cannot do its job properly if its editors are involved in a perpetual popularity contest. Often, the ethical choice will be the unpopular choice. This fact makes reliance on one-shot measures extremely dangerous. However, the survey method can be useful if its measurements are taken as indicating temporary conditions that have long-term meaning only in the context of a large collection of measures. The weather report is a good analogy. If the weatherman tells us that it rained 2 inches yesterday, we do not assume that we must wear raincoats in perpetuity. But a large number of those daily measures can be studied for patterns that will tell us a good deal about our climate and the subtle changes being made in it as the polar ice cap melts or the ionosphere thickens or other suspected sinister influences do their work. Survey research to monitor newspaper ethics can be useful only if such repeated measures are made, and editors, publishers, and newspaper staff members must be secure enough in their own ethical stands to care more about the long-term climate of public opinion than about any one day's storms and calms.

Another possible application of survey research to an ethical audit would be to do what the ASNE survey did and question the management and staff of the newspaper itself. As the survey showed, a certain sensitivity to ethical issues is associated with relatively high morale and a mutual respect between editor and publisher. Direct measurement of the latter is not feasible for individual newspapers, because the survey technique depends on the confidentiality that can be provided only by aggregating responses in reasonably large groups. Staff morale can be measured, however, and the staff's level of confidence in the ethical judgments of the editor and publisher would be worth knowing about.

An ethical audit should also include an inventory of real and potential conflicts of interest. The survey method would be appropriate here without any need for confidentiality. Each person who has a hand in creating the newspaper's content should list all his or her associations and financial interests that could be helped or harmed by what went into the newspaper. Here the purpose is not to quantify or even evaluate so much as to disclose. The listing could be used by supervisors to steer reporters clear of serious conflicts or to provide a basis for disclosure to readers when the conflicts are unavoidable.

The sum of all these data could be an annual ethical audit report published in the newspaper or printed as a separate supplement to be made available to readers interested enough to inquire. The centerpiece of such a report would be the accuracy measurement, showing subjective, objective, and total error rates reported separately for those parts of the paper where stories are written under deadline pressure and those where the writers have more time. The second annual report would compare the current error rates with those for the previous year. If the paper's standards were deteriorating, everyone would know about it and have the evidence, and that would greatly enhance the odds that action would be taken.

Quantifiable aspects of the ethics audit should also be built into MBO packages for senior managers. Virtue may be its own reward, but tying it to compensation is more effective. Increase accuracy by so many points, and your reward is a specific number of dollars. Money is a great remedy for ambiguity. Like the infant mortality rate, the accuracy rate should improve simply through the virtue of being made measurable. And the psychological side effects could lead to improved performance in other areas, just as a football team that has mastered blocking and tackling is free to work on more subtle and interesting problems. An obsessive concern for accuracy might lead not only to better facts but to a heightened concern for what the Hutchins commission called "the truth about the fact."[12]

It will be argued that the ethical problems of journalism go beyond anything that can be measured by such a simple evaluation. But improvement must begin somewhere, and if it cannot begin at that simple and fundamental level, perhaps news people should face the possibility that it cannot be achieved at all. Fairness, balance, objectivity, and the defense of unusual methods are all empty without the basic capacity to gather and report the facts. Your newspaper owes you at least that much.

NOTES

1. Walter Lippmann, *Public Opinion* (New York: Free Press, 1965), p. 239.

2. Robert W. Ackerman and Raymond A. Bauer, *Corporate Social Responsiveness: The Modern Dilemma* (Reston, Va.: Reston Publishing, 1976), p. 15.

3. Mitchell V. Charnley, "Preliminary Notes on a Study of Newspaper Accuracy," *Journalism Quarterly,* December 1936; 394–401.

4. William B. Blankenburg, "News Accuracy: Some Findings on the Meanings of the Errors," *The Journal of Communication* (December 1970): 375–386; William A. Tillinghast, "Newspaper Errors: Reporters Dispute Most Source Claims," *Newspaper Research Journal* (July 1982): 15–23; William A. Tillinghast, "Source Control and Evaluation of Newspaper Inaccuracies," *Newspaper Research Journal* (Fall 1983): 13–24.

5. Ibid., p.379.

6. Ibid. See also Charles H. Brown, "Majority of Readers Give Papers an A for Accuracy," *Editor & Publisher,* February 13, 1965, p. 13; Michael Singletary, "Accuracy in News Reporting: A Review of the Research," *ANPA News Research Report,* no. 25, January 25, 1980.

7. Tillinghast, "Newspaper Errors."

8. Blankenburg "News Accuracy."

9. Angus Campbell, "Social Accounting in the 1970s," *Michigan Business Review* 23, no. 1 (1971): 2–7.

10. Daniel A. Katz, Barbara A. Gutek, Robert L. Kahn, and Eugenia Barton, *Bureaucratic Encounters: A Pilot Study in the Evaluation of Government Services* (Ann Arbor, Michigan: Institute for Social Research, University of Michigan, 1975).

11. Seymour Martin Lipset and William Schneider, *The Confidence Gap* (New York: Free Press, 1983).

12. Commission on Freedom of the Press, *A Free and Responsible Press* (Chicago: University of Chicago Press, 1947), p. 22.

ASNE Survey on Newspaper Ethics: Frequencies

The tables on the following pages show the response frequencies for each of the questions asked in the ASNE survey. Percentages are weighted by circulation. (see Appendix II for details of the weighting scheme.) Numbers in parentheses show, without weighting for circulation, how many newspaper responses contributed to the percentages in columns headed "total." The percentages are weighted by circulation so that readers rather than news people are represented. Because the information in Part Two of this survey was sought from a publisher, an editor, and a staff member from each paper, there is a potential for three responses from each paper.

Part One: Editors Only

V005. Does this market have just one daily newspaper or is there more than one?

Only one	27%	(113)
More than one	73%	(211)

V006. (If more than one) Does your company own more than one paper in this market?

Yes	43%	(97)
No	57%	(112)

V007. (If company owns more than one) Are you the editor for just one paper, or more than one?

One	64%	(53)
More	36%	(46)

V008. Does the publisher live in your circulation area or does he/she live somewhere else?

In area	94%	(303)
Somewhere else	6%	(19)

V009. Does the company which owns your newspaper(s) also own newspapers in other markets, or is this the only one?

Owns others	78%	(242)
Only one	22%	(82)

V010. Is the company privately owned, or is its stock traded publicly?

Privately owned	68%	(232)
Stock traded	32%	(92)

V011. Does your paper have a regular ombudsman column?

Yes	15%	(36)
No	85%	(288)

V012. (If regular column) Is the ombudsman chosen by you or by someone independent of you?

By editor	58%	(23)
By someone else	36%	(8)
Written by editor	7%	(3)

V013. (If regular column) Do you read the ombudsman's copy before it is published?

Yes	37%	(15)
No	63%	(16)

V014. (If regular column) Do you read it for information or to approve it?

Information	89%	(10)
Approve	11%	(2)

V015. I am going to read a list of different ways that newspapers handle corrections and amplifications. Please tell me which one comes closest to your paper's policy.

    1. Corrections appear under a standing head, anchored to a specific place in the paper.

    2. Corrections appear under a standing head which floats as needed.

    3. Corrections are run as needed, without a standing head or a particular location in the paper.

4. Corrections are normally not made. The most we'll do is run another version of the story to get a correct version in the paper, but without acknowledging that it is a correction.

5. No correction of any kind is made.

Statement 1	55%	(171)
Statement 2	21%	(67)
Statement 3	24%	(82)
Statement 4	0%	(1)
Statement 5	0%	(1)

I am going to read a list of ethical questions that newspapers sometimes face. For each one, I would like you to estimate how often cases of that type are discussed at your paper. The first type of ethical question involves. . .

V016. News gathering methods—using false identity; stolen documents; concealed recording; eavesdropping.

Never	28%	(106)
Less than once a year	19%	(59)
About once or twice a year	28%	(76)
Several times a year	18%	(52)
About once a month	4%	(10)
2–3 times a month	2%	(5)
Nearly every week	2%	(4)
Several times a week	0%	(1)

V017. Protection of sources; granting and preserving confidentiality; disguising the nature of a source with a vested interest or otherwise withholding relevant information from the reader.

Never	6%	(23)
Less than once a year	8%	(28)
About once or twice a year	16%	(61)
Several times a year	35%	(111)
About once a month	16%	(39)
2–3 times a month	9%	(24)
Nearly every week	7%	(20)
Several times a week	4%	(9)

V018. Invasion of privacy: causing injury to feelings; disclosing embarrassing private facts.

Never	5%	(14)
Less than once a year	8%	(25)
About once or twice a year	16%	(53)

Several times a year	33%	(106)
About once a month	18%	(44)
2–3 times a month	12%	(34)
Nearly every week	6%	(21)
Several times a week	3%	(7)

V019. Economic temptations: accepting trips, meals, favors, loans, gifts, from sources or suppliers, or heavy socializing with sources.

Never	28%	(91)
Less than once a year	10%	(27)
About once or twice a year	31%	(95)
Several times a year	18%	(58)
About once a month	12%	(29)
2–3 times a month	1%	(4)
Nearly every week	1%	(2)
Several times a week	1%	(2)

V020. Government secrecy: grand jury leaks; national security problems, including military secrets and diplomatic leaks.

Never	15%	(61)
Less than once a year	14%	(50)
About once or twice a year	32%	(99)
Several times a year	21%	(66)
About once a month	12%	(21)
2–3 times a month	2%	(8)
Nearly every week	2%	(4)
Several times a week	2%	(4)

V021. Civil disorder: publicizing rioters, terrorists, bomb threats, at the risk of encouraging imitators.

Never	13%	(47)
Less than once a year	26%	(66)
About once or twice a year	32%	(102)
Several times a year	24%	(73)
About once a month	3%	(8)
2–3 times a month	3%	(6)
Nearly every week	1%	(2)
Several times a week	0%	(0)

V022. Photos: violence, obscenity, hurt feelings.

Never	9%	(20)
Less than once a year	4%	(15)
About once or twice a year	19%	(65)
Several times a year	39%	(113)

About once a month	14%	(49)
2–3 times a month	5%	(15)
Nearly every week	6%	(21)
Several times a week	4%	(7)

V023. Pressure from advertisers: blurbs, business office musts, keeping things out of the paper or getting them in.

Never	21%	(59)
Less than once a year	6%	(18)
About once or twice a year	26%	(73)
Several times a year	20%	(68)
About once a month	11%	(38)
2–3 times a month	6%	(18)
Nearly every week	6%	(24)
Several times a week	3%	(12)

V024. Fairness, balance and objectivity: allocating space to opposing interest groups or political candidates. Providing right of reply to criticism.

Never	2%	(9)
Less than once a year	2%	(9)
About once or twice a year	6%	(20)
Several times a year	25%	(82)
About once a month	15%	(52)
2–3 times a month	13%	(35)
Nearly every week	14%	(53)
Several times a week	22%	(51)

V025. Conflict of interest: interest group activity by editors and publishers; service on boards and committees; campaign donations; stories involving financial interests of newspaper staff or management; spouse involvement.

Never	17%	(49)
Less than once a year	16%	(44)
About once or twice a year	38%	(116)
Several times a year	22%	(71)
About once a month	4%	(17)
2–3 times a month	2%	(6)
Nearly every week	1%	(2)
Several times a week	1%	(2)

V026. Use of reporters for non-news tasks; writing advertising supplements, gathering data for the company's financial decisions or labor relations objectives.

Never	62%	(192)
Less than once a year	15%	(40)

About once or twice a year	15%	(50)
Several times a year	7%	(23)
About once a month	1%	(5)
2–3 times a month	0%	(0)
Nearly every week	1%	(5)
Several times a week	0%	(0)

V027. Suppression of news to protect the community, factory relocations, school closings, highway expansion, etc.

Never	55%	(159)
Less than once a year	12%	(39)
About once or twice a year	18%	(56)
Several times a year	5%	(19)
About once a month	8%	(28)
2–3 times a month	1%	(5)
Nearly every week	2%	(5)
Several times a week	0%	(0)

Part Two: Publishers, Editors and Staff Members

V029. Have you seen the movie "Absence of Malice"?

	Publishers	Editors	Staff Members	Total	
Yes	54%	54%	50%	53%	(357)
No	46	46	50	47	(373)

V030. (IF YES TO V029) Which of the following four statements about "Absence of Malice" comes closest to the way you, yourself, feel about the movie?

  a. The movie gives an accurate portrayal of problems that sometimes occur in the newspaper business.

  b. The movie makes some valid points about problems in the newspaper business, but it does so with situations that were exaggerated and not true to life.

  c. The situations and people in the movie bear hardly any resemblance to the newspaper business as I know it, and its moral points have little value.

  d. The movie is an unfair and inaccurate attack on the newspaper profession.

	Publishers	Editors	Staff Members	Total	
Statement a	25%	21%	18%	22%	(72)
Statement b	63	70	76	70	(254)
Statement c	9	9	4	8	(27)
Statement a	3	0	1	1	(3)

V031. Was any formal action taken in response to "Absence of Malice" at your newspaper in the way of discussion groups, committees, or actions to put ethics on your policy agenda?

	Publishers	Editors	Staff Members	Total	
Yes	8%	9%	4%	7%	(50)
No	92	91	96	93	(662)

V032. (IF YES TO V031) Was that action based more on the publisher's initiative or more on the editor's initiative?

	Publishers	Editors	Staff Members	Total	
Publisher's	62%	7%	10%	26%	(15)
Editor's	38	93	90	74	(34)

V033. Newspapers vary greatly in the amount of involvement that publishers have in the news operations. Here are four statements describing different levels of publisher involvement. Regardless of how things work at your paper, which of the following statements comes closest to describing the way you think *publishers* ought to operate:

a. The publisher should always be involved in deciding what appears in his or her newspapers on a day-to-day basis.

b. The publisher should generally be involved in deciding what appears in his or her newspaper over the long run, but not on a daily basis.

c. The publisher should be involved in hiring good people to run the news operation, but not in deciding what appears in the paper; his only intervention in the news operation should be to hire or fire the editor.

d. The publisher should have nothing whatever to do with the news operation.

	Publishers	Editors	Staff Members	Total	
Statement a	4%	2%	1%	2%	(18)
Statement b	79	58	54	63	(465)
Statement c	18	36	53	32	(229)
Statement d	0	5	2	3	(16)

V034. Now that you have told us how publishers *should* operate, please indicate which of the four comes closest to the way things actually work at your paper.

a. The publisher is always involved in deciding what appears in his or her newspaper on a day-to-day basis.

b. The publisher is generally involved in deciding what appears in the newspaper over the long run, but not on a daily basis.

c. The publisher is involved in hiring good people to run the news operation, but not in deciding what appears in the paper; his only intervention in the news operation is to hire or fire the editor.

d. The publisher has nothing whatever to do with news operation.

	Publishers	Editors	Staff Members	Total	
Statement a	5%	3%	9%	5%	(42)
Statement b	74	61	53	63	(465)
Statement c	21	32	29	27	(181)
Statement d	0	4	9	5	(33)

V035. One issue in some companies is how much editors should be involved in the company's marketing and financial plans. Which of the following statements best describes the role you think the *editor* should have at your company?

a. The editor should participate fully in financial planning and marketing decisions.

b. The editor should be kept fully informed in financial planning and marketing decisions, but should participate only when questions related to his specific expertise are involved.

c. The editor should be kept informed of financial planning and marketing decisions on a "need-to-know" basis, i.e., whenever his help is needed in carrying out the decisions.

d. The editor should be insulated from all financial planning and marketing decisions so that he can concentrate on putting out the paper.

	Publishers	Editors	Staff Members	Total	
Statement a	42%	45%	20%	36%	(239)
Statement b	34	39	54	43	(340)
Statement c	23	14	21	19	(132)
Statement d	1	2	6	3	(19)

V036. Which comes closest to describing the actual situation at your company?

a. The editor participates fully in financial planning and marketing decisions.

b. The editor is kept fully informed in financial planning and marketing decisions.

c. The editor is kept informed of financial planning and marketing decisions on a "need-to-know" basis, i.e., whenever his help is needed in carrying out the decisions.

d. The editor is insulated from all financial planning and marketing decisions so that he can concentrate on putting out the paper.

	Publishers	Editors	Staff Members	Total	
Statement a	27%	28%	11%	22%	(162)
Statement b	38	33	38	36	(259)
Statement c	34	35	45	38	(270)
Statement d	1	4	6	4	(29)

V037. Newspaper people have different ideas about respecting pledges of confidentiality. Which of the following statements comes closest to your view:

a. A pledge of confidentiality to a source should always be kept no matter what the circumstances, even if it means a long jail term for the reporter and heavy financial cost to the newspaper.

b. A pledge of confidentiality should always be taken seriously, but it can be violated in unusual circumstances, as when it is learned the source lied to the reporter.

c. A pledge of confidentiality can be broken if the editor and the reporter agree that the harm done by keeping it is greater than the damage caused by breaking it.

d. Pledges of confidentiality are largely rhetorical devices and not intended to be taken seriously.

	Publishers	Editors	Staff Members	Total	
Statement a	18%	20%	40%	25%	(179)
Statement b	65	71	51	62	(447)
Statement c	18	9	9	12	(99)
Statement d	0	0	0	0	(2)

V038. Under which of the following circumstances should a newspaper publish material from leaked grand jury transcripts:

a. Whenever the material is newsworthy.

b. Whenever the importance of the material revealed outweighs the damage to the system from breaching of its security.

c. Only if the material exposes flaws in the workings of the grand jury system itself, e.g., it shows the prosecutor to be acting improperly.

d. Never.

	Publishers	Editors	Staff Members	Total	
Statement a	11%	19%	32%	20%	(145)
Statement b	62	60	49	57	(396)
Statement c	23	15	13	17	(140)
Statement d	3	7	7	6	(42)

V039. A reporter is assigned to find out about the activities of a political action group whose objectives are in sharp contrast to his own strongly held views. To get the story he needs the cooperation of group members. Should the reporter:

a. Ask the editor to assign someone else to the story.

b. Take care to explain his own views to the sources so that they can take them into account in deciding how to deal with him.

c. Keep quiet about his own views, but be frank and forthcoming if asked.

d. Adopt the stance of a sympathetic neutral.

e. Pose as an advocate of the action group's objectives.

	Publishers	Editors	Staff Members	Total	
Statement a	28%	35%	16%	26%	(200)
Statement b	5	1	1	2	(20)

	Publishers	Editors	Staff Members	Total	
Statement c	53	45	53	50	(360)
Statement d	15	20	29	21	(145)
Statement e	0	0	0	0	(0)

V040. The first refugees from the Falkland Islands come to stay with relatives in your town. You know from the Iranian hostage experience that they are likely to be harassed and intimidated by competing news persons striving for the last detail. Already, reporters and camera persons are setting up camp in their front yard. Should the editor:

a. Organize pool coverage to reduce the burden on the family.

b. Make a public plea for all media to use restraint.

c. Avoid public pronouncements, but order his own staff to use restraint.

d. Do nothing, on the theory that competitive news coverage is best for society in the long run.

	Publishers	Editors	Staff Members	Total	
Statement a	8%	7%	16%	10%	(86)
Statement b	4	4	2	3	(31)
Statement c	65	70	51	62	(447)
Statement d	23	20	31	24	(164)

V041. A prominent citizen is vacationing alone in Key West, and his hotel burns down. The wire service story lists him among those who escaped uninjured and identifies the hotel as a popular gathering place for affluent gays. The citizen says he'll commit suicide if you publish his name in the story. Should the editor:

a. Publish the story in full.

b. Publish the story, but without mentioning the gay angle.

c. Publish the story, but without mentioning the local citizen.

d. Kill the story.

	Publishers	Editors	Staff Members	Total	
Statement a	39%	41%	46%	42%	(286)
Statement b	50	52	43	49	(370)
Statement c	10	7	10	9	(65)
Statement d	1	0	0	0	(4)

V042. In making the decision indicated above, who should be involved?

a. The editor only.

b. The editor, in consultation with the publisher.

c. The publisher, in consultation with the editor.

d. The publisher only.

	Publishers	Editors	Staff Members	Total	
Statement a	39%	60%	57%	52%	(339)
Statement b	50	38	39	42	(344)

	Publishers	Editors	Staff Members	Total	
Statement c	11	2	4	6	(50)
Statement d	0	0	0	0	(0)

V043. An investigative reporter uses a computer to analyze criminal court records and writes a prize-winning series. A major computer manufacturer then offers to pay him $500 to speak at a seminar for reporters which it is sponsoring at a university. Which of the following best describes your view?

a. The reporter should be allowed to make the speech and accept the $500 from the computer manufacturer.

b. The reporter should be allowed to make the speech, but accept the $500 only if the honorarium is paid through the university.

c. The reporter should be allowed to make the speech but not to accept the honorarium.

d. The reporter should not be allowed to make the speech.

	Publishers	Editors	Staff Members	Total	
Statement a	28%	24%	38%	30%	(232)
Statement b	19	18	16	17	(147)
Statement c	48	51	41	47	(310)
Statement d	5	8	5	6	(43)

V044. In making the decision indicated above, who should be involved?

a. The editor only.

b. The editor, in consultation with the publisher.

c. The publisher, in consultation with the editor.

d. The publisher only.

	Publishers	Editors	Staff Members	Total	
Statement a	37%	72%	76%	62%	(422)
Statement b	50	27	20	32	(258)
Statement c	12	2	4	6	(49)
Statement d	1	0	1	1	(5)

V045. An investigative reporter discovers a former city employee now living in another state who has evidence of a kickback scheme involving the mayor and half the city council. He appears interested in cooperating with your investigation, but indicates that he will want money. Should your paper:

a. Pay an honorarium based on the news value of the story.

b. Put him on the payroll for the time that he spends working with your staff in gathering and documenting the facts, plus expenses.

c. Pay his out-of-pocket expenses only.

d. Pay nothing.

	Publishers	Editors	Staff Members	Total	
Statement a	8%	7%	4%	6%	(49)
Statement b	14	5	7	8	(65)

	Publishers	Editors	Staff Members	Total	
Statement c	33	32	33	33	(226)
Statement d	46	56	56	53	(392)

V046. An investigative reporter does a thorough and praiseworthy exposé of inequalities in tax assessment practices. In the course of investigating for the story, he looks at his own assessment records and finds that a value-enhancing addition to his property was never recorded, and as a result, his taxes are $300 less than they should be. He reports this fact in the first draft of his story, but, later, at the urging of his wife, takes it out. Should the editor:

    a. Insist that he leave the information in, even though it will raise the reporter's taxes.

    b. Talk to the wife and try to persuade her that the reporter's honesty at leaving it in will be rewarded, someday.

    c. Leave it to the reporter to decide, but appeal to his conscience.

    d. Don't interfere.

	Publishers	Editors	Staff Members	Total	
Statement a	63%	74%	58%	65%	(456)
Statement b	2	4	2	3	(23)
Statement c	29	17	29	25	(184)
Statement d	6	5	11	7	(58)

V047. A just-nominated presidential candidate is meeting with state party chairpersons to discuss his choice for vice presidential candidate. The meeting is closed to the press. A reporter, pretending to be a party staff person, hands a briefcase to one of the people going into the meeting and asks him to leave it on the table for his boss. The briefcase contains a tape recorder, and the reporter retrieves it after the meeting. Should the editor:

    a. Admonish the reporter and kill the story.

    b. Admonish the reporter, but use the information as background for conventional reporting.

    c. Admonish the reporter, but use the story.

    d. Reward the reporter and use the story.

	Publishers	Editors	Staff Members	Total	
Statement a	40%	45%	43%	43%	(332)
Statement b	45	29	32	35	(255)
Statement c	3	7	5	5	(32)
Statement d	12	20	20	17	(103)

V048. Suppose the meeting was of the local party central committee. Which action should the editor take?

    a. Admonish the reporter and kill the story.

    b. Admonish the reporter, but use the information as background for conventional reporting.

c. Admonish the reporter, but use the story.
d. Reward the reporter and use the story.

	Publishers	Editors	Staff Members	Total	
Statement a	41%	45%	43%	43%	(340)
Statement b	43	28	32	34	(248)
Statement c	4	7	6	6	(37)
Statement d	12	20	19	17	(101)

V049. The city manager has proposed a one-way street plan which adds a mile and a half to the route your newspaper's circulation trucks must take to reach the major freeways. The circulation manager proposes an alternate plan, and top management agrees to have the company's lawyer present it to city council. In covering the story, should the editor:
a. Give no special instructions to the city desk.
b. Tell the desk to cover the story fully, take special precautions to get the facts straight.
c. Have a free-lance writer, whose livelihood does not depend on the paper, cover the story.
d. Use the wire story.

	Publishers	Editors	Staff Members	Total	
Statement a	27%	32%	41%	33%	(258)
Statement b	72	66	57	65	(458)
Statement c	1	1	1	1	(9)
Statement d	1	1	1	1	(8)

V050. In making the decision indicated above, who should be involved?
a. The editor only.
b. The editor, in consultation with the publisher.
c. The publisher, in consultation with the editor.
d. The publisher only.

	Publishers	Editors	Staff Members	Total	
Statement a	50%	71%	73%	65%	(459)
Statement b	40	27	25	31	(236)
Statement c	10	2	2	4	(37)
Statement d	0	0	0	0	(2)

V051. The company that owns a major metropolitan newspaper also owns a major sports franchise in that town. Should the paper:
a. Try to build up local interest in the team it owns, because it is good for community spirit as well as profitable to the company.
b. Treat the team exactly as it treats any other team.
c. Bend over backwards to be fair and treat the company-owned team with more skepticism and outright criticism than are accorded other teams.
d. Sell the franchise.

	Publishers	Editors	Staff Members	Total	
Statement a	2%	3%	3%	3%	(20)
Statement b	80	79	70	77	(560)
Statement c	3	0	1	1	(7)
Statement d	15	18	26	20	(141)

V052. The business manager of the company has developed close friendships with Canadian newsprint suppliers, reinforced by regular hunting trips in the north woods as their guest. The company decides to prohibit managers from accepting favors from suppliers. The business manager continues to take the trips. Should the publisher:

a. Fire the business manager.

b. Impose discipline short of firing and extract a promise that it will not happen again.

c. Advise the business manager to pay his own way on these trips or reciprocate by hosting the suppliers on equivalent outings.

d. Decide that the no-favor rule should not apply to such long-standing and clearly benign activities.

	Publishers	Editors	Staff Members	Total	
Statement a	20%	28%	18%	22%	(145)
Statement b	58	51	48	52	(391)
Statement c	17	18	32	22	(169)
Statement d	5	3	2	3	(23)

V053. Your company receives a special rate from a major hotel chain for your traveling employees. A staff member goes out of town for a three-day business meeting and, because the site of the meeting is a major cultural center, decides to stay through the week at his own expense. He pays his own hotel bill for Friday and Saturday nights, but at the special commercial rate. Your company has a conflict of interest policy against employees accepting any kind of favor or reward from suppliers. Should your company.

a. Fire the traveling employee.

b. Require him to reimburse the hotel for the difference between the commercial and regular rate and warn him not to repeat the practice.

c. Warn him not to repeat the practice, but not worry about reimbursement because the amount is so small.

d. Make a ruling that such discounts are not considered favors or rewards under the conflict-of-interest policy.

	Publishers	Editors	Staff Members	Total	
Statement a	0%	1%	0%	1%	(5)
Statement b	24	44	65	44	(347)
Statement c	27	16	14	19	(125)
Statement d	49	40	21	37	(247)

V054. The restaurant reviewer at your paper has become friendly with a local restaurant operator and, working without pay, has helped his friend to design and plan a new restaurant with a continental theme—the exact sort of restaurant whose absence in your town he has decried in his column. Should the editor:

a. Fire the restaurant critic.

b. Admonish the critic not to get so close to sources, and ban any mention of the new restaurant in his column.

c. Advise the critic not to do it again, but take no further action.

d. Do nothing.

		Publishers	Editors	Staff Members	Total	
Statement	a	4%	12%	8%	8%	(62)
Statement	b	48	58	49	52	(335)
Statement	c	32	20	27	26	(204)
Statement	d	16	10	16	14	(116)

V055. Easter Sunday is approaching, and the editor plans the traditional page-one recognition of the holiday: A banner, "He Is Risen." Then a new publisher, who happens to be an agnostic, points out that the latest religious census shows the community to be six percent non-Christian. Should the editor:

a. Keep the Easter banner.

b. Reduce the size of the headline in deference to the non-Christians in the community.

c. Limit the paper's coverage to specific religious-oriented events scheduled for that day.

d. Avoid any mention of Easter.

		Publishers	Editors	Staff Members	Total	
Statement	a	62%	50%	42%	51%	(398)
Statement	b	5	4	4	4	(30)
Statement	c	30	46	53	43	(286)
Statement	d	3	1	1	2	(9)

V056. What percent non-Christian should the community reach before you would choose a different response?

	Publishers	Editors	Staff Members	Total
Mean Percent	50.4%	44.4%	47.4%	47.3% (477)

V057. Your Washington correspondent has spent years developing friendships with the key people now in power, and it is paying off. He knows the town well, and they are relative newcomers, so he is frequently consulted by the White House staff and the President's political operatives before key decisions are made. Should the editor:

    a. Fire the Washington correspondent.

    b. Move the correspondent to another city.

    c. Admonish the Washington correspondent to maintain a reasonable distance from his sources.

    d. Reward the Washington correspondent for developing such a good knowledge of his subject and such loyal sources.

		Publishers	*Editors*	*Staff Members*	*Total*	
Statement	a	1%	1%	1%	1%	(10)
Statement	b	10	6	16	10	(78)
Statement	c	75	77	71	75	(521)
Statement	d	14	16	12	14	(114)

V058. The publisher is convinced that a downtown amusement park is just what the community needs. The editor of the editorial page opposes it. Should the publisher:

    a. Order the editor to support the amusement park.

    b. Drop some gentle hints to the editor, but avoid a direct order.

    c. Avoid discussing the issue with the editor at all.

    d. Encourage the editor to call the issue as he sees it.

		Publishers	*Editors*	*Staff Members*	*Total*	
Statement	a	35%	29%	15%	26%	(192)
Statement	b	27	19	15	21	(170)
Statement	c	2	3	10	5	(39)
Statement	d	36	49	58	48	(312)

V059. A scandal is unfolding in city government, and your paper is getting more than its share of the news beats. But, today, your paper is beaten by a competing medium on a key element of the story. Should your paper:

    a. Treat the new element just as though the competition had never mentioned it.

    b. Acknowledge the competition's beat in print and cover the story according to its intrinsic news value.

    c. Downgrade the importance of the new element.

    d. Ignore the new element.

		Publishers	*Editors*	*Staff Members*	*Total*	
Statement	a	44%	39%	41%	41%	(324)
Statement	b	56	61	59	59	(406)
Statement	c	0	1	0	0	(2)
Statement	d	0	0	0	0	(0)

V060. The chief photographer moonlights as a wedding photographer. The father of a bride calls the editor and says the photographer has made a sales pitch to his daughter and included a sly hint that if he is hired for the job, her picture has a better chance of making the society page. The editor investigates and confirms that this is the photographer's regular practice. Should the editor:

a. Fire the photographer.

b. Impose lesser discipline and order the photographer to stop moonlighting.

c. Allow the photographer to continue moonlighting but order him not to use—or pretend to use—his position to gain favored treatment for clients.

d. Ask the photographer to be more discreet.

		Publishers	Editors	Staff Members	Total	
Statement	a	44%	47%	49%	47%	(327)
Statement	b	13	16	15	15	(116)
Statement	c	43	36	37	39	(287)
Statement	d	0	0	0	0	(1)

V061. A business writer discovers that TV sets with built-in videotex decoders will be on the local market within 60 days, greatly increasing convenience and reducing costs for people who sign up for the local videotex service—which, incidentally, is not owned by your paper. The advertising manager calls the publisher and says local TV dealers are afraid they will be stuck with an oversupply of obsolete TV sets if the word gets out. Should the publisher:

a. Order the story killed.

b. Explain the problem to the editor with a recommendation that the story be delayed.

c. Suggest to the editor that the story be double-checked for accuracy.

d. Help the ad manager pacify the retailers, but say nothing to the editor.

		Publishers	Editors	Staff Members	Total	
Statement	a	0%	0%	0%	0%	(0)
Statement	b	3	2	2	3	(20)
Statement	c	47	36	34	39	(297)
Statement	d	50	62	64	59	(405)

V062. A local boy who grew up in poverty makes good by educating himself, working hard, and becoming a successful businessman. This effort culminates in the opening of the fanciest restaurant the town has yet seen. His younger brother has also made good, in a way, by becoming an editorial writer, and he salutes his brother's Horatio Alger story in a folksy and appealing signed column. To ward off any charge of conflict of interest, he identifies himself as the brother of the subject of the piece in the opening paragraph. Should the editor:

a. Kill the column.

b. Have the column rewritten to eliminate the brother's name and the name of the restaurant.

c. Move the piece to some less conspicuous part of the paper.

d. Let it stand.

		Publishers	Editors	Staff Members	Total	
Statement	a	23%	22%	20%	21%	(128)
Statement	b	4	0	4	3	(22)
Statement	c	5	3	8	5	(42)
Statement	d	68	75	69	71	(535)

V063. Your paper's city hall reporter has gotten so close to the mayor and his staff that they frequently consult him before making major decisions. Should the editor:

a. Fire the reporter.

b. Move the reporter to a different beat.

c. Admonish the reporter to maintain a reasonable distance from his sources.

d. Reward the reporter for developing a reasonable knowledge of his subject and such loyal sources.

		Publishers	Editors	Staff Members	Total	
Statement	a	1%	1%	1%	1%	(7)
Statement	b	30	21	38	30	(219)
Statement	c	61	67	55	61	(428)
Statement	d	9	11	6	9	(69)

V064. In making the decision indicated above, who should be involved?

a. The editor only.

b. The editor, in consultation with the publisher.

c. The publisher, in consultation with the editor.

d. The publisher only.

		Publishers	Editors	Staff Members	Total	
Statement	a	49%	86%	84%	73%	(524)
Statement	b	46	15	14	25	(187)
Statement	c	4	0	1	2	(17)
Statement	d	0	0	0	0	(1)

V065. Some newspaper companies in Florida donated money to a campaign to defeat a statewide referendum which, if passed, would have legalized gambling. Which of the following statements comes closest to your view on this action?

a. A newspaper that takes an editorial stand on an issue has a right, and possibly even a duty, to back up its belief with its money.

b. The contributions are justified if the referendum would have a detrimental effect on the business climate in which the newspaper operates.

c. The contributions should not have been made because they might lead readers to question the objectivity of the papers' news coverage.

d. No political contributions should ever be made by newspapers; the news and editorial columns make us powerful enough already, and adding money only indicates inappropriate hunger for more power.

	Publishers	Editors	Staff Members	Total	
Statement a	22%	11%	6%	13%	(105)
Statement b	11	2	4	5	(39)
Statement c	23	31	34	30	(224)
Statement d	44	56	57	53	(347)

V066. If an editor could set any rule he or she wanted for defining the relationship with the publisher, which of the following possible rules would result in the best newspaper?

a. Don't ever talk to me about what I put in the paper.

b. Make suggestions about the content if you want, but don't give orders, unless to fire me.

c. Play a major role in the big decisions—creating new sections, targeting new markets, and major design changes, for example—but don't get involved in individual stories.

d. Be the boss, all the way.

	Publishers	Editors	Staff Members	Total	
Statement a	0%	0%	2%	1%	(5)
Statement b	11	26	36	24	(171)
Statement c	82	72	61	72	(520)
Statement d	8	2	1	4	(33)

V067. Which of the above rules comes closest to describing what actually happens at your newspaper?

a. Don't ever talk to me about what I put in the paper.

b. Make suggestions about the content if you want, but don't give orders, unless to fire me.

c. Play a major role in the big decisions—creating new sections, targeting new markets, and major design changes, for example—but don't get involved in individual stories.

d. Be the boss, all the way.

	Publishers	Editors	Staff Members	Total	
Statement a	0%	2%	2%	1%	(11)
Statement b	13	25	29	23	(146)
Statement c	80	63	50	64	(459)
Statement d	7	11	19	12	(99)

V068. How often, according to your best estimates, does the publisher of your paper ask for special handling of an article about a company or organization which has some economic clout over your newspaper?

a. Never
b. Less than once a year
c. About once or twice a year
d. Several times a year
e. About once a month
f. 2–3 times a month
g. Nearly every week
h. Every week

	Publishers	Editors	Staff Members	Total	
Statement a	58%	54%	32%	48%	(320)
Statement b	10	12	18	13	(94)
Statement c	18	19	20	19	(149)
Statement d	10	11	23	14	(118)
Statement e	2	1	3	2	(16)
Statement f	1	1	3	2	(14)
Statement g	1	1	1	1	(7)
Statement h	0	0	0	0	(1)

V069. How often, according to your best estimate, does the publisher ask for special handling of an article about an organization or individual with whom he has strong social ties?

a. Never
b. Less than once a year
c. About once or twice a year
d. Several times a year
e. About once a month
f. 2–3 times a month
g. Nearly every week
h. Every week

	Publishers	Editors	Staff Members	Total	
Statement a	58%	48%	31%	46%	(302)
Statement b	8	14	10	11	(85)
Statement c	23	19	24	22	(162)
Statement d	9	16	23	16	(121)
Statement e	1	1	5	2	(21)
Statement f	1	2	4	2	(20)
Statement g	0	0	2	1	(8)
Statement h	0	0	0	0	(1)

V070. How often does the publisher ask the editor to send a reporter on a non-news mission for the company: to influence legislation, for example, or gather information on competition?

a. Never
b. Less than once a year
c. About once or twice a year
d. Several times a year

e. About once a month
f. More than once a month

		Publishers	*Editors*	*Staff Members*	*Total*	
Statement	a	90%	81%	82%	84%	(612)
Statement	b	7	12	10	10	(65)
Statement	c	2	5	6	4	(33)
Statement	d	1	2	2	2	(13)
Statement	e	0	0	0	0	(0)
Statement	f	0	0	0	0	(1)

V071. Do you think it is a good idea or a bad idea for a newspaper publisher to serve on the board of another local company?

	Publishers	*Editors*	*Staff Members*	*Total*	
Good idea	11%	6%	9%	9%	(73)
Bad idea	65	71	71	69	(476)
No difference	24	23	21	22	(181)

V072. (IF BAD IDEA TO V071) What if the company is non-profit, like a hospital or a symphony orchestra? Would the publisher's serving on such a board be a good idea or a bad idea?

	Publishers	*Editors*	*Staff Members*	*Total*	
Good idea	59%	27%	21%	35%	(164)
Bad idea	18	51	57	43	(205)
No difference	23	23	22	23	(105)

V073. (IF BAD IDEA TO V072) What if it was the board of a charitable enterprise like United Way or a local foundation?

	Publishers	*Editors*	*Staff Members*	*Total*	
Good idea	27%	7%	4%	8%	(21)
Bad idea	50	87	91	84	(164)
No difference	24	6	5	8	(19)

V074. (IF BAD IDEA TO V073) How about a church vestry or PTA board?

	Publishers	*Editors*	*Staff Members*	*Total*	
Good idea	0%	5%	1%	3%	(6)
Bad idea	77	38	56	49	(84)
No difference	24	57	44	48	(73)

V075. Do you think it is a good idea or a bad idea for a newspaper editor to serve on the board of another local company?

	Publishers	*Editors*	*Staff Members*	*Total*	
Good idea	5%	3%	3%	4%	(33)
Bad idea	80	92	88	87	(614)
No difference	15	6	9	10	(83)

V076. (IF BAD IDEA TO V075) What if the company is non-profit, like a hospital or a symphony orchestra? Would the editor's serving on such a board be a good idea or a bad idea?

	Publishers	Editors	Staff Members	Total	
Good idea	26%	10%	13%	16%	(100)
Bad idea	55	78	74	70	(418)
No difference	19	12	12	14	(92)

V077. (IF BAD IDEA TO V076) What if it was the board of a charitable enterprise like United Way or a local foundation?

	Publishers	Editors	Staff Members	Total	
Good idea	9%	2%	1%	4%	(19)
Bad idea	82	92	91	89	(363)
No difference	9	6	8	7	(33)

V078. (IF BAD IDEA TO V077) How about a church vestry or PTA board?

	Publishers	Editors	Staff Members	Total	
Good idea	11%	9%	5%	8%	(33)
Bad idea	47	48	63	53	(182)
No difference	42	43	33	39	(144)

Suppose that your paper's performance was being graded by different groups. Each year, each group would send you a report card. For each group listed, please indicate whether you would be extremely interested, very interested, somewhat interested, or not interested at all in that group's report card on your paper.

V079. Readers

	Publishers	Editors	Staff Members	Total	
Extremely	93%	87%	86%	89%	(658)
Very	6	8	12	8	(57)
Somewhat	1	5	3	2	(17)
Not	0	0	0	0	(0)

V080. Politicians

	Publishers	Editors	Staff Members	Total	
Extremely	25%	34%	27%	29%	(194)
Very	23	25	25	25	(196)
Somewhat	45	34	43	41	(300)
Not	6	6	4	5	(41)

V081. Retail advertisers

	Publishers	Editors	Staff Members	Total	
Extremely	47%	36%	29%	37%	(263)
Very	31	27	19	26	(202)
Somewhat	21	33	41	32	(231)
Not	0	4	12	5	(35)

V082. Potential investors in your company

	Publishers	Editors	Staff Members	Total	
Extremely	29%	29%	27%	28%	(193)
Very	22	17	20	19	(148)
Somewhat	25	32	32	30	(217)
Not	25	22	21	23	(163)

V083. National advertisers

	Publishers	Editors	Staff Members	Total	
Extremely	35%	31%	28%	32%	(210)
Very	37	17	15	23	(169)
Somewhat	23	40	42	35	(282)
Not	4	13	15	11	(69)

V084. People who put out other newspapers

	Publishers	Editors	Staff Members	Total	
Extremely	41%	45%	49%	45%	(315)
Very	36	31	33	33	(252)
Somewhat	21	20	18	20	(150)
Not	1	4	1	2	(13)

V085. Journalism school faculties

	Publishers	Editors	Staff Members	Total	
Extremely	24%	30%	39%	31%	(236)
Very	37	26	30	31	(234)
Somewhat	31	36	28	32	(219)
Not	8	8	4	7	(43)

V086. Security analysts

	Publishers	Editors	Staff Members	Total	
Extremely	18%	22%	17%	19%	(129)
Very	20	12	9	14	(102)
Somewhat	41	40	47	42	(309)
Not	21	26	27	25	(188)

V087. Journalism students

	Publishers	Editors	Staff Members	Total	
Extremely	21%	26%	26%	25%	(173)
Very	31	22	24	26	(179)
Somewhat	42	44	44	43	(327)
Not	6	8	6	7	(53)

V088. Classified advertisers

	Publishers	Editors	Staff Members	Total	
Extremely	42%	33%	24%	33%	(233)
Very	29	22	18	23	(181)
Somewhat	28	34	35	33	(241)
Not	1	12	23	12	(76)

V089. Your own editorial staff

	Publishers	Editors	Staff Members	Total	
Extremely	78%	81%	75%	78%	(559)
Very	19	17	20	19	(148)
Somewhat	3	2	4	3	(23)
Not	0	0	1	0	(2)

For each of the following statements, please tell me whether you agree or disagree.

V090. When there is disagreement between editor and publisher over the endorsement of a political candidate, the editor should have the final say.

	Publishers	Editors	Staff Members	Total	
Agree	22%	37%	47%	36%	(245)
Disagree	78	63	53	64	(482)

V091. An editor should not be a director or an officer of the company he works for.

	Publishers	Editors	Staff Members	Total	
Agree	16%	25%	57%	32%	(255)
Disagree	84	75	43	68	(471)

V092. It's okay for the lawyer who advises the newspaper on the legal risks it takes to sit on the company's board.

	Publishers	Editors	Staff Members	Total	
Agree	65%	55%	39%	53%	(392)
Disagree	35	45	61	47	(336)

V093. There are situations, like the Pentagon Papers case, where it is more loyal to the nation to violate security rules than to follow them.

	Publishers	Editors	Staff Members	Total	
Agree	79%	87%	92%	86%	(611)
Disagree	21	13	8	14	(114)

V094. Public concern over newspaper ethics is caused less by the things newspapers do than by their failure to explain what they do.

	Publishers	Editors	Staff Members	Total	
Agree	68%	72%	60%	67%	(503)
Disagree	32	28	40	33	(223)

V095. Sometimes the letters to the editor at our paper are really written by the staff.

	Publishers	Editors	Staff Members	Total	
Agree	1%	0%	2%	1%	(10)
Disagree	99	100	98	99	(718)

V096. An adversarial relationship between the government and newspapers is healthy for the country in the long run.

	Publishers	Editors	Staff Members	Total	
Agree	78%	91%	87%	85%	(606)
Disagree	22	9	13	15	(121)

V097. A state news council, modeled after the National News Council, would be a good idea.

	Publishers	Editors	Staff Members	Total	
Agree	21%	29%	49%	33%	(252)
Disagree	79	71	51	67	(439)

V098. A reporter who has promised confidentiality to a source should, if asked, reveal that source to his editor.

	Publishers	Editors	Staff Members	Total	
Agree	91%	91%	70%	84%	(595)
Disagree	9	9	30	16	(136)

Several possible "yardsticks" for evaluating newspaper companies are listed below. On a scale of 1 to 10, how important is each of these indicators to you? A score of 1 means the indicator is unimportant; a score of 10 means the indicator is extremely important.

V099. Earnings consistency

	Publishers	Editors	Staff Members	Total	
1	0%	5%	2%	3%	(10)
2	0	0	3	1	(10)
3	2	2	3	2	(16)

	Publishers	Editors	Staff Members	Total	
4	2	1	2	2	(14)
5	5	6	15	8	(68)
6	6	7	8	7	(47)
7	19	18	19	19	(116)
8	21	20	21	21	(161)
9	13	12	12	13	(85)
10	31	29	16	25	(196)

V100. Management quality

	Publishers	Editors	Staff Members	Total	
1	0%	1%	1%	1%	(3)
2	0	0	0	0	(0)
3	0	0	0	0	(1)
4	0	0	1	0	(3)
5	0	0	2	1	(6)
6	0	0	1	1	(5)
7	1	3	4	3	(25)
8	10	11	13	11	(86)
9	16	16	17	16	(126)
10	74	69	61	68	(476)

V101. Readiness to adopt new production technology

	Publishers	Editors	Staff Members	Total	
1	0%	1%	0%	0%	(1)
2	0	0	1	0	(1)
3	0	0	2	1	(4)
4	0	1	1	1	(6)
5	4	7	8	6	(42)
6	11	8	10	10	(59)
7	13	11	16	13	(100)
8	22	19	19	20	(159)
9	18	18	14	17	(126)
10	32	35	30	33	(231)

V102. Involvement with new electronic information systems

	Publishers	Editors	Staff Members	Total	
1	1%	6%	1%	3%	(8)
2	1	0	3	1	(8)
3	0	2	3	2	(12)
4	3	3	1	2	(20)
5	21	5	8	11	(71)
6	12	10	9	10	(80)
7	17	11	12	14	(104)

	Publishers	Editors	Staff Members	Total	
8	13	21	19	18	(138)
9	12	16	14	14	(107)
10	20	26	30	25	(180)

V103. Community service orientation

	Publishers	Editors	Staff Members	Total	
1	0%	1%	3%	1%	(7)
2	0	0	0	0	(2)
3	1	2	4	2	(9)
4	1	1	3	1	(11)
5	8	13	13	11	(60)
6	6	9	13	9	(63)
7	15	10	15	13	(95)
8	20	21	18	20	(151)
9	18	13	10	13	(106)
10	33	31	22	29	(225)

V104. Newspaper editorial quality

	Publishers	Editors	Staff Members	Total	
1	0%	1%	0%	0%	(2)
2	0	0	1	0	(2)
3	0	0	0	0	(0)
4	0	0	1	0	(1)
5	0	0	1	1	(6)
6	0	0	0	0	(2)
7	1	1	0	1	(8)
8	11	2	6	6	(47)
9	11	5	13	9	(78)
10	77	91	77	82	(584)

V105. Overall product quality

	Publishers	Editors	Staff Members	Total	
1	0%	1%	1%	0%	(2)
2	0	0	0	0	(1)
3	0	0	0	0	(0)
4	0	0	0	0	(0)
5	0	0	0	0	(2)
6	0	0	1	0	(3)
7	2	1	1	1	(11)
8	8	2	7	6	(48)
9	15	10	11	12	(91)
10	76	86	79	80	(571)

V106. Overall company image

	Publishers	Editors	Staff Members	Total	
1	0%	1%	1%	1%	(4)
2	0	0	1	0	(2)
3	0	0	0	0	(2)
4	0	1	1	1	(5)
5	1	4	9	5	(35)
6	5	4	7	5	(36)
7	16	16	16	16	(99)
8	29	23	17	23	(171)
9	11	15	14	13	(106)
10	37	37	35	36	(269)

V107. Financial health as represented by the balance sheet

	Publishers	Editors	Staff Members	Total	
1	1%	0%	1%	0%	(4)
2	0	0	1	0	(1)
3	0	0	4	1	(7)
4	0	1	1	1	(6)
5	2	3	11	5	(45)
6	2	5	8	5	(43)
7	14	10	17	14	(90)
8	21	31	24	26	(176)
9	24	15	12	17	(122)
10	36	35	21	31	(232)

V108. Readiness to introduce new products

	Publishers	Editors	Staff Members	Total	
1	0%	1%	5%	2%	(14)
2	0	1	3	1	(10)
3	0	1	3	1	(10)
4	0	2	3	2	(15)
5	4	7	14	8	(62)
6	4	5	7	6	(48)
7	22	15	20	19	(125)
8	20	28	17	22	(159)
9	21	18	14	18	(121)
10	28	22	14	22	(162)

V109. Readiness to expose wrongdoing

	Publishers	Editors	Staff Members	Total	
1	0%	1%	1%	0%	(3)
2	0	0	1	0	(1)
3	0	0	0	0	(1)
4	0	0	0	0	(0)

	Publishers	Editors	Staff Members	Total	
5	1	2	0	1	(11)
6	1	1	1	1	(8)
7	8	2	3	4	(27)
8	14	8	11	11	(77)
9	26	17	17	20	(147)
10	50	69	67	62	(454)

How important is *newspaper editorial quality* to each of the following goals:

V110. Helping maintain staff morale

	Publishers	Editors	Staff Members	Total	
Very Important	91%	95%	90%	92%	(679)
Somewhat Important	9	5	8	7	(50)
Not Important	0	0	2	1	(4)

V111. Helping maintain circulation

	Publishers	Editors	Staff Members	Total	
Very Important	82%	79%	62%	75%	(533)
Somewhat Important	17	21	35	24	(193)
Not Important	1	0	3	1	(7)

V112. Helping maintain service to the community

	Publishers	Editors	Staff Members	Total	
Very Important	68%	79%	70%	72%	(538)
Somewhat Important	32	20	28	26	(186)
Not Important	0	1	2	1	(9)

V113. Helping maintain advertising revenues

	Publishers	Editors	Staff Members	Total	
Very Important	54%	58%	33%	49%	(344)
Somewhat Important	44	37	53	44	(336)
Not Important	2	5	14	7	(53)

V114. Helping keep the public informed

	Publishers	Editors	Staff Members	Total	
Very Important	93%	96%	95%	95%	(689)
Somewhat Important	7	3	4	5	(42)
Not Important	0	0	0	0	(2)

Listed below are some of the things publishers do to influence editorial content. For each one, please indicate how often it happens—to your knowledge—at your newspaper.
1. Never
2. Less than once a year
3. About once or twice a year
4. About once or twice a month
5. 2–3 times a month
6. Nearly every week
7. Every week
8. Several times a week
9. Daily

V115. The publisher orders the editors to undertake a major investigation or series of articles on a specific subject.

	Publishers	Editors	Staff Members	Total	
Statement 1	45%	61%	41%	50%	(333)
Statement 2	24	18	22	21	(152)
Statement 3	22	18	30	23	(181)
Statement 4	8	3	5	5	(43)
Statement 5	0	0	1	0	(4)
Statement 6	1	0	1	1	(6)
Statement 7	0	0	0	0	(1)
Statement 8	0	0	0	0	(1)
Statement 9	0	0	0	0	(1)

V116. The publisher suggests a major investigation or series of articles, but leaves the final decision to the editor.

	Publishers	Editors	Staff Members	Total	
Statement 1	9%	17%	29%	18%	(127)
Statement 2	16	26	25	23	(157)
Statement 3	51	50	35	46	(329)
Statement 4	18	6	9	11	(79)
Statement 5	3	1	1	2	(14)

	Publishers	Editors	Staff Members	Total	
Statement 6	1	0	0	0	(4)
Statement 7	1	0	0	0	(3)
Statement 8	1	0	1	0	(4)
Statement 9	0	0	0	0	(0)

V117. The publisher demonstrates by his actions, such as public speeches, backing of causes, and civic activities what areas he would like the paper to investigate.

	Publishers	Editors	Staff Members	Total	
Statement 1	64%	71%	62%	66%	(450)
Statement 2	10	10	16	12	(95)
Statement 3	19	15	15	16	(123)
Statement 4	4	3	3	3	(28)
Statement 5	1	1	1	1	(10)
Statement 6	0	0	1	1	(6)
Statement 7	1	0	0	0	(2)
Statement 8	0	0	0	0	(0)
Statement 9	0	0	1	0	(2)

V118. The publisher demonstrates, by selective use of praise or criticism, what he wants the editor to do.

	Publishers	Editors	Staff Members	Total	
Statement 1	23%	22%	22%	22%	(151)
Statement 2	6	8	11	8	(59)
Statement 3	20	27	21	23	(168)
Statement 4	27	20	19	22	(147)
Statement 5	7	11	13	11	(69)
Statement 6	7	9	4	7	(52)
Statement 7	6	2	4	4	(30)
Statement 8	4	2	1	2	(18)
Statement 9	0	1	5	2	(13)

V119. In setting ethical standards for a newspaper, which is more important for a *publisher* to do:
    a. Choosing and articulating the standards, or
    b. Choosing the right editor and trusting him to set and carry out the standards?

	Publishers	Editors	Staff Members	Total	
Statement a	31%	25%	25%	27%	(204)
Statement b	69	75	75	73	(513)

Listed below are some of the things a publisher might do to influence the news content of the paper. For each one, please indicate whether it is a good idea, a bad idea, or whether it is neither good nor bad.

V120. Call the desk with tips on news stories.

	Publishers	Editors	Staff Members	Total	
Good idea	69%	69%	56%	65%	(499)
Bad idea	12	18	24	18	(114)
Neither	19	14	21	18	(116)

V121. Catch errors in grammar and spelling and let the editor know about them.

	Publishers	Editors	Staff Members	Total	
Good idea	71%	76%	48%	65%	(496)
Bad idea	3	9	28	13	(86)
Neither	26	16	25	22	(147)

V122. Catch factual errors and let the editor know.

	Publishers	Editors	Staff Members	Total	
Good idea	99%	95%	86%	94%	(684)
Bad idea	0	1	5	2	(12)
Neither	1	4	8	4	(35)

V123. Spot stories that will offend advertisers and let the editor know.

	Publishers	Editors	Staff Members	Total	
Good idea	11%	11%	3%	9%	(69)
Bad idea	60	75	86	74	(524)
Neither	29	14	11	18	(138)

V124. Spot stories that will offend civic leaders and let the editor know.

	Publishers	Editors	Staff Members	Total	
Good idea	10%	10%	4%	8%	(67)
Bad idea	58	73	82	71	(509)
Neither	32	18	13	21	(155)

V125. Make suggestions about improving the writing in the paper.

	Publishers	Editors	Staff Members	Total	
Good idea	87%	86%	63%	79%	(591)
Bad idea	4	3	18	8	(48)
Neither	9	11	19	13	(92)

V126. Make suggestions about changing the design of the paper.

	Publishers	Editors	Staff Members	Total	
Good idea	84%	77%	67%	76%	(563)
Bad idea	1	5	8	5	(30)
Neither	14	18	25	19	(138)

V127. As closely as you can estimate, how often does the publisher of your paper walk into the newsroom?
   a. Never
   b. Less than once a year
   c. About once or twice a year
   d. About once a month
   e. 2–3 times a month
   f. Nearly every week
   g. Every week
   h. Several times a week
   i. Daily
   j. More than once a day

	Publishers	Editors	Staff Members	Total	
Statement a	0%	3%	5%	3%	(16)
Statement b	0	1	0	1	(4)
Statement c	4	7	13	8	(58)
Statement d	6	12	15	11	(60)
Statement e	5	13	12	10	(63)
Statement f	9	12	8	10	(58)
Statement g	4	5	3	4	(34)
Statement h	24	16	17	19	(143)
Statement i	27	15	14	19	(141)
Statement j	22	17	13	17	(145)

V128. Different newspapers have different rules for deciding what is acceptable in advertising copy. At your newspaper, how often does the publisher ask the editor's advice when a question of acceptability arises?

	Publishers	Editors	Staff Members	Total	
Always	2%	6%	1%	3%	(19)
Most of the time	12	8	6	9	(63)
Some of the time	35	35	14	29	(184)
Almost never	52	51	79	60	(431)

One of the topics that often comes up in the newsroom is whether a reporter with a history of personal activity in a given area is more or less qualified to cover a related field because of that history. Here are some examples, and in each one, please assume that the reporter is otherwise well qualified. Please decide whether the reporter's personal history or circumstances are likely to be a help, a hindrance, or make any difference in covering the indicated field.

V129. A reporter with a history of vigorous union activity is assigned to cover big business.

	Publishers	Editors	Staff Members	Total	
Help	3%	7%	19%	9%	(65)
Hindrance	75	73	63	71	(528)
No difference	22	19	19	20	(134)

V130. A black is assigned to cover civil rights.

	Publishers	Editors	Staff Members	Total	
Help	42%	47%	50%	46%	(305)
Hindrance	20	14	13	16	(133)
No difference	38	38	38	38	(287)

V131. An assistant city editor who has married an heiress and undertaken the task of managing her investments has been promoted to business editor.

	Publishers	Editors	Staff Members	Total	
Help	31%	30%	30%	30%	(215)
Hindrance	32	35	36	34	(233)
No difference	38	35	34	35	(279)

V132. A Washington bureau chief's daughter becomes secretary to a cabinet officer.

	Publishers	Editors	Staff Members	Total	
Help	19%	24%	22%	22%	(144)
Hindrance	31	35	33	33	(233)
No difference	50	42	45	45	(347)

V133. A reporter whose best friend is elected mayor is assigned to cover city hall.

	Publishers	Editors	Staff Members	Total	
Help	9%	12%	8%	10%	(75)
Hindrance	84	81	88	84	(601)
No difference	6	7	5	6	(50)

V134. A reporter whose parents run an independent oil exploration business is assigned to cover energy.

	Publishers	Editors	Staff Members	Total	
Help	25%	31%	31%	28%	(208)
Hindrance	41	46	42	43	(315)
No difference	34	23	28	28	(203)

V135. A copy editor whose wife runs a public relations firm sometimes edits stories which mention his wife's clients.

	Publishers	Editors	Staff Members	Total	
Help	1%	1%	0%	1%	(5)
Hindrance	81	74	70	75	(525)
No difference	18	25	30	24	(194)

V136. A reporter who took a leave of absence to work in the vice president's successful election campaign is assigned to the Washington Bureau.

	Publishers	Editors	Staff Members	Total	
Help	30%	23%	22%	25%	(195)
Hindrance	56	64	66	62	(423)
No difference	14	13	12	13	(106)

V137. A reporter who was raised on a farm is assigned to cover agriculture.

	Publishers	Editors	Staff Members	Total	
Help	94%	95%	94%	95%	(689)
Hindrance	1	0	1	1	(4)
No difference	5	5	4	5	(34)

V138. An atheist is assigned to cover religion.

	Publishers	Editors	Staff Members	Total	
Help	2%	8%	13%	8%	(34)
Hindrance	69	59	50	59	(450)
No difference	29	33	37	33	(240)

V139. A reporter with a law degree is assigned to cover local courts.

	Publishers	Editors	Staff Members	Total	
Help	97%	97%	94%	96%	(699)
Hindrance	1	1	3	2	(11)
No difference	2	2	3	2	(18)

V140. A reporter who has served on the current mayor's staff returns to the paper to cover local politics.

	Publishers	Editors	Staff Members	Total	
Help	30%	23%	29%	27%	(202)
Hindrance	61	66	63	63	(439)
No difference	9	12	8	10	(78)

V141. How often does the publisher at your newspaper question or otherwise participate in the assignment of a particular reporter to a story or beat?
   a. Never
   b. Less than once a year
   c. About once or twice a year
   d. Several times a year
   e. About once a month
   f. 2–3 times a month
   g. Nearly every week
   h. Every week
   i. Several times a week
   j. Daily

	Publishers	Editors	Staff Members	Total	
Statement a	46%	55%	56%	52%	(367)
Statement b	21	21	20	21	(149)
Statement c	14	15	9	13	(93)
Statement d	14	6	8	10	(67)
Statement e	2	1	3	2	(17)
Statement f	1	1	2	1	(11)
Statement g	0	1	0	0	(3)
Statement h	1	0	1	1	(5)
Statement i	0	0	1	1	(5)
Statement j	0	0	0	0	(1)

V142. How often, to the best of your knowledge, does your paper publish editorial matter controlled by the business office on behalf of advertisers in the news columns (commonly known as "blurbs" or "business office musts")?
   a. Never
   b. Less than once a year
   c. About once or twice a year
   d. Several times a year
   e. About once a month
   f. 2–3 times a month
   g. Nearly every week
   h. Every week
   i. Several times a week
   j. Daily

	Publishers	Editors	Staff Members	Total	
Statement a	79%	76%	61%	72%	(491)
Statement b	5	3	9	6	(43)
Statement c	4	5	6	5	(41)
Statement d	5	9	12	9	(74)
Statement e	2	1	3	2	(18)
Statement f	1	2	3	2	(17)
Statement g	1	2	3	2	(19)
Statement h	1	0	3	1	(10)
Statement i	0	1	1	1	(8)
Statement j	1	0	0	0	(2)

V143. As you know, some newspaper companies are privately owned, and some are at least partly owned by investors who buy and sell stock on public exchanges. Do you think that whether a company is publicly or privately owned makes any difference in the way it serves its local community?

	Publishers	Editors	Staff Members	Total	
Yes	40%	38%	39%	39%	(294)
No	60	62	61	61	(432)

V144. (IF YES TO V143) How frequently would you say the pressures of being publicly owned hinder a newspaper's ability to serve the local community: often, sometimes, rarely, or never?

	Publishers	Editors	Staff Members	Total	
Often	12%	16%	10%	13%	(40)
Sometimes	50	53	60	54	(157)
Rarely	27	19	26	24	(62)
Never	10	12	4	9	(27)

V145. Do you think that it is a good idea or a bad idea to use polls and surveys to find out what readers want to read?

	Publishers	Editors	Staff Members	Total	
Good idea	97%	92%	94%	94%	(698)
Bad idea	3	8	6	6	(31)

V146. Suppose that there were an issue that really meant a lot to the health and safety of people in your community, but people weren't very interested in it. Should the paper try to get people interested, or should it wait until their interest is aroused in some other way?

	Publishers	Editors	Staff Members	Total	
Try to get interest	100%	99%	100%	100%	(728)
Wait	0	1	0	0	(3)

V147. Suppose the issue were the effect of seat belt use in reducing deaths and injuries from auto accidents. If people aren't very interested in using seat belts, should the paper try to get them interested or wait until their interest is aroused in some other way?

	Publishers	Editors	Staff Members	Total	
Try to get interest	85%	95%	87%	89%	(653)
Wait	15	5	13	11	(76)

V148. Suppose the issue were the effect of diet on disease. If people weren't very interested, should the paper try to get them interested or wait until their interest is aroused in some other way?

	Publishers	Editors	Staff Members	Total	
Try to get interest	89%	95%	86%	90%	(662)
Wait	11	5	14	10	(67)

V149. Some newspaper people believe that every newspaper should have a written code of ethics or set of guidelines that its staff could consult when problems came up. Others say that every situation is different, and each ethical problem needs to be considered on its own merits. Which comes closest to your belief?

	Publishers	Editors	Staff Members	Total	
Written code	59%	63%	63%	62%	(427)
Case by case	41	37	37	38	(295)

V150. Does your newspaper have a written code of ethics or set of guidelines?

	Publishers	Editors	Staff Members	Total	
Yes	55%	51%	35%	47%	(319)
No	45	49	65	53	(404)

V151. (IF YES TO V150) Could you put your hands on it right now if you wanted to, or would you have to look around for a while to find it?

	Publishers	Editors	Staff Members	Total	
Now	78%	91%	65%	80%	(242)
Have to look	22	9	35	20	(66)

Here are a few questions about people in general.

V152. Do you think most people would try to take advantage of you if they got a chance, or would they try to be fair?

	Publishers	Editors	Staff Members	Total	
Most try to take advantage	9%	18%	16%	14%	(112)
Most try to be fair	91	82	84	86	(615)

V153. Generally speaking, would you say that most people can be trusted or that you can't be too careful in dealing with people?

	Publishers	Editors	Staff Members	Total	
Most can be trusted	86%	83%	65%	78%	(558)
You can't be too careful	14	17	35	22	(169)

V154. These are two statements about ethics. Please tell me which one of them comes closest to your view:

a. In deciding ethical questions, one should refer to certain universal truths about right and wrong which never change.

b. There are few, if any, universal truths, and each question should be decided according to what benefits the community in the long run.

	Publishers	Editors	Staff Members	Total	
Statement a	68%	68%	58%	65%	(462)
Statement b	32	32	42	35	(256)

V155. How would you rate the morale in your newsroom during the past few months? On a scale of 1 to 10, with 10 being the happiest possible newsroom and 1 being the least happy, where would you put yours?

	Publishers	Editors	Staff Members	Total	
1	1%	1%	5%	2%	(14)
2	1	1	4	2	(15)
3	1	1	10	4	(32)
4	1	3	12	5	(41)
5	9	7	25	14	(106)
6	11	20	14	15	(98)
7	33	27	19	27	(180)
8	35	35	8	27	(192)
9	6	5	2	5	(39)
10	0	0	1	1	(5)

(EDITORS AND STAFF ONLY.)

V156. On a scale of A to F, with A being the highest grade and F being a failing grade, how would you rate the ability of your publisher to deal with ethical matters?

	Editors	*Staff Members*	*Total*	
A	47%	26%	37%	(169)
B	31	31	31	(159)
C	15	26	21	(92)
D	2	7	4	(25)
E	5	5	5	(25)
F	0	5	3	(15)

(PUBLISHERS ONLY.)

V157. On a scale of A to F, with A being the highest grade and F being a failing grade, how would you rate the ability of your editor to deal with ethical matters?

	Publishers	
A	64%	(136)
B	29	(68)
C	4	(10)
D	1	(4)
E	2	(5)
F	0	(1)

V158. We'd like to know how involved *you* are in civic affairs. About how many local, voluntary organizations do you belong to? Include churches, civic clubs, charitable organizations, veterans groups, and the like.

	Publishers	*Editors*	*Staff Members*	*Total*	
Mean	7.0	2.3	1.2	3.5	(697)

V159. Now just a few questions so we'll know the kinds of people we've surveyed. In what year were you born? [Thus, age equals 1982 minus year born.]

	Publishers	*Editors*	*Staff Members*	*Total*	
Mean age	51.4	49.2	37.4	46.1	(713)

V160. And how many years of school have you completed?

	Publishers	*Editors*	*Staff Members*	*Total*	
Mean	16.3	15.9	15.9	16	(720)

V161. Have you ever served in the Armed Forces?

	Publishers	*Editors*	*Staff Members*	*Total*	
Yes	69%	68%	28%	56%	(396)
No	31	32	72	44	(332)

V162. (IF YES TO V161) Are you still active in the reserve?

	Publishers	Editors	Staff Members	Total	
Yes	1%	3%	0%	1%	(7)
No	99	97	100	99	(374)

V163. Are you black, white, or something else?

	Publishers	Editors	Staff Members	Total	
Black	0%	1%	2%	1%	(721)
White	100	99	97	99	(4)
Other	0	0	1	0	(2)

V164. Please indicate your sex.

	Publishers	Editors	Staff Members	Total	
Male	97%	95%	69%	87%	(627)
Female	3	5	31	13	(101)

V165. What is your religious preference?

	Publishers	Editors	Staff Members	Total	
Protestant	67%	62%	44%	58%	(429)
Catholic	13	16	23	17	(136)
Jewish	6	7	11	8	(40)
Other	4	1	4	3	(21)
None	9	14	19	14	(100)

V166. How often do you attend religious services?
   a. Never
   b. Less than once a year
   c. About once or twice a year
   d. Several times a year
   e. About once a month
   f. 2–3 times a month
   g. Nearly every week
   h. Every week
   i. Several times a week

	Publishers	Editors	Staff Members	Total	
Statement a	10%	18%	18%	15%	(92)
Statement b	12	19	19	17	(108)
Statement c	17	10	12	13	(97)
Statement d	23	15	16	18	(121)
Statement e	7	4	7	6	(48)
Statement f	10	7	7	8	(66)

	Publishers	Editors	Staff Members	Total	
Statement g	10	12	10	11	(85)
Statement h	9	14	11	11	(96)
Statement i	2	1	1	1	(12)

(PUBLISHERS ONLY.)
V167. How many years have you spent in the newspaper business?

26.5 average years   (229)

V168. Does that include any time on the news-editorial side?

Yes   66%   (144)
No   34   (79)

V169. (IF YES TO V168) How many years did you spend in news-editorial work?

15.7 average years   (141)

(EDITORS ONLY.)
V170. How many years have you spent in the newspaper business?

25.4 average years   (245)

V171. Does that include any time on the business side?

Yes   13%   (32)
No   87   (211)

V172. (IF YES TO V171) How many years did you spend on the business side?

4.1 average years   (32)

APPENDIX II

The ASNE Survey Method

The ASNE survey is about the relationships of editors and publishers and how they work together to set and enforce ethical standards on daily newspapers. As its practitioners know, the newspaper business is complicated. Any plan to study it must be complicated, too, and the investigator who fails to define terms and establish clear procedures risks drowning in ambiguity. This study counts and measures things, and it is meant to be replicable. If this good intention is realized, the study's procedures should be so clear and its interpretations so sharply defined that some future investigator could take the same steps, ask the same questions, and know from the results whether or not the industry had changed in the intervening time.

Two design issues had to be resolved at the beginning. One was the very basic question of to whom or what the results should be generalized. The other was the procedural issue of how to define the main actors in the study. The first problem was aggravated by the tremendous variation in newspaper size and a resulting paradox: the vast majority of newspapers are relatively small, i.e., under 50,000 daily circulation, but the majority of newspaper readers are served by the larger papers. Two percent of the newspapers (the 31 with circulation over 250,000) account for about a quarter of the total daily circulation in the United States.

If this study were primarily concerned with making life easier for editors and publishers, it would be fashioned so that newspapers in general were the population under study, and it would be based on a representative sample of them, with smaller papers constituting the great bulk of the units in the sample, just as they do in real life. If, on the other hand, the study is to be concerned with social responsibilities, it is readers, not newspapers, that need to be equally represented.

The latter option was chosen in this case. Newspapers were chosen for study at random—but with the probability of selection made proportionate to the size of their daily circulation. The sample is therefore representative of the population of newspaper users. It is as though we had taken a pure random sample of persons who buy newspapers, either by subscription or single copy, asked them what papers they read, and selected those papers into our study.

The execution of this process was easier than it sounds. Statisticians at the Research Triangle Institute used a computer to examine the circulation numbers in the 1981 *Editor & Publisher Yearbook* and determined that the desired sample size of 333 newspapers could be obtained by choosing the paper represented by approximately every 140,000th newspaper buyer. Imagine the total paid press runs of all the daily newspapers on an average day in 1981 piled in a single stack. Now, from a random start somewhere among the first 140,000, peel them off one at a time and set aside every 140,000th paper. Those are the newspapers in our sample.

One other step is necessary, however, to make these 333 newspapers truly representative of all newspaper buyers. Some are so large that their selection is automatic, and some of the very largest will be selected more than once. To complete the requirement of equal representation for all consumers of daily newspapers, it is necessary to count these extra-large newspapers more than once—in proportion to their size. This task was accomplished by the simple means of duplicating responses from those newspapers enough times to give them their proportional weight.

The numbers in this survey are therefore circulation-adjusted whenever they refer to editors, publishers, or staff members. When they refer to readers, they are simple projections to all daily newspaper readers in the United States—with circulation used as a universal indicator of readership. Aside from giving readers their just recognition with this procedure, the method has the effect of producing very powerful generalizations. The news people reponding to this survey produce more than half of all daily circulation in the United States. As a result, sampling error is quite small— and representativeness quite good—for editors and publishers. For staff members, however, the numbers are only crudely representative. This difference occurs because an editor or a publisher represents himself or herself. Chance plays no part in the selection once the newspaper is chosen. A single staff member, on the other hand, represents all of the diversity of the staff at his or her newspaper, and that selection is subject to chance. The problem is probably minor when the whole population of newspaper readers is considered, but it may not be so minor when only parts of that population are examined. This report therefore considers staff attitudes in less detail than those of editors and publishers.

Even though this study is reader-oriented rather than editor- or publisher-oriented, the actual number of newspapers behind each of the main categories of response is reported with the responses so that you can check if you ever suspect that an unexpected result is too thinly supported by real life.

The second major problem, defining the actors in the study, is solved more straightforwardly. Because this is a study about editors and publishers, we must make very clear at the outset what we mean by the terms "editor" and "publisher." Again, in the interests of replicability, we must make the definitions so clear that another researcher could follow them and come out in the same place.

It was evident from the start that titles in the newspaper business are too variable and ambiguous to be of much help. It was more important to keep functions rather than titles uniform. Our procedure, therefore, began with the editor. For the purpose of this study, the editor was defined as the highest-ranking person with full-time responsibility for the news operation at the paper. This definition held regardless of title, and it prevented an editor-publisher from being defined as the editor. It also ruled out the selection of editors whose only responsibility was the editorial page. A person who was the top editor of two papers had his responses counted twice in the few cases where both papers fell into the sample.

Finding the person to define as publisher was fairly easy once the editor had been identified. The publisher, in this study, is that person to whom the highest-ranking editor reports. If an editor found the concept of "reporting" ambiguous—and some did—he or she was asked who did the hiring, firing, salary adjustment, and budget approval for the editor. In certain group situations, that person was a corporate officer in some other city, but was nevertheless defined as the publisher. An editor-publisher was defined as the publisher if he or she was the person to whom the highest-ranking full-time editor reported. Anyone who was the publisher of more than one paper in the sample had his or her responses counted for each of those papers.

Selection of a person to represent the staff at each newspaper was done as randomly as possible but still kept within a fairly limited range of writers, desk people, and lower management. Seven job descriptions were written and rotated so that each editor was asked to match a staff name to a randomly selected position. This provided the researchers with staff names without their selection being left entirely to the editors. If more than one person fit the description, the full list was obtained, and selection made according to alphabetical order.

Data were collected in two stages. Editors were contacted by telephone and their eligibility verified. Once this was done, the editor was asked questions to establish the identity of the publisher and the eligible staff person. Some substantive questions on the frequency of certain kinds of ethical problems were also asked at this stage. A follow-up self-administered form was then sent to the editor, his or her publisher, and a staff member at each newspaper.

Response rates were quite high for a survey of any type, much less a complicated, two-stage, mail-and-telephone procedure. Fully 97.6 percent of the editors (325 our of 333) supplied data for the first stage. Six editors refused and two were dropped from the sample because their newspapers closed while the study was in progress. Raw response rates for the mail survey, based on the 331 newspapers still in the sample, were 78.2 percent for editors, 71 percent for publishers, and 72.5 percent for staff members. Only 22 of the 331 newspapers produced no response from any of the three persons contacted.

Field work for this project was performed by the Research Triangle Institute of North Carolina under the supervision of Don Jackson, project director, and Jennifer J. McNeil, survey specialist. James R. Chromy supervised the sampling. J. Walker Smith, School of Journalism, University of North Carolina at Chapel Hill, managed the data file, searched the literature and checked the facts. This project was conceived and supervised by the Ethics Committee of the American Society of Newspaper Editors under the chairmanship of Robert H. Phelps of the *Boston Globe*.

Others who offered helpful advice include Robert L. Burke, Malcolm F. Mallette, Carol Reuss and Donald Shaw. The project was financed by the John and Mary R. Markle Foundation. All errors, careless interpretations, and non sequiturs are the sole responsibility of the author.

Four Codes of Ethics

American Society of Newspaper Editors, Canons of Journalism

Adopted by the ASNE Committee on Ethics, 1923.

The primary function of newspapers is to communicate to the human race what its members do, feel, and think. Journalism, therefore, demands of its practitioners the widest range of intelligence, of knowledge, and of experience, as well as natural and trained powers of observation and reasoning. To its opportunities as a chronicle are indissolubly linked its obligations as teacher and interpreter.

To the end of finding some means of codifying sound practice and just aspirations of American journalism these canons are set forth:

I

Responsibility.   The right of a newspaper to attract and hold readers is restricted by nothing but considerations of public welfare. The use a newspaper makes of the share of public attention it gains serves to determine its sense of responsibility, which it shares with every member of its staff. A journalist who uses his power for any selfish or otherwise unworthy purpose is faithless to a high trust.

II

Freedom of the Press.   Freedom of the press is to be guarded as a vital right of mankind. It is the unquestionable right to discuss whatever is not explicitly forbidden by law, including the wisdom of any restrictive statute.

III

Independence.   Freedom from all obligations except that of fidelity to the public interest is vital.

1. Promotion of any private interest contrary to the general welfare, for whatever reason, is not compatible with honest journalism. So-called news communications from private sources should not be published without public notice of their source or else substantiation of their claims to value as news, both in form and substance.

2. Partisanship in editorial comment which knowingly departs from the truth, does violence to the best spirit of American journalism; in the news columns it is subversive of a fundamental principle of the profession.

IV

Sincerity, Truthfulness, Accuracy. Good faith with the reader is the foundation of all journalism worthy of the name.

1. By every consideration of good faith a newspaper is constrained to be truthful. It is not to be excused for lack of thoroughness or accuracy within its control or failure to obtain command of these essential qualities.

2. Headlines should be fully warranted by the contents of the articles which they surmount.

V

Impartiality. Sound practice makes clear distinction between news reports and expressions of opinion. News reports should be free from opinion or bias of any kind.

1. This rule does not apply to so-called special articles unmistakably devoted to advocacy or characterized by a signature authorizing the writer's own conclusions and interpretations.

VI

Fair Play. A newspaper should not publish unofficial charges affecting reputation or moral character without opportunity given to the accused to be heard; right practice demands the giving of such opportunity in all cases of serious accusation outside judicial proceedings.

1. A newspaper should not invade private rights or feelings without sure warrant of public right as distinguished from public curiosity.

2. It is the privilege, as it is the duty, of a newspaper to make prompt and complete correction of its own serious mistakes of fact or opinion, whatever their origin.

VII

Decency. A newspaper cannot escape conviction of insincerity if while professing high moral purpose it supplies incentives to base conduct, such as are to be found in details of crime and vice, publication of which is not demonstrably for the public good. Lacking authority to enforce its canons, the journalism here represented can but express the hope that deliberate pandering to vicious instincts will encounter effective public disapproval or yield to the influence of a preponderant professional condemnation.

American Society of Newspaper Editors Statement of Principles

Adopted by the ASNE board of directors, Oct. 23, 1975; this code supplants the 1923 Code of Ethics ("Canons of Journalism").

Preamble

The First Amendment, protecting freedom of expression from abridgment by any law, guarantees to the people through their press a constitutional right, and thereby places on newspaper people a particular responsibility.

Thus journalism demands of its practitioners not only industry and knowledge but also the pursuit of a standard of integrity proportionate to the journalist's singular obligation.

To this end the American Society of Newspaper Editors sets forth this Statement of Principles as a standard encouraging the highest ethical and professional performance.

Article I—Responsibility

The primary purpose of gathering and distributing news and opinion is to serve the general welfare by informing the people and enabling them to make judgments on the issues of the time. Newspaper men and women who abuse the power of their professional role for selfish motives or unworthy purposes are faithless to that public trust.

The American press was made free not just to inform or just to serve as a forum for debate but also to bring an independent scrutiny to bear on the forces of power in the society, including the conduct of official power at all levels of government.

Article II—Freedom of the Press

Freedom of the press belongs to the people. It must be defended against encroachment or assault from any quarter, public or private.

Journalists must be constantly alert to see that the public's business is conducted in public. They must be vigilant against all who would exploit the press for selfish purposes.

Article III—Independence

Journalists must avoid impropriety and the appearance of impropriety as well as any conflict of interest or the appearance of conflict. They should neither accept anything nor pursue any activity that might compromise or seem to compromise their integrity.

Article IV—Truth and Accuracy

Good faith with the reader is the foundation of good journalism. Every effort must be made to assure that the news content is accurate, free from bias and in context, and that all sides are presented fairly. Editorials, analytical articles and commentary should be held to the same standard of accuracy with respect to facts as news reports.

Significant errors of fact, as well as errors of omission, should be corrected promptly and prominently.

Article V—Impartiality

To be impartial does not require the press to be unquestioning or to refrain from editorial expression. Sound practice, however, demands a clear distinction for the reader between news reports and opinion. Articles that contain opinion or personal interpretation should be clearly identified.

Article VI—Fair Play

Journalists should respect the rights of people involved in the news, observe the common standards of decency and stand accountable to the public for the fairness and accuracy of their news reports.

Persons publicly accused should be given the earliest opportunity to respond.

Pledges of confidentiality to news sources must be honored at all costs, and therefore should not be given lightly. Unless there is clear and pressing need to maintain confidences, sources of information should be identified.

These principles are intended to preserve, protect and strengthen the bond of trust and respect between American journalist and the American people, a bond that is essential to sustain the grant of freedom entrusted to both by the nation's founders.

Associated Press Managing Editors Association Code of Ethics

Adopted by the APME board of directors, April 15, 1975.

This code is a model against which newspaper men and women can measure their performance. It is meant to apply to news and editorial staff members, and others who are involved in, or who influence, news coverage and editorial policy. It has been formulated in the belief that newspapers and the people who produce them should adhere to the highest standards of ethical and professional conduct.

Responsibility

A good newspaper is fair, accurate, honest, responsible, independent and decent. Truth is its guiding principle.

It avoids practices that would conflict with the ability to report and presents news in a fair and unbiased manner.

The newspaper should serve as a constructive critic of all segments of society. Editorially, it should advocate needed reform or innovations in the public interest. It should expose wrongdoing or misuse of power, public or private.

News sources should be disclosed unless there is clear reason not to do so. When it is necessary to protect the confidentiality of a source, the reason should be explained.

The newspaper should background, with the facts, public statements that it knows to be inaccurate or misleading. It should uphold the right of free speech and freedom of the press and should respect the individual's right of privacy.

The public's right to know about matters of importance is paramount, and the newspaper should fight vigorously for public access to news of government through open meetings and open records.

Accuracy

The newspaper should guard against inaccuracies, carelessness, bias or distortion through either emphasis or omission.

It should admit all substantive errors and correct them promptly and prominently.

Integrity

The newspaper should strive for impartial treatment of issues and dispassionate handling of controversial subjects. It should provide a forum for the exchange of comment and criticism, especially when such comment is opposed to its editorial positions. Editorials and other expressions of opinion by reporters and editors should be clearly labeled.

The newspaper should report the news without regard for its own interests. It should not give favored news treatment to advertisers or special interest groups. It should report matters regarding itself or its personnel with the same vigor and candor as it would other institutions or individuals.

Concern for community, business or personal interests should not cause a newspaper to distort or misrepresent the facts.

Conflicts of Interest

The newspaper and its staff should be free of obligations to news sources and special interests. Even the appearance of obligation or conflict of interest should be avoided.

Newspapers should accept nothing of value from news sources or others outside the profession. Gifts and free or reduced-rate travel, entertainment, products and lodging should not be accepted. Expenses in connection with news reporting should be paid by the newspaper. Special favors and special treatment for members of the press should be avoided.

Involvement in such things as politics, community affairs, demonstrations and social causes that could cause a conflict of interest, or the appearance of such conflict, should be avoided.

Outside employment by news sources is an obvious conflict of interest, and employment by potential news sources also should be avoided.

Financial investments by staff members or other outside business interests that could conflict with the newspaper's ability to report the news or that would create the impression of such conflict should be avoided.

Stories should not be written or edited primarily for the purpose of winning awards and prizes. Blatantly commercial journalism contests, or others that reflect unfavorably on the newspaper or the profession, should be avoided.

No code of ethics can prejudge every situation. Common sense and good judgment are required in applying ethical principles to newspaper realities. Individual newspapers are encouraged to augment these guidelines with locally produced codes that apply more specifically to their own situations.

Society of Professional Journalists, Sigma Delta Chi, Code of Ethics

Adopted by the 1973 annual convention of Sigma Delta Chi.

The Society of Professional Journalists, Sigma Delta Chi, believes the duty of journalists is to serve the truth.

We believe the agencies of mass communication are carriers of public discussion and information, acting on their Constitutional mandate and freedom to learn and report the facts.

We believe in public enlightenment as the forerunner of justice, and in our Constitutional role to seek the truth as part of the public's right to know the truth.

We believe those responsibilities carry obligations that require journalists to perform with intelligence, objectivity, accuracy, and fairness.

To these ends, we declare acceptance of the standards of practice here set forth.

Responsibility

The public's right to know of events of public importance and interest is the overriding mission of the mass media. The purpose of distributing news and enlightened opinion is to serve the general welfare. Journalists who use their professional status as representatives of the public for selfish or other unworthy motives violate a high trust.

Freedom of the Press

Freedom of the press is to be guarded as an inalienable right of people in a free society. It carries with it the freedom and the responsibility to discuss, question, and challenge actions and utterances of our government and of our public and private institutions. Journalists uphold the right to speak unpopular opinions and the privilege to agree with the majority.

Ethics

Journalists must be free of obligation to any interest other than the public's right to know the truth.

1. Gifts, favors, free travel, special treatment, or privileges can compromise the integrity of journalists and their employees. Nothing of value should be accepted.

2. Secondary employment, political involvement, holding public office, and service in community organizations should be avoided if it compromises the integrity of journalists and their employers. Journalists and their employers should conduct their personal lives in a manner which protects them from conflict of interest, real or apparent. Their responsibilities to the public are paramount. That is the nature of their profession.

3. So-called news communications from private sources should not be published or broadcast without substantiation of their claims to news value.

4. Journalists will seek news that serves the public interest, despite the obstacles. They will make constant efforts to assure that the public's business is conducted in public and that public records are open to public inspection.

5. Journalists acknowledge the newsman's ethic of protecting confidential sources of information.

Accuracy and Objectivity

Good faith with the public is the foundation of all worthy journalism.

1. Truth is our ultimate goal.

2. Objectivity in reporting the news is another goal, which serves as the mark of an experienced professional. It is a standard of performance toward which we strive. We honor those who achieve it.

3. There is no excuse for inaccuracies or lack of thoroughness.

4. Newspaper headlines should be fully warranted by the contents of the articles they accompany. Photographs and telecasts should give an accurate picture of an event and not highlight a minor incident out of context.

5. Sound practice makes clear distinction between news reports and expressions of opinion. News reports should be free of opinion or bias and represent all sides of an issue.

6. Partisanship in editorial comment which knowingly departs from the truth violates the spirit of American journalism.

7. Journalists recognize their responsibility for offering informed analysis, comment, and editorial opinion on public events and issues. They accept the obligation to present such material by individuals whose competence, experience, and judgment qualify them for it.

8. Special articles or presentations devoted to advocacy or the writer's own conclusions and interpretations should be labeled as such.

Fair Play

Journalists at all times will show respect for the dignity, privacy, rights, and well-being of people encountered in the course of gathering and presenting the news.

1. The news media should not communicate unofficial charges affecting reputation or moral character without giving the accused a chance to reply.

2. The news media must guard against invading a person's right to privacy.

3. The media should not pander to morbid curiosity about details of vice and crime.

4. It is the duty of news media to make prompt and complete correction of their errors.

5. Journalists should be accountable to the public for their reports and the public should be encouraged to voice its grievances against the media. Open dialogue with our readers, viewers, and listeners should be fostered.

Pledge

Journalists should actively censure and try to prevent violations of these standards, and they should encourage their observance by all newspeople. Adherence to this code of ethics is intended to preserve the bond of mutual trust and respect between American journalists and the American people.

Index